Praise for *The Singing Guru*

"Kamla Kapur has created a Sikh parallel of Homer's *Odyssey* in the re-imagining of its founder's spiritual journey, cleverly recounted in the voice of a mercurial acolyte. As with that work, the prose melts into mellifluous poetry, music to the soul. In company with the Sikh spiritual leader, Guru Nanak, we travel from magical place to magical place throughout India and are reminded again and again of what values should inform our life. You wait until the saga is over to exhale and still wish there were more. A ripping read."

—THOMAS HOOVER, author of *Zen Culture* and *The Moghul*

"Kamla Kapur chooses an innovative and wondrous way of retelling the eternal truths contained in the life and teachings of Guru Nanak. Her simple, melodious narrative depicts common human frailties and deep philosophical complexities with equal ease: *The Singing Guru* will delight the mind even as it enlightens the spirit."

—NAVTEJ SARNA, author of *The Book of Nanak* and *The Exile*

"Rich imagination, anchored by the spirit of the Janamsakhi tradition, brings alive the story of Guru Nanak Dev, the founder of Sikhism. Kamla Kapur has written a gripping book in a style that is both simple and lucid. Her reinterpretation of the Janamsakhis should find wide resonance among readers."

—ROOPINDER SINGH, author of *Guru Nanak: His Life and Teachings*

"*The Singing Guru* is simply superb!"

— SURJIT PATAR, renowned Punjabi poet

"*The Singing Guru* is a fascinating reconstruction of the Purantan Janamsakhi tradition. I teach a course on South Asian Literary Cultures and a work like this would make an engaging text for students to read."

— HARPREET SINGH, Department of South Asian Studies, Harvard University

"I am filled with utmost happiness in my heart going through *The Singing Guru* and discovering a way to enlightenment. We can only imagine Guru Nanak singing 500 years ago and I congratulate the author on her wonderful, enthusiastic story and the underlying music that fills it."

— HANS RAJ HANS, Punjabi Rock star and Sufi singer

"*The Singing Guru* is indeed a remarkable work of imagination through which Kamla Kapur brings alive the story of Guru Nanak in the voice of his lifelong companion Bhai Mardana. This retelling of Janam-sakhi narratives is breathtaking in scope, refreshingly innovative and written in accessible style. It will make an interesting read for both academic and popular audiences. The author deserves our compliments for her rare achievement."

— PASAHURA SINGH, Author of *The Bhagats of the Guru Granth Sahib* and Jasbir Singh Saini, Endowed Chair in Sikh and Punjabi Studies, University of California, Riverside

Into the great heart

Legends and Adventures of Guru Angad

the Second Sikh Guru

KAMLA K. KAPUR

JAICO PUBLISHING HOUSE

Ahmedabad Bangalore Bhopal Bhubaneswar Chennai
Delhi Hyderabad Kolkata Lucknow Mumbai

Published by Jaico Publishing House
A-2 Jash Chambers, 7-A Sir Phirozshah Mehta Road
Fort, Mumbai - 400 001
jaicopub@jaicobooks.com
www.jaicobooks.com

To be sold only in India, Bangladesh, Bhutan,
Pakistan, Nepal, Sri Lanka and the Maldives.

INTO THE GREAT HEART
ISBN 978-93-87944-10-7

First Jaico Impression: 2018

Page design and layout:
Special Effects Graphics Design Company, Mumbai

Printed by
Thomson Press (India) Limited

For my late mother,
Laj, as the earth
full of darkness and light,
shrew and saint,
and for all the mothers present
past, and future
who populate our planet
including myself
who did not give birth
yet are fecund.

Acknowledgments

I wish to thank all those in my family who have been an enduring emotional support: foremost among them my husband, Payson R. Stevens; my sister, Harmesh Kaur Khatri, my brother-in-law, Maj. General Kuldip Singh Khatri, their sons, Jaipdeep Singh and his family, Sheeba, Anhad and Ameera; Ramandeep Singh, Perry, Ajuni, and Ajoojh; and my intentional family, Gajendra Singh and Priti Kumari of Khimsar.

Contents

Introduction

When I started writing *The Singing Guru*, the first volume of the Sikh saga, my agenda was to finish Guru Nanak's story and move on to book two, about Bhai Lehna, who later became the second guru of the Sikhs under the name of Guru Angad. The writing process, however, is happily irreverent about agendas and plans, and *The Singing Guru* ended midway through Guru Nanak's journey on this planet, with the establishment of Kartarpur, the city he founded and which became the cradle of Sikhism. Lehna only made his appearance in the epilogue as the prologue to the next book in the series.

Not having learnt my lesson the first time around, my intention when I began writing book two in the series, *Into the Great Heart*, was to center the book on Lehna/Guru Angad. But *The Singing Guru*, though it was done and published, was still incomplete. I hadn't dealt with Guru Nanak's death, or Mardana's, nor with the entire story of how and why Lehna came to Kartarpur, his deep and abiding service and love for Guru Nanak, the jealousy of Nanak's sons towards him, the unfolding of the rest of the narrative all the way to the deaths of Guru Nanak and Mardana, the main protagonist in the first book, and the transformation of Lehna into Guru Angad. The history and story is so complex and intertwined that my intention was once again, happily muscled aside. I say happily because these books ended up being what they needed to be even though they involved more time and labor to complete. And this labor was immensely sweetened by the lesson – prone to frequent, if not hourly, forgetting – to get out of my own way and let the story unfold the way it wanted and needed. Agendas and intentions, wonderful as they are as organizing and production tools, depend largely on the ego and its attendant will. All the gurus and bhagats in the Sri Guru Granth Sahib (SGGS) sing of the imperative to hold the ego in abeyance so a space is created for the universe to go to work in. They call this process and the rewards thereof, *sehaj*.

Into the Great Heart is about the second Sikh guru's arc from Lehna to Guru Angad. Though it begins and ends with him, it does not cover his 13 years as the guru of the Sikhs after Guru Nanak's death in 1539, for which another book is underway. It is also about the parts of Guru Nanak's stories that remain untold in *The Singing Guru,* and about the many contemporaneous women in Sikh history whose stories were not related in the first volume.

Not many people, including Sikhs, know much about Guru Angad (1504 – 1552). Here are some accepted anecdotes, facts, history of his life; born in Harike in Punjab; married a woman called Khivi; had two sons, Dasu and Datu, and a daughter, Amro; moved to Khadur when the Mughals sacked his hometown; was a devoted priest of a Durga temple in Khadur, where he danced to his Goddess, wearing ankle bells; took an annual party of pilgrims to Jwalamukhi, meaning 'the deity of flaming mouth,' a temple in the Himalayas built over some natural jets of combustible gas, believed to be the manifestation of the Goddess; heard a friend in Khadur, Bhai Jodha, singing one of Guru Nanak's songs, and was ignited with a desire to meet its author; interrupted his journey to Jwalamukhi to meet Guru Nanak, abandoned his faith and his priesthood, and never left him.

Together with Guru Nanak, Lehna invented and perfected an alphabet and script called *Gurmukhi.* Guru Nanak wanted to serve the common people of Punjab by inventing a language understood by them for Sikh scripture. Hindu sacred writing was in Sanskrit – a language no one could read or understand. *Gurmukhi,* the language of the Sikh holy text, *The Sri Guru Granth Sahib,* means '*from the mouth of the Guru.*' The word *Gurmukh,* a central concept in Sikhism, means '*one whose face is turned towards the Guru.*' (As a relevant aside, the arch Guru in Sikhism is 'God himself' in 'his' role as instructor speaking to the soul of one who is attuned to that Voice.)

One of my agendas in this book, mercifully fulfilled, was to make it more female-centric. *The Singing Guru* had mainly male protagonists and the many historical women – Guru Nanak's wife, Mata Sulakhni, his sister, Bebe Nanaki, Mata Khivi, Bibi Amro, Guru Angad's wife and daughter, respectively, Nihali, the woman who gave Lehna shelter – who form part of this enduring saga, were only mentioned in it. Their stories remained unimagined and untold and I had to harken to their voices that spoke to my soul, my gender and the female question that has always existed and continues down to our times, affecting the lives of both genders, societies and cultures at large whose members have been reared, and influenced, by the happiness, peace, or lack thereof, of women. We cannot neglect one half of the equation and hope for wholeness.

There are many hints in accounts of Guru Nanak's life of Mata Sulakhni being a shrew. As the invented character, Shai Tani, says at one point in the book, 'shrews are made, not born.' We have to remember the consequences on Guru Nanak's wife of his being an absent husband and father for many years while he was on his *udaasis,* or journeys. For those years, Sulakhni was a single mother. Guru Nanak's absence impacted their children as well, one of whom, Baba Sri Chand, was brought up by Guru Nanak's sister, Bebe Nanaki. We know from advances in psychology and from sheer common sense that this arrangement must have had emotional consequences for all involved. If we are to bring history up to date, make it relevant for ourselves, we need to see it in the light of contemporary insights, still quite limited, about human nature. Simply put, Guru Nanak's journeys, and his invaluable and lasting message, had its casualties.

This is not a criticism of Guru Nanak who had to follow his own path in order to leave humankind the message that has resounded for five and a half centuries and will continue to do so till the end of time. It is rather a recognition of the fact that one person's destiny impacts another's. This is especially true when it comes to women whose destinies are yoked to the destinies of their husbands. This sort of causal connection, of course, has its exceptions. Bebe Nanaki, by all accounts, was a very saintly person, as was Bibi Amro, who went on to become a preacher.

The feminine question cannot be raised without dealing with the question of patriarchal concepts of God in most religions. The human tendency to anthropomorphize and personify in terms of race and gender, comforting as it may be for many, has the inherent peril of misrepresentation. Personification of the energy we call God, so necessary for sense-bound humanity, is not only erroneous but dangerous without the understanding that it is only a convenient representation of the inherent mystery, awesome energy and power we sense all around and within us. Evidence of the dangers of such falsification is visible on the political, social, domestic, individual/psychic arenas. This misguided and mainly unconscious tendency has taken many lives and caused much suffering throughout history.

Failure of language and the inadequacy of translation are mainly to blame for our images of 'God' as male. Language is not only an expression of thought, it influences thought, and thereby our realities, culture, social and political thought and structures. Gurmukhi uses far fewer words than English, which is heavily dependent on all sorts of pronouns, specifically, personal pronouns (he, she, it), possessive pronouns (his, hers), and reflexive pronouns (herself, himself). No gender-neutral pronouns exist for those energies that have no gender. The world awaits a coinage that will free us of these misleading divisions. Translations of Gurmukhi into English compound the problem and add to the misconception.

Sikhism's root prayer, the *Japji,* contains very few pronouns. The words *tis, toon, tudh, tisai, aap,* sparingly used, are gender neutral, and address the Supreme Entity as 'You,' but 151 instances of personal, possessive and reflective pronouns of he, him, himself, are used in the online version of the *Japji,* translated by Singh Sahib Sant Singh Khalsa. All translators of Gurbani follow this convention.

In the *Japji* alone Guru Nanak sings the universal feminine energy three times. In speaking of the all-encompassing guru, he says the guru includes the Hindu trinity of Shiva, Vishnu, Brahma *and* Mother Parvati. In the middle of the prayer he says many gods and goddesses sing to the guru; towards the end of the prayer he again reiterates that the Great Mother generated the gods and thereby, all humanity. The guru, he makes clear in another *shabad,* is gender free: *naar naa purkh, kahoo ko kaisai* – neither female nor male. How shall one call it?

That said, I too continue to use 'He' and 'Him' in this book. I am as bound by the limits of language as the rest of us. 'She' and 'Her' simply didn't work in the Sikh context. Convinced as I am of the gender neutrality of the Mystery we call God, I am equally comfortable using the masculine pronouns for the sake of convenience. But I use qualifiers whenever I can.

Beyond these gender issues, beyond the limits of language and translation, lies the greatest barrier to our comprehension of what we name 'God.' It is the failure of our imaginative powers to conceptualize that which lies outside our sense-shackled experience. The word refers to something so abstract, so all encompassing, pervading, present and transcendent, like air, that we can have no image for it. Guru Nanak stresses our utter inability to comprehend the Mystery: I am just a fish in the Ocean that is you; how can I know your extent?

On the human level, however, where gender perceptions matter to material beings like us, perhaps there is hope in the splintering of our concepts of gender in our own times of sex-change realities and all the possibilities between the traditional heterosexual poles. Hopefully it will broaden our minds and expand our hearts to include all, regardless of apparent differences. Hopefully it will set us on the path to transcending divisions and conflicts caused by narrow habits of thought, morality and behavior.

I would like to end this introduction with a manifesto of sorts in defense of a writer's need to invoke the imagination to recreate history. The lacunas in it are particularly fecund for a writer. Sikhs, like the Muslims, are overly sensitive about personifications and representations not only of God but also the Gurus and all the historical people associated with them – probably for the reasons stated above. Yet they allow posters and portraits of the Gurus to adorn their temples and homes. The human need for representation goes hand in hand, paradoxically, with its attendant dangers.

Representation is also the very meat of art, and freedom its very breath. A writer must have freedom if she is going to create a narrative that coheres and evokes some sense of times past. I am less interested in recreating an age than in making the narrative relevant to our times. Although I have been reverent about the main facts and legends in the Sikh Saga, my books are not hagiographies but fictional recreations. I have not tampered with the stories that history has bequeathed me. I have used them as suspensions bridges from which to hang the airy web of my fictions. I take comfort from the fact that the word 'history' has 'story' in it.

Though our gurus and guides were extraordinary individuals who continue to guide us through centuries, their lives and the lives of their families and associates were undoubtedly embedded in a human, creaturely, secular context. I have tried, to the best of my ability, with the help of several invented characters, particularly the family of Mardana, Guru Nanak's historic minstrel and companion, his wife, Fatima, and granddaughter, Aziza among them, to present my own version of this matrix.

Part I

The Dancing Guru: Lehna

Prologue

Guru Nanak survived longer than anyone thought he would. Even at sixty-three, he passionately wrote, composed, and preached his message through songs, and engaged with every aspect of life in the township that he had founded, Kartarpur, the City of God. From working in the fields to the common kitchen called Langar, he was constantly involved in the lives of his devotees. Over time, Kartarpur become the focal point of the Sikhs, expanding and growing through the emigrations of thousands of devotees, each contributing labor, love, food supplies and wealth.

But Guru's Nanak's two sons, Sri Chand and Lakhmi Das, were openly at war with each other for succession to the guruship. The populace, too, had taken sides. While Lakhmi Das was eying the wealth of the position, Sri Chand, shunning material wealth, wanted the power and prestige of being *the* guru of the Sikhs.

Sri Chand was already a guru of sorts. He had started a sect of Sikhism quite different from his father's, called the Udaasis.[1] Though his followers came from different castes, classes, and races, contrary to his father's preference that his devotees engage wholeheartedly in all aspects of the life that human nature needs and demands while being detached from outcomes and desires, Sri Chand mandated that his followers be celibate, vegetarian,

1 From Sanskrit, udasin: one who is above worldly attachments.

and abstain from alcohol. He did, however, allow smoking and eating intoxicants, such as bhang, charas,[2] and opium. Most of his followers went naked while some wore loincloths, smeared ashes from crematoria on their bodies and hair, wore brass chains around their necks, and cords across their bodies.

Lakhmi Das, on the other hand, was married, and though he engaged in all aspects of life except manual labor, he barely had a spiritual spark. Pleasure-seeking, hotheaded, impulsive, his passion was hunting, eating and living well. Neither of Guru Nanak's sons believed in honest labor, though they both made a pretense of it to win their father's favor, who believed exercise of the body was essential for spiritual progress. Sri Chand's purpose was renunciation, meditation, control of the mind through physical restraints, severe austerities like abstinence from food and drink, hanging upside down from trees for days and weeks, sitting on beds of nails, and acquisition of occult powers. Lakhmi Das, in addition to spending most of his waking life hunting, liked expensive horses, fancy outfits and good food.

A vanguard of Sri Chand's followers trooped into Kartarpur one day in a cloud of smoke from their smoldering pipes. They had come to announce, with the blowing of horns and beating of drums, the arrival of their guru.

People from the township gathered around them and listened to the miraculous stories recounted by Sri Chand's followers, who called him Baba Sri Chand, stories of how he could disappear before their eyes, appear at different places at the same time, bring dead people to life, materialize things out of air, and even levitate and fly.

Then Sri Chand himself arrived, wearing a red loincloth, looking like Shiva[3]. His body strong, muscular and lean from his many austerities, smeared with ash, hair matted like snakes, eyes sharp

---

2 Hashish.

3 The Hindu god of destruction and creation.

and piercing. People bowed to him, touched his feet, told him about their troubles and sought his advice. They believed he was Guru Nanak's true heir.

Soon, like a destined entrance, Lakhmi Das– short, a little plump, fine-featured, clad in expensive woolen clothes, leather boots –rode in on his Arabian horse, wearing a cap with feathers and singing a secular song. The hunting party carried the bloody carcasses of deer and various birds slung on their saddles. Lakhmi Das rolled his eyes at the sight of his older brother, dismounted, barely acknowledged Sri Chand's presence whose visits to Kartarpur had become more frequent in order to stake his claim to his inheritance.

Sri Chand's eyes sparked fire as he saw the dead animals and birds; he walked up to his younger brother and slapped him so hard that Lakhmi Das stumbled back and fell in the slush of the recent rains. Lakhmi Das's companions leapt from their horses, weapons drawn; Sri Chand's followers, their muscles bulging with strength, tackled the other side. A battle ensued, in which many an injury was inflicted on both sides.

It didn't take long for word to reach their mother, Sulakhni, and Nanaki, their father's sister, to run out of the house screaming and shouting at them to 'Stop! Stop! Stop! You are brothers!'But their pleas for truce were muffled in the turbulence of both parties' inflamed and pent up rage.

The women ran into the dogfight, parrying the blows and getting hurt in their attempt to separate the brothers. In her rage and fear that her sons may kill each other, Sulakhni began to hit Sri Chand with her fists, convinced that it was he who had started the fight. Their presence brought a temporary halt to the hostilities. However, the brothers still shouted abuses at each other. Nanaki ministered to Sri Chand and Sulakhni to Lakhmi Das. Though Nanaki bestowed a great deal of tenderness and loving care on Sri Chand, wiping his wounds with her veil, Sri Chand's gaze was riveted on the sight of his mother wailing, cooing over and kissing Lakhmi Das. He pulled away from Nanaki, ran to his mother, pulled her away from his younger brother with force, shook her up and shouted,"Witch! You gave me away as a child!"

—

Into this battlefield that Kartarpur had become came a stranger, a pilgrim, priest, dancer with bells on his ankles, and feathers in his cap. He was a worshipper of fire, a spark seeking to obliterate itself in a flame, a singer with Nanak's songs reverberating in the chambers of his heart. The stranger, with a little girl astride on the saddle of his white horse, rides joyously into the scenes of our story, his greatest longing about to be fulfilled.

CHAPTER 1

Lehna Comes to Give and Take

The sun, setting after a blazing display of color, has left behind a luminous sky awash with gentle clouds seemingly without plan, purpose and symmetry, yet with a beauty so stunning as to captivate the eye of the beholder riding towards it, making him marvel at the miracle of light and the succeeding darkness in which seeds quicken, take root, germinate. The stars appear to him like seeds of light scattered in the field of an indigo firmament in which the barely visible luminous arc of the new moon floats like a feather.

In the cobbled streets of Kartarpur, the stranger meets an old farmer in mud-stained clothes and a beard the color of the moon, accompanied by a young boy.

"Could you please show me the way to Guru Nanak's house?" He asks. The old man and young boy smile at each other in complicity. Silently, they take the reins of the stranger's horse and lead him on.

"Do you know Guru Nanak?" the little girl sitting on the saddle before her father asks excitedly.

"A little bit," the old man replies. "He is not easy to know. The older he becomes, the more eccentric he gets. Almost like a fool."

"That's not true!" the young boy responds. "I don't think he is eccentric at all, but becoming more and more divinely mad. I am Guru Nanak's slave. He calls me Buddha, the Ancient One, herder of cows and buffaloes."

"You? Ancient?" the girl laughs.

"Guru Nanak has slaves?" The stranger asks disappointedly.

"Voluntary ones that have given all of themselves to him."

"Buddha," says the old man, "if you give everything to that man, Nanak, what do you give to your Maker?"

"Nanak is the Maker's slave. So to be Nanak's slave is to be His slave's slave," the young boy says, skipping along the horse and stroking his muzzle.

The old man smiles affectionately and puts his arm across the young boy's shoulders. The rider, too, is impressed by the boy who could not have been more than twelve or thirteen years of age. So childlike and so wise.

"I've been waiting a long, long time to meet Guru Nanak," the stranger says with barely concealed excitement.

"Why?" the old man asks.

"I am a priest and dancer in the temple of Durga[4] Ma in Khadur, which is a village by the river Beas. Takht Mal, the head of the city, has constructed a beautiful temple made of marble, with niches for idols of all the various manifestations of Durga."

"The Warrior Goddess! Kali! Sati! Chandi![5] They all wear such pretty clothes and necklaces and rings and bangles! Bee Jee[6] says she will buy some more bangles for me," the child prattles, jangling them on her arm.

"You worship idols?' the boy asks. "Then why do you want to see Guru Nanak? He is the breaker of idols!"

"One evening, I had just finished washing the utensils for my *aarti*,[7] scrubbing the sacred silver salver clean with soft ash till I

4 The Goddess Durga from Hindu mythology, also called Kali; the destructive aspect of the feminine godhood, the counterpart of Lord Shiva.

5 Various names of Durga.

6 One of the many Punjabi words for 'mother.'

7 A form of prayer, explained later.

could see my face in it, then filled the lamps with oil and wick, lit them and scattered some hibiscus in the plate."

"They are red flowers and have thin yellow tongues with a *bodi*[8] at the end of them," the girl adds.

Every one laughs and then the stranger continues.

"It was that time in the evening which is the portal between day and night, the sky neither light nor dark, but both, a sapphire blue fabric embroidered faintly with flowers of light. Crossing the courtyard towards the temple I heard the enchanting strains of a song pouring into my ears like ambrosia. The youthful, feminine voice of the singer was so alluring that every string of my heart pulled me in its direction. The salver fell from my hands, and like a *gopi*[9] crazed by Krishna's flute, I left the temple and went in search of the song and the angel who was singing it. It was Jodha, the young son of my neighbor."

"Bhai[10] Jodha! He is my friend! He comes to the dera whenever he can and teaches me archery and swordsmanship! He is a singer *and* a warrior," Buddha cries excitedly. "There are some people in whose company the world vibrates on a high, clear, pure note, like Guru Nanak, Nanaki, Aziza, and Bhai Jodha! Everything that happens in their presence is magic!"

"I stood at his open door, enraptured, as if I had found the source of all my searching. When the song tapered into silence I asked, 'Whose music, whose words?' and he replied, 'my guru, Baba Nanak's.'

Whenever I met Jodha in the gully, he would tell me about Guru Nanak and Kartarpur but his descriptions didn't mean anything to me. But the words 'Baba Nanak' and 'Kartarpur' burst into life

---

8 Bodi: A tuft, or tail of hair on top of a shaved head.

9 Gopi: A lover of Krishna, one of the Gods in the Hindu pantheon who elicits everyone's love.

10 From Sanskrit, 'bhratr', meaning 'brother' in the literal sense but also used as an honorific.

with Jodha's song. The descriptions began to breathe. Ever since then I have been on fire to meet him."

"What were the words?" The old man asks.

"It was a long song but I have memorized a stanza." The young man clears his throat and sings:

Har charan kamal makarand lobhit mano
Andi no mohair ae epiyasa
Kirpa jal dai Nanak sarang ko
Hoi ja terai naam vaasaa

The stranger's voice is full of passion and feeling. Though a bit untrained, his audience senses a power waiting to be released.

"It means," the stranger explains, 'I am thirsty for the nectar of your Lotus Feet, Beloved! Give Nanak *sarang,*[11] your songbird, a drop of your rain of mercy. Captivate him; put him in the cage of your Love!"

His singing and explanation are so impassioned that it is followed by a lull in the conversation. Then, in a gentle voice, the stranger resumes his story.

"I was dumbstruck by the coincidence. Just the same day in a different context I had asked a scholar the meaning of *sarang.* It is a mythic songbird, somewhat like our own cuckoo that sings so very sweetly and plaintively at night before the monsoon. It is the symbol of the pain of love, and when separated lovers hear it, their hearts bleed anew. The mythic *sarang,* also called *chatrik*, is a symbol of divine love. It is always thirsty, like Nanak, and waits, its head tilted backwards, mouth open for not just any rain, but for that special drop of water called *swati,* that falls only when the moon is near the bright star called Arcturus."

"Yes, but the *swati* can fall anytime, whether the moon is full or in the house of Arcturus, or whether it is the monsoon. Don't take

---

11 A mythic bird that only drinks ambrosia. Described further on the next page.

myth too literally," the old man says to the stranger. "I think Nanak lies in that stanza. Who can be always thirsty? We are human and need what we need. But I think, from his *shabads*, he is beginning to learn that separation and union are the same thing."

"But to burn like Nanak burns in those words!" the stranger said.

"He was younger, still traveling all over the world. He composed that song for a priest in the temple of Jagannath. So I am told," the old man adds.

"Tell me the story!" The stranger says, eagerly.

"I will tell you!" Buddha replies instantly. He loves telling stories and has gathered many of them from Bhai Mardana, the aged, retired Minstrel who accompanied Guru Nanak on all his journeys.

"In their many wanderings they came upon the large, ancient and extremely wealthy temple of Jagannath."

"Jagannath means the Lord of this whole big universe, stars and horses and everything!" the girl explains, patting the rippling neck of the horse.

"In the sanctum was a statue of the Lord of the World, all dressed up in the finest clothes, with a crown of gold studded with shimmering diamonds. Devotees were lighting lamps and praying. The pandit[12] was just about to do *aarti.*"

"I know how to do aarti," the girl chimes in. "Take a plate, put a lamp on it; soak the wick in ghee, light it, pluck some pretty flowers, put them on the tray. Ask Bee Jee for rice, grains, lentils, and put them on it. Take an incense stick and light it. Put the plate in your hand, like this, and take the bell in the other hand, stand before Ma Durga's statue, look into her eyes, ring the bell, make circles around her, and sing the words of the aarti!"

"Except the plate in Jagannath was made of solid gold and so were the lamps and incense holder and the bell. Together with jasmines and marigolds, there were pearls, diamonds and other

---

12 High caste priest.

precious stones on the plate."

"Really?" the girl exclaims, wonder-eyed.

"Baba and Bhai Mardana stood and watched. And when the *aarti* was over, the priest, who had heard of Baba, said to him, 'If you truly believe there is no Hindu and no Muslim, that God can be approached through all religions, why didn't you pray with us?'

Baba told him to come at night to their camp outside town and he would tell him why. Baba prefers being in nature, under the trees and stars. A breeze had perfused the night with the smell of sandalwood and wild jasmine; the sky was brilliant with planets, stars and the crescent moon. In answer to the priest's query, Baba sang this *shabad*, his version of the *aarti* to the Lord of the Universe. The stanza you sang was the last stanza of that *shabad*.[13]

You'll hear this *shabad* again today.[14] Baba Nanak and the community sing it every evening. Here we are," Buddha says, coming to a halt before a wide-open double wooden door with iron studs. The rider alights, holds out his arms to the young girl who leaps into them.

"Go on in, make yourself comfortable. I'll tie your horse near the water trough and feed him some hay," the old man says.

Buddha ushers the travelers in, brings in a *manji*,[15] covers it with a clean sheet, asks the strangers to take a seat, and fetches two tumblers of water. As they sit and wait for Guru Nanak, Buddha quietly sweeps the courtyard.

"I want to sweep, too!" the girl says, and Buddha fetches her a broom. Soon the old man returns and asks if they are hungry. The strangers says 'no,' but the girl says, 'yes, very.' The old man goes into the house, returns and sits on the floor by the *manji*.

"No, no, come sit here with me," the stranger says, moving over.

---

13 A hymn, a sacred poem.

14 Explained below.

15 A strung wooden cot.

"I'm fine here. And what's your name?" The old man asks the little girl.

"Amro," she replies. "What will you give me to eat? Will you give me some *halwa*?"[16]

"Amro!" the stranger admonishes indulgently.

"We always have *kadaa parshaad*[17] ready. You can have it after your meal. And what is your name?" the boy asks the stranger.

"Lehna."

"Lehna. And what have you come to take, Lehna?"[18] The old man asks.

The stranger, who has never before been made aware of this twist to his name, laughs loudly and the old man joins him till the courtyard rings with laughter.

"Everything," Lehna jokes.

"You can't take everything without giving everything," Buddha says, joining in the laughter that is spontaneous, pure and vibrant under the luminescent, starry sky.

"Did you come to meet Guru Nanak or are you on your way somewhere else?" Buddha asks when the laughter quiets down.

"We are on a pilgrimage to Jwalamukhi[19] to dance and sing in the temple of Ma Durga," the girl adds.

"What is Jwalamukhi?" the boy asks.

"Don't you know?" The girl says. "It is where Ma Durga's blue tongues come out as fire from the rocks! She has nine tongues, and we give them milk and water to drink. Ma Durga is very powerful and if we don't go she will get angry with us, and then bad things

---

16 A sweet dish.

17 Made of flour, sugar and ghee, offered as Prasad, or blessing, to everyone who comes to the Gurdwara, the Sikh temple. It is a halwa.

18 'Lehna' also means 'to take.'

19 Jwalamukhi is a famous temple to the goddess Jwalamukhi, the deity of flaming mouth, also an epithet of Durga, built over some natural jets of combustible gas, believed to be the manifestation of the Goddess.

will happen. So we sing and dance to her to make her happy."

"Every year I take a group of pilgrims to Jwalamukhi. They didn't want to interrupt the journey to come to Kartarpur, but they are camped for the night and I have come to meet Nanak," Lehna explains.

"You should have brought them here. We have a *dharamsala*[20] to house and feed travelers."

"The pilgrims are not happy with me for wanting to meet Guru Nanak! They see it as a desertion and betrayal of Ma Durga. They fear she will punish me for looking elsewhere for spiritual guidance. To tell you the truth, I have also had some fears, but my longing to see Nanak is so intense I have to follow it. I adore Ma Durga, of course, as the embodiment of the feminine energy of the universe, but I have to admit that something in me is unfulfilled." Lehna stops, and then asks eagerly, "When will he be here?"

"Not long now," Buddha replies, looking at the old man. "Have you informed him?"

"He knows, but I will go and remind him." The old man disappears into a room in one corner of the courtyard.

"Dance and sing for us. Show us what you do at the temple," Buddha requests.

Amro looks at her father, who looks at her encouragingly.

"Come Phapa jee, do it with me." Shyly at first, but loosening up as her father joins her, she does a little dance and sings in praise of the Goddess, repeating the first and the last phrase between musical permutations of the lines:

Jai ambe gauri, mayya jai shyama gauri
Tum ko nish-din dhyavat, hari brahma shivji
Jai ambe gauri

The old man, dressed in white clothes, his long, white hair falling

20 A place of refuge, dwelling.

in curls about his shoulders, comes in and watches them silently. Lehna's strong supple body undulates lyrically, like a wave of energy. He is so surrendered to the dance as to be unaware of his audience.

The dance over, Lehna turns towards the old man, his face turning crimson in a flash of insight. At once embarrassed and delighted, he falls at his feet. Imitating him, Amro does the same.

"I am so blind!" Lehna stammers. "What a fool I am! Please forgive me… to let you lead my horse while I was on it… water and feed my animal… forgive me!" Lehna pleads.

"Come, come," Baba Nanak says, lifting him up and embracing him warmly. "We shouldn't have tricked you like this. Forgive *me.* But there is no fault anywhere. You are here, I am here, what more could we ask for?"

Several people trooping in through the door interrupt their interaction: musicians with their instruments, *rababs*[21] and *dholaks*,[22] children with their blankets, infants in their mothers' embrace, young boys and girls riding the shoulders of their fathers or being carried piggy back.

"Now you'll see and hear our *aarti*," Buddha says to Amro as he joins the others in spreading sheets and woven *darees*[23] on the floor.

"But where are the plates, the lamps, the flowers, the incense, the whisk to fan her with? Where is Ma Durga's statue?" Amro asks, holding the corners of the sheets and helping Buddha lay them down.

"We don't need those things for the type of *aarti* we're going to do. We pray to Akaal Purukh[24] who doesn't have clay noses and

---

21 A musical instrument, either plucked or played with a bow, also called rebec.

22 A round Indian drum with two heads.

23 Woven mats.

24 Akal means beyond time; Purukh is the Sikh variant of the Vedic Purush, the primeval, creative spirit embodied and personified by the human imagination, but not limited by it.

fake eyes like your idols."

"No hands and feet and face! Then how do you see her and touch her feet?"

"Akaal Purukh has many feet and faces and hands, but no hand, or feet or face. Akaal Purukh's faces and feet are the faces of every human and creature that lives in the universe."

"Even my feet are Akaal Purukh's feet?" Amro asks, looking at her mud-stained feet.

"Yes, and mine, too."

While Amro stands staring at her feet, stunned with awe, the musicians tune their instruments, clear their throats, and begin. With the first sounds of the vibrating strings, a silence falls in the courtyard.

In the night sky above the courtyard the orange hued bowl of the crescent moon lingers before setting; stars sparkle brightly; the *aarti* begins, everyone joining in, their voices ringing and rising in adoration.

"The sky is the plate; the moon and stars are the lamps and jewels; the forests of sandal wood are the temple incense; all the plants and flowers of the earth are offerings to you, O luminous Beloved, Lord of the Universe, destroyer of fear!"

CHAPTER 2

In the Kitchen

Mata[25] Sulakhni and Bebe Nanaki, silently washing the dishes in the kitchen after the evening meal, hear the sounds of a horse's hooves clattering on the cobbled street. Nanaki, the older of the two women, her grey hair tied into one long braid behind her, looks out of the window and exclaims,

"Guests! A young man and a lovely little girl! Vir[26] Jee and Buddha are leading them here!"

"Guests!" Sulakhni scoffs. "When we've just finished with the kitchen for the day! Just wait, he's going to come in here and say we have to feed them! And there are no left overs!"

Having washed, dried and shelved the dishes, they are about to leave the kitchen when Nanak comes in. Sulakhni says curtly:

"Dinner is finished. We've cleaned up. There's nothing left."

"But we can make more," Nanaki volunteers.

"The little girl is hungry and though the father won't admit it, he is too."

"We'll make something. Lakhmi hasn't returned from the hunt, and he'll be hungry too."

---

25 Mother.

26 An affectionate word for 'brother.' Generally, it is the word used for older brothers, but Nanaki calls Nanak by this name even though she is five years older than him.

Nanak leaves. Sulakhni says to Nanaki. "You offered. You cook."

"Okay, but could you please send Dhanvanti?"[27]

"Dharam[28] has a fever and she's taking care of him. You are on your own. You want to be good, be good yourself, Bebe. Don't drag others into your goodness."

"You can be bad and still help me a little?" Nanaki asks, very sweetly.

"No," Sulakhni says, leaving the kitchen.

Nanaki gathers her ingredients, flour and lentils from earthenware jars, a few small red onions, potatoes, tomatoes, cloves of garlic, ginger and an eggplant from a basket, and goes to work lighting a fire with cow dung patties. Jairam, Nanaki's husband, always tuned into her needs, comes into the kitchen and quietly begins to help her wash and chop the vegetables.

Shortly thereafter Sulakhni enters the kitchen, reaches for the bowl with the flour in it, pours some water into it, and begins to mix and kneed it aggressively.

"See?" Smiles Nanaki. "You do have a streak of goodness in you, Bhabi."[29]

"Don't you believe it," Sulakhni says. "I'm in the habit of doing my duty as a wife whether I feel like it or not, whether I'm tired or not."

"Jairam is helping me now. Go take your rest. I'm sure your husband won't say anything if you don't cook."

"Go ahead, believe the best of your Guru brother, and thank God you're not married to him. It is impossible to be the wife of a guru. You have to live up to his standards; become what he wishes you to be when you're made very differently; talk sweetly when what you really want to do is bark."

---

27 Lakhmi's wife.

28 Lakhmi and Dhanvanti's son.

29 Name for brother's wife.

"I'm sure you can bark sometimes! But tell me, does he speak sweetly to you, Bhabi?"

"You heard him. 'We have guests, cook dinner even though you have just finished cleaning up and are tired.'"

"It was a request. He asked sweetly, I thought. He was thinking of the strangers."

"But not of his wife. I'm sick of being sweet. All my life I've had a lock on my mouth."

"I don't remember that!" Nanaki laughs good-humoredly.

"Boiling water has to speak to let us know it is speaking, or it will burn down the pot and set your home on fire."

Jairam listens and marvels at the aptness of yet another of Mata Sulakhni's metaphors, of her expressive face and her wide gestures.

"What do you know what I have had to endure as his wife from the very beginning?" Sulakhni continues.

"I do know," Nanaki says.

"You were there at the wedding and saw how he made me the butt of jokes when he took only four *pheras*[30] around the fire and stopped the ceremony! I think it is because he didn't want to get married from the start!"

"Bhabhi, you are so wrong!"

"Yes, I'm always wrong and everyone else is always right!"

"Nanak's quarrel was with the ceremony itself! He wanted the whole universe to witness your wedding, not just fire! Vir Jee had said, 'I marry her with all of Nature as my witness.' He did the same thing during his *janeu*[31] ceremony. The *pandits* were all there, the goats had been sacrificed, the guests had arrived and he refused to wear it! They are just meaningless rituals, he said."

---

30 Circumambulations around fire during a Hindu wedding. The prescribed number is 7.

31 Strands of a sacred thread tied as a coming of age ceremony for a boy. Only high caste Hindus can do this ceremony which is supposed to make them pure.

"I understand your point of view, Mata Sulakhni," Jairam says.

"Yes, I'm the one who had to suffer the ridicule of the entire village. 'She's marrying a madman! She's marrying a madman!' They said. And when he went off on his journeys with Mardana and left me all alone in Sultanpur, without a roof over my head, with two little boys to take care of and feed, with everyone whispering 'He's left her! He's left her!' How do you know what I felt? Only my heart knows and it will shout and scream its story when it bursts in the fire of my pyre, and the whole world will hear what happened to the Guru's wife!"

Jairam and Nanaki go over to her to hug her, but Sulakhni's body is armored, rigid. Memory, in all its presence, its wounds still bleeding, has obliterated time and has her in its unyielding grip. In the absence of a pleasant present, she clings to the past, pressing its thorns against the pulp of her heart.

"But I did help out by adopting Chand," Nanak offers.

"By taking away my child, you mean! By making me choose which one I should give away!"

"Bhabi, you know it was your mother's decision to give us one of the boys, and you agreed. Who were we to demand or insist on it?" Jairam says softly.

"You couldn't make a child of your own and wanted to grab one of mine!" Sulakhni, with flour on her face, turns towards them with rage.

"I hadn't even thought about adopting one of your children, Bhabhi, I swear. I had been through my quarrels with Akal Purakh for not giving us a child, and surrenderedto Him the heavy burden of what He chose not to give me. I had already begun to see my barrenness as a gift when you and your mother came to us and made the suggestion. From resisting it initially, I came to see the rearing of Chand, too, as a gift."

"None of this would have happened if your Guru hadn't

abandoned me!"

"And I was there when Vir jee told you before he left that he would be faithful to you," Nanaki reminds.

"Faithful! It is worse to have a husband who is married to Akaal Purukh! God is his first wife and my rival! He only loves Her."

Jairam's laughter disperses some of the gravity in the air.

"He calls Akaal Purukh his husband," Nanaki corrects.

"Of course! It has to be a husband. If Akaal Purukh was a wife, your brother would have abandoned her long ago. Only a male can be Akaal Purukh. If it was Akal Istri, she would have made a better life for us females."

Jairam and Nanaki laugh together.

"It is so very sweet to love the way only a woman can love," Nanaki says.'That's why so many saints think of themselves as females in their devotion to Him who is both male and female and neither."

"Yes, yes, you know so much. Whatever or whoever he is married to I am her rival. Now he is upset at the boys for not being what he wants them to be. He had very little to do with their upbringing so why is he complaining now? And I am to pretend to myself that everything God does is for the best when I want to scream, "It's not right; it's not fair!" Sulakhni says, clattering the metal bowl rather loudly on the stone floor as she pounds the dough with both her fists.

Nanaki says, "Shhh! Our guests will hear you and feel unwelcome."

"Good! Let them hear this *kirtan*[32] of life."

Nanaki and Jairam laugh again, delightedly.

"He doesn't like his sons."

"Not true!" Nanaki says quickly. "What a loving father he was in Sultanpur before he left on his journeys, playing *gulidanda* and

32 Hymns sung to accompaniment.

kabaddi[33] with them, teaching them to swim in the Beini River."

"Yes, yes, but was isn't is. Now he doesn't like that they have turned out so different from him. He insists that Chand and Lakhmi get up early in the morning, meditate, yoke the bullocks to their plows and till the fields. They don't want to. Neither of them is obedient enough for him."

"We have to admit they're not," Nanaki replies. "Vir Jee believes we have to carry our own weight and do whatever needs to be done."

"You should take some responsibility for their turning out the way they did."

Nanaki, hurt to the quick, says with an edge to her voice: "You think I am to blame? I only... loved them."

"You spoilt them. You let them do what they liked."

"Children must be allowed to become what they are. They were like this even as infants. Chand was always serious, disciplined, aloof, and Lakhmi naughty, haughty, quick-tempered, but also loving. You had a hand in their upbringing, too."

"But they always ran to you. They only did their duty by me."

"That's not true! You can't feel like that!"

"Who are you to tell me how I can't feel? What do you know? Nothing!" Sulakhni shouts back.

They work in silence for a while, chopping, cutting, stoking the fire, rolling the bread and baking it on the skillet to the strains of the *aarti* coming in through the courtyard. When the meal is almost ready, Nanaki says, "It's true."

"What?"

"I know nothing. I have to keep coming back to this place: I know nothing. It's actually a great place to be; very liberating."

"Why did the two of you move to Kartarpur? Couldn't you have stayed in your own house in Sultanpur? What was the need?"

---

33 A game with a bat and stick, and wrestling.

"He invited us, Bhabhi," Jairam says, softly.

"We moved to be near him. And you. And the children," Nanaki explains.

"Why don't you just say 'him' and the 'children'? No, don't give me a hug. Your hands are dirty."

"I'm sorry if I gave you the impression that I leave you out of my affections."

"You do."

Nanaki is quiet a long time. While her hands are in the dough, pinching off bits of the lump and shaping it between her hands into a ball, then rolling it out on a floured board with the pin, she has withdrawn deeply into herself as she thinks:

She is right, Nanaki, admit it. You've always thought she was unenlightened and coarse compared to him. Meditate on this, Nanaki. Meditate on this deeply.

"I'm sorry, Bhabhi. I'll pay attention to what you said. Forgive me."

The door opens and Lakhmi, with four dead partridges strung over his shoulder, strides in.

"I'm hungry!" he says, looking into the pot. "Oh the same old food every day! I'm in the mood for meat!"

"Cook it yourself, then," Sulakhni says.

"Bhua?"[34] he asks, giving Nanaki a hug.

Nanaki wasn't about to offer cooking the partridges after her recent encounter with Sulakhni, and turns away. "It's too much work right now."

"I'll do it," Jairam volunteers, reaching for the partridges and beginning to pluck them.

"Oh you're such a special man!" Lakhmi says, putting his arm around his shoulders.

"I want to eat them too," Jairam chuckles.

---

34 Name for father's sister.

"I also brought two homeless puppies from the street and they are hungry. I've put them in the barn."

"Puppies!" cries Nanaki, excitedly.

"Puppies! As if we don't have enough to do! More mouths to cook and slave for," Sulakhni says. "Give them away!"

"No. One is for Dharam. Where is he? Where is Dhanvanti? Why isn't she helping you?"

"Dharam has a fever and Dhanvanti is taking care of him."

"A fever! Have you called the Hakim?"[35]

"He's fine, don't worry so much," Nanaki assures him.

Lakhmi leaves hurriedly to check on his young son while Nanaki and Sulakhni bring out the plates, place bowls on them into which they pour the different dishes, stack up the bread smeared with ghee, and place a gob of thick yogurt near it.

"Do you have to give so much ghee to strangers?" Sulakhni asks. "The old cow isn't giving milk."

"It's already melted," Nanaki says, a bit annoyed with Sulakhni.

They carry the plates of food to the courtyard where the congregation has left after having generous helpings of *kadaa prasad*, and place them before their guests.

---

35 Doctor.

CHAPTER 3

A Birth

"Amro," Lehna calls his daughter, "Come, eat."

"What is this?" she asks, pointing at the rabab[36] leaning against the wall, touching the strings. Her father admonishes her.

"It's all right," Baba Nanak says. "We encourage children to learn the instrument. It is called a rabab."

"The food will get cold," Sulakhni scolds.

"Come, eat first, Amro," Baba Nanak says, "and then you can play with it."

Amro and Lehna eat heartily and quietly while Sulakhni and Nanaki fetch glasses of water, help Buddha fold the sheets, *darees* and stack them in the corner again.

"Baba jee," Amro asks Baba Nanak between bites, "Will you give me a rabab?"

"*I'll* give you one," Nanaki says. "Bhai Phiranda, the rabab maker, brought many *rababs* for the congregation, including some smaller ones for children."

"Wait till she's done eating," Sulakhni says.

"Can girls play rababs and sing?" Buddha asks. "Aziza's mother says girls mustn't do such things. They are not pure enough."

"Not pure enough!" Nanaki says. "How can they not be pure when, as Baba Nanak says, they birth emperors and saints! They

36 A musical instrument, either plucked or played with a bow, also called rebec.

birth the world!"

"Ma Durga is a girl," Amro adds.

Just as Lehna and Amro finish eating, Baba Nanak fetches a hoe from the cowshed and hands it to Lehna, saying, "There is work to be done."

"At this time of the night? Is this the way to treat a guest?" Sulakhni asks her husband, not very politely.

"Don't question him," Nanaki says. "He has his reasons."

"Reasons! He's losing his reason! Where is there any reason for going to the field at night!"

Lehna quietly follows Baba Nanak out of the courtyard into the starlit night.

"He's gone mad!" Sulakhni says, beating her head with her fist as she leaves the courtyard.

Nanaki goes into the house and fetches a small rabab.

"You never gave *me* a rabab," Buddha complains.

"You asked for a bow and arrow, not a rabab. But of course, if I only had one rabab you would get it first, Buddha jee." Nanaki says, handing it to him. "But we have enough, Amro. I'll get one for you, too."

"One for Aziza, too?" Buddha asks.

"Of course."

"Can I have a bow and arrow, too?" Amro asks.

"You're a girl," Buddha says.

"Girls must be warriors, too," Nanaki says as she goes inside to fetch the items, returns with another rabab, a small children's set of bow, quiver, arrows and gives them to Amro.

"Hold the rabab like this, the bow goes in this hand, and leave the wrist that holds the bow loose, like this," Nanaki demonstrates.

The two children, very excited, make some screechy sounds while Nanaki instructs them further about the positioning of the instrument and fingering.

"And," she says, producing two, small, hand-made *pothis*[37] from the pockets in her *kameez*,[38] "These are for you as well. But you must wash your hands before I give them to you. They are very precious and must be handled with love and care."

The two children go off to wash their hands from the water jars in the courtyard, and return.

"What is it?" Amro asks.

"I've been sewing them and writing Baba Nanak's *Japji*[39] in them."

"What does it say?" Amro asks, opening it in awe.

"The first word in it is 'One.' Just learn that."

"But I already know 'one.' I know two and three and four all the way to one hundred."

"Good. But just remember, 'One.' That is your homework, Amro. And next time we'll learn some more, but you always have to keep coming back to the first lesson, 'One.'"

"One," repeat the children in unison.

"And, we have another surprise. There are two little puppies in the barn!"

"Puppies!" cry the children.

"Take them home with you," Sulakhni says to Amro, poking her head through the door.

"But we already have two dogs," Amro says.

Eager to see them, the children and Nanaki go to the barn carrying two bowls of milk with cream in them. They spot two fuzzy little fawn colored puppies with black noses, black paws and ears, cuddled up on a pile of straw.

"Let them sleep a little. This is the pregnant buffalo that is going to give birth any day now," Nanaki says, pointing to a huge black

---

37 A pothi is a handmade notebook. For the Sikhs it means a sacred book.

38 A long shirt worn by both men and women.

39 The first composition of Sikh scripture.

buffalo, covered in dry mud. Beneath a broad forehead from which two large horns curve down then spiral up, her eyes are round and dilated. The buffalo looks at the visitors and bellows. Nanaki pats her forehead.

"Is she a girl buffalo? Because only girls can have babies. Can I have babies? Do all girls have babies?" Amro asks.

"No. Not all. I didn't."

"Why?"

"I don't know why," Nanaki replies.

The sound of a little bark tells them the puppies are awake. They feed them milk and watch as they slurp it all up. Then they pick them up and play with them in the straw.

"Bebe Nanaki, Amro doesn't know who Akaal Purukh is," Buddha says.

"I don't know who Akaal Purukh is, either!" Nanaki says. "Nobody does!"

"No, tell!"

Nanaki puts Amro on her lap and asks,

"Have you ever been frightened and alone?"

"Ummm… let me think. When I got lost in town when Phapa jee took me one day. I went into a street and looked at red, yellow and blue bangles, and when I stopped looking, he wasn't there and I was frightened and alone. I was afraid a bad man and a witch were going to carry me away, like they carried away my friend, Sukhi, and I couldn't find my owner anywhere and I started to cry."

"Owner?" Nanaki asks, full of surprise that a child would use such a word. "And then what happened?"

"Then I don't know how but I knew I would find my house. I started walking and when I reached the fields and there were two roads and I didn't know which one to take, I was frightened again."

"And then?"

"Something, I don't know what, told me if I took this road I would find home. And I ran and ran and saw the bridge on the river and there was our village! Bee Jee was there to give me a hug, and I told her everything, and Phapa jee also came after a long time looking for me, looking worried but when he saw me, he dropped everything he was carrying and picked me up!"

"That something that told you which road to take is Akaal Purukh, Amro. You can never see Akaal Purukh because..."

"...He has no face but many faces and no feet but many feet, like mine and the feet of ants and insects," Amro says eagerly.

"Very good!"

"*I* told her that," Buddha boasts.

"Akaal Purukh is our Companion when we are alone and frightened. He is the Friend who brings us home when we are lost. Above all Akaal Purukh is our Owner, Amro."

"Like Phapa jee and Bee jee are mine?"

"Yes, except Akaal Purukh is your father and mother's owner, too, and everyone else's. Your parents love you, don't they?"

Amro nods vigorously.

"Akaal Purukh is our Owner and loves us like they love us."

"Once Bee jee slapped me when I didn't want to go to school for a long time, not ever."

"Why didn't you want to go to school?" Nanaki asks Amro.

"My teacher doesn't like me."

"Oh, my little one," Nanaki says, stroking her hair. "How can anyone not like you?"

Amro cries a little, then says, "She's a witch. I don't like witches. They frighten me. "

"Akaal Purukh gives us courage to defeat witches."

"Is He Ma Durga's husband?" Amro asks. "She is dressed like a bride in a red sari and wears earrings and bangles that are very pretty. Ma Durga protects us, too."

"Does she move and dance like you?" Buddha asks.

"Are you stupid? Statues don't move," Amro explains.

"My Akaal Purukh moves. He is the movement of the world. We wouldn't move if we didn't have His movement," Buddha says proudly.

Nanaki marvels at Buddha's words.

"How can you love someone who doesn't have a face? Ma Durga has a face."

"Then love Ma Durga," Nanaki says. "Ma Durga is also Akaal Purukh. But know that a statue of Ma Durga is only an image, a reminder of Akaal Purukh."

"What is an image?"

"I can explain that," Buddha says, picking up a stick and drawing a vertical line on the dirt floor, and a circle around the line. He leaves one side of the divided circle blank, and on the other half he draws little stick animal and human figures, a tree and a house.

"On this side," he says, pointing to the side he has left blank, "is the Land of the Invisible. You can't see anything. This is the Land from which we come. As soon as we cross the line from the invisible to the visible, we start to see and be seen. The things we see are images. This side is the Land of Images, the things we see, touch, hear, smell and taste. Images only live for a short time and then die. You and I and everything we see are images. When we die, we go back to the Land of the Invisible. That is why dead people cannot be seen or heard, but they are there, back where they came from."

He draws some figures returning across the line, and then rubs them out again with his foot. "But in the Land of the Invisible they have no bodies because they are not images anymore, and are invisible to our eyes."

Nanaki looks at him in awe, and then asks again, "Very clever. Are you sure?"

"Yes, I am."

Nanaki rubs out Buddha's drawing, and says, "But maybe there is no line. Maybe there is no circle. Truth is beyond our imagination though our imagination can take us a little closer to it. The Awakened Ones have glimpses of it, but they can't tell about it because though words are lovely, they stop at the threshold of Truth which is beyond words, lines and circles."

"How do you know?" Buddha asks.

"I don't know. I don't know anything," Nanaki says. "Maybe it is better not to think we know. Maybe it's all so big and boundless, so magical and far more mysterious than our brains can imagine."

Buddha is silent and confused by her words.

"But I think I am right," he says.

"Maybe you are!"

"And Baba is right when he says that Akaal Purukh is everything."

"Even this puppy? Is this puppy Akaal Purukh?"

"Yes!" Says Nanaki, cuddling the puppy close.

"Look, look," Buddha exclaims, pointing to the buffalo, which has turned her back to them, and lifted up her tail. Something white, like a sack, protrudes out of her. The children, puppies in their arms, stand and watch in holy silence the primeval drama happening before their eyes.

"The calf is coming into the Land of Images!" Buddha says, pleased at the synchronicity of the event.

The translucent sack, with something dark inside it, becomes larger and longer till finally it falls to the ground with a gush and a splash of water and blood. The calf's long, folded legs poke out of the sack like two stiff black sticks with hooves at the end of them.

Nanaki begins to remove the white sack surrounding the tiny calf.

"Come, help me," she says to the children, who are kneeling down and removing parts of the caul still clinging to the tiny calf which looks like a big mouse with its eyes closed. Mewing like a cat it calls its mother who licks it lovingly. For a short while it struggles to stand up, falling and stumbling many times, but as they watch, it stands up on wobbly legs and walks haltingly to seek its mother's udders and begins to suckle.

CHAPTER 4

Worms and Butterflies

"Bhai Mardana jee! Aziza!" Buddha calls, skipping into the courtyard of Bhai Mardana's house, carrying his *rabab*, bow and arrows, the puppy following him stumbling over the threshold.

Bhai Mardana, face wrinkled, eyes sunken into their sockets, a few front teeth missing, sits up on his cot under the guava tree in the courtyard and smiles broadly.

"My friend! And who is this?" He asks, extending his arms to the puppy. Buddha picks her up and hands her to him. When she begins to lick his face, Bhai Mardana laughs in happy, childlike delight.

"Bhai Lakhmi rescued two puppies from the street and Mata Sulakhni doesn't want to keep any, but Bhai Lakhmi kept one for Dharam and this one is for Aziza."

"What's her name?" Bhai Mardana asks.

"We haven't named her yet."

"Motia. Yes, let's call her Motia!" Mardana says, excitedly.

His wife, Fatima, comes into the courtyard carrying a basket of fleece. Seeing the puppy, she exclaims, "Moti has come back to you as a female!"

"Yes, she does sort of look like him!"Mardana says.

"Moti died the day after you came back from your travels and both of you were so sad at yet another separation that he reincarnated to come back to love you some more!" Fatima says.

"*Kabir kookar ram ko, Motia mera naam, galay hamaree jayvaree, jah khinchai tah jaon*," Mardana recites, then explains Kabir's[40] verse to Buddha: "Kabir says, I am my Beloved's dog, Motia. I wear his collar and follow him wherever he takes me."

"How are you doing, Mardana jee?" Buddha asks, bouncing a ball up and down.

"I say to God, I will go where you take me. I will stay where you make me stay. I will live if you make me live, and die when you kill me," Mardana answers.

Buddha stops playing with his ball, bows his head and touches Mardana's feet. "I will pray this prayer, too, Mardana jee. Thank you."

"Buddha! Buddha! Buddhu! Guddhu!" Aziza says, skipping into the courtyard with an armload of cow patties. She drops the patties at the sight of the puppy in her grandfather's lap.

"Is this ours?" She asks hopefully, picking it up. The puppy licks her face all over. Aziza sees the *rabab* that Buddha has left standing by the bed, and drops the puppy on the ground so suddenly, she whelps.

"Where did you get this? Whose is this?" She stammers.

"Bebe Nanaki gave it to me. She said Bhai Phiranda made a few small ones for children. They are very good quality," Buddha explains.

"They couldn't be otherwise. He's the best *rabab* maker in the world," Mardana says.

"Bebe Nanaki gave one to Amro. She said girls are pure enough to play them. They are pure because they give birth to the whole world! Bebe has one for you, too, Aziza, just like this one. Why don't you take this and I'll take the other one. Here."

---

40 A saint whose dates of birth and death are uncertain, but generally accepted to be 1440 – 1518. Over 450 of Kabir's compositions are included in the Sri Guru Granth Sahib (SGGS), the Sikh holy book.

Buddha holds it out to her and Aziza, stunned with a feeling greater than delight or joy, reaches for it gently, lovingly, and cradles it in her arms. She looks up at her grandfather, her eyes wide and brimming with tears, and says quietly, "See? This is the message, Daadu Jaan."[41]

Buddha looks at her questioningly, and she explains, "Daadu said if God sends me a strong message, I can play the *rabab*. It couldn't be stronger than this!"

"Tell Bebe Nanaki to keep her rabab. Aziza can't have one," Nasreen, Aziza's mother, shouts from the corner of the courtyard where she squats on the *thadaa*,[42] vigorously scrubbing pots and pans with ash.

Aziza's face screws up in sudden, spontaneous anger. She stomps her foot and says, "I want it."

"You will go into purdah[43] soon so how are you going to play the *rabab*? And who is going to feed the dog?"

Nasreen washes her hands quickly, grabs the *rabab* out of her daughter's hands and thrusts it back into Buddha's arms. "And we can't keep the dog either. Take it back." Aziza bursts into tears and runs screaming into her grandmother, Fatima's, arms.

"I will feed the dog," Fatima says, looking at her husband holding the puppy near his heart.

"And say something about the *rabab*, too, Daadi Jaan!"[44] Aziza shouts.

---

41 Daadu is an affectionate variation of "dada" or "paternal grandfather," and Jaan means "my life," an affectionate endearment.

42 A stone or slate portion in the courtyard of a house where dishes are washed and which also serves, with a curtain around it, as a bathing area, or a small area on the ground, in doors or out, that is well worn, its soil pounded down by use, and used as a floor to sit upon.

43 Purdah literally means curtain. Here it means the dress Muslim girls wear when they come of age. Also called a burqua, or a baya.

44 Paternal grandmother.

"She has a few years left before she goes into purdah," Fatima adds.

"Better be careful," Mardana whispers to Fatima. "Ask her father first."

"Haven't I already told you?" Nasreen says, beginning to scrub the utensils even more vigorously.

"As the elder in the house I insist on it," Fatima says, taking the *rabab* from Buddha and giving it to Aziza.

"You don't know what you are starting," Mardana warns his wife, his features contorted with worry.

"When will things start to *change*?" Fatima says, her voice verging on a scream.

Aziza takes the *rabab* from her grandmother with extreme reverence, and goes into the loom room to be alone with it, as with a long, long lost friend. She has keenly observed and heard her father and relatives playing it all her life, and doesn't need to be told how to hold it. Even her first, tentative tuning of it has a measure of mastery, so when she starts to play it a bit, everyone in the courtyard stops in brief wonder.

"*Hukum. Hukum, Hukum,*"[45] says Mardana, nodding his head as if to nobody, and calming down with each repetition. "So, tell me, Buddha jee, what's happening at the dera?"

"A stranger, a dancer came to the *dera* yesterday with his daughter, Amro. We played a joke on them!"

Buddha recounts the story of the previous night in great detail, emphasizing the things that impressed him most, especially Amro asking for and getting a bow and arrow from Bebe Nanaki.

"A bow and arrow to a girl!" Nasreen says in a very audible whisper.

"Is she pretty, this Amro?" Aziza asks.

---

45 A very rich word in Sikh philosophy meaning "Divine Law," but in this instance meaning, "Your will, Your will."

"Not as pretty as you, but her hair is neater," Buddha replies.

Nasreen drops an earthenware jar full of water on the bricked floor with a loud crash. As Buddha continues with his tale after a pause, Daulatan Masi,[46] who hardly ever participates in family matters, hobbles over to Mardana's bed and listens intently, the whites of her half-blind eyes rolling in her head.

"Mists, mists," Daulatan intones, waving her arms about her head, as if removing cobwebs from her face. "I can see very little very clearly. Fire, cool fire full of jewels, so many,… orange, red, blue, rising like a wave, water from a spring gushing from the fire. Two… no, three… such kind flames, so kind, so kind, so kind. He will bring salt and take saffron. His clothes will be so beautifully dirty," she laughs her face relaxed deeply. "Wait for the gold! Eat the dead man!" She pretends to chew. "Tasty, tasty! *Kadaa parshad!* When the wall made of sand falls it will be built again and never fall down again. Never, never, never."

"Bhai Mardana jee, will you tell me the story of what happened to Daulatan Masi?" Buddha asks when Daulatan Masi retreats into her corner again and becomes still.

"I'll tell you, I've heard it so many times, though it happened so many, many years ago when Daadu was just ten years old," Aziza says, coming over with the rabab, and playing chords as she tells the story.

"You know, Masi was the midwife at Baba Nanak's birth, though she didn't have to do anything because Nanaki, Mata Tripta[47] and Baba's grandmother did everything. Masi wasn't allowed to hold Baba Nanak when he was an infant; she was not allowed to touch him, perhaps because we are Muslims, who are considered low caste people by Hindus."

---

46 Masi means mother's sister. Also used for an elderly lady. Here it means Mardana's Masi.

47 Guru Nanak's mother. Mata means mother but is also used as an honorific.

"But Baba…" interrupts Buddha.

"I know Baba has changed a lot of that, though it still lives on in the minds and hearts of people," Mardana says.

"Back then Muslims were not allowed to eat with high caste people, like the Bedis. Baba is a Bedi. Masi could only wash his clothes and rock him in his cradle. One day Daulatan Masi came home from their house, her hair was wild, her eyes crazy, as if she had seen a ghost, or gone mad. She didn't speak, couldn't speak, and the family thought she had become dumb. Daadu's mother, Masi's older sister, went to the Bedis' house to find out what happened. Mata Tripta didn't know anything but Bebe Nanaki seemed to know something, though she's never told us what. Bebe Nanaki went to Masi's house – she used to live alone then, she never married, never wanted to marry. After she got old we brought her to our house to take care of her. Bebe Nanaki embraced her, touched her head, and Masi calmed down. But she was never the same again. She lost most of her eyesight, but she sees things inside her head. She doesn't speak except in bursts like this, which make no sense to us."

"Did you ever find out what happened?"

"Bebe Nanaki said one day she saw Masi kissing the baby Nanak's feet. We didn't understand why this would cause her to go mad."

Buddha is silent a long time. Mardana reaches for Aziza's rabab and inspects it. "Very well made."

"You can't have it Daadu. It's mine. But you can play it sometime. Come, Buddha, I want to show you something," Aziza says, skipping over to the guava tree in the courtyard and lifting up a few leaves. Buddha sees three silken cocoons, some larva spinning shrouds from filaments and a few caterpillars feeding ravenously.

"You know, these ugly worms go into their fortress, which is their cocoon, and they come out with wings!" Aziza says with amazement and delight, her arms spread wide as she skips around the courtyard.

"Fortress!" Buddha exclaims.

"Inside our bodies is a city," Aziza explains.

"Oh, you are using images from Baba's *shabads*," says Mardana, who has sung Baba's *shabads* repeatedly so his entire family knows them well.

"Yes, and inside the city is a fortress with locked gates. When you say the name of the Nameless Beloved, the doors swing wide open. You can go inside, crawling on your many legs, like a caterpillar, and find Allah. Then your skin bursts like a mango full of juice and you become a beautiful butterfly with colored wings that can go anywhere at all!" Aziza exclaims.

Mardana and Fatima look at each other and smile.

CHAPTER 5

Proof in the Dream

Lehna walks through the large wooden door into the courtyard of his house in Khadur. For a moment he stands and watches his wife, Khivi, her back towards him, teaching some village children and their two sons, Dasu and Datu,[48] how to read and write. As they write the visible equivalent of the vowels on their wooden tablets, they recite it aloud.

"A aaa, e eee, o ooo, aw awe."

"Bee Jee, Bee Jee," Amro bursts in, holding up the rabab, a bow, and a quiver full of tiny arrows. "Look what Bebe Nanaki gave me. I love her and we saw a girl cow give birth, and there was blood and snot, long strands of it, and because I am a girl I am going to give birth, too, only it will be a girl or a boy, and not a calf."

Khivi turns around, surprised at her daughter and husband's presence in the house. He and Amro were supposed to be at Jwalamukhi for the yearly festival of Ma Durga. But she withholds her questions to hug her daughter.

The household dogs, too, run in from the street to greet them.

"And I met Akaal Purukh, too, and he is a puppy," Amro adds.

Dasu and Datu run up to their father and hug him, though their attention is riveted on the bow and arrow, and before long the

48 Bhai Lehna's sons.

children are squabbling over it. Datu forcefully takes them away, and Dasu the rabab, leaving Amro in tears.

"Give them back to her," Khivi says calmly and firmly. "They are hers."

"She is not a boy and bows and arrows are for boys," Datu says, running away with his loot.

"And she didn't get anything for us," Dasu adds, not knowing what the rabab is or whether he even wanted it, but holding it tightly in his hands, anyway.

"Give them back to her," Lehna says. "Bebe Nanaki is a very kind woman who loves children and she will give you bows, arrows and rababs, too."

"I want this one," Datu says, trying to fit an arrow into the bow but because he has only a rudimentary knowledge about stringing it, he aims it downwards and succeeds in hurting his own foot and screaming in pain.

"Come, give it back to her or you'll hurt yourself further."

"No! No! I won't!" he screams, limping around the courtyard.

Dasu reluctantly returns the rabab to Amro after trying and failing to figure out what to do with it.

"Good boy!" Lehna says, "Come, I'll wrestle with you." The boys charge their father, Dasu in delight, and Datu in rage, and the other children who had been watching the drama, join in, and for a while everything is playful and very merry in the courtyard.

Khivi quietly picks up the rabab, the toy weapon and goes into the *kothari*[49] that serves as a family room. Amro, wiping away her tears, tiny sobs still escaping her grimaced face, follows her.

"And she's going to teach me how to play the rabab. See, you hold it like this," she demonstrates. "And this is how you play *sa*."[50]

Later in the evening, after supper, when the children are asleep,

49 A dark room made of mud walls in which kitchen supplies are stored.

50 The first note in the Indian musical scale.

Khivi turns eagerly to Lehna.

"Something has happened to you," she said. "I can see it in your eyes. You have never looked like this before, except when you told me you had heard Bhai Jodha singing. That day, too, you had the same look in your eyes that I can't describe. They are glowing with fire. And where are your ankle bells?"

"O Khivi," Lehna begins, tears gathering in his eyes. "I have taken them off to dance to the Invisible Lord and Lady of the Galaxies! I danced for the goddess in the temple, but now my whole existence will be a dance!" He is silent a long time and Khivi sits quietly by his side.

"I have found what my soul has been searching for, what I didn't even know I was looking for!"

After another silence, he narrates to his wife the events of the last few days.

"When I started out with the pilgrims I had hoped I could persuade them to make a stop in Kartarpur so I could meet the author of the song that so moved me. I didn't think they would agree, but I hoped anyway. We were delayed upon starting out, as you know, on account of some of the pilgrims being late, and by the time we broke our journey for the night I realized I was very near Kartarpur. I mounted my horse, took Amro with me, and arrived at Kartarpur just as the new moon shone brightly in the evening sky. I asked an old man and a young boy…"

And here Lehna bursts into tears. "I am so blind and full of pride! I let him lead me on as if he were my servant while I sat like a lord on my horse! I let him feed and water my horse! That's how humble he is!"

It was a while before he could tell his wife the rest of the story about the evening he had spent in Kartarpur, the meal, Nanaki, and Sulakhni. After he tells her about the *aarti,* and sings a few lines, he stops his narrative once more to explain the impact the meeting with Nanak has had on him.

"My skull blew off and infinity poured in. No, Khivi, I cannot explain the experience. It felt like I had been living in a small, dark, sunless cave all my life and Baba's voice and words blew off the roof of my brain, crumbled the walls and something unbounded, immeasurable and utterly mysterious poured in."

Khivi sits quietly in his silence.

"I experienced a different way of being, of living in such an open, spacious way… my little version of 'god' was blown apart to include the universe and everything in it. I saw another way of dancing, Khivi, with my whole being, as if 'I' didn't dance but was danced… do you know what I mean?"

"I think so. Sometimes I think *I* do not live but am lived through."

"Exactly. Baba calls this *sehaj*,[51] that which is natural, spontaneous, like a flower, folding from the inside out. I know with absolute certainty that this is the path for me now. I have given my small self away."

"You've abandoned Ma Durga?" Khivi asks after her husband grows silent. Her heart is full of trepidation and fear for her husband, herself, her entire family. Their families had worshipped Durga as far back as she can remember.

"Don't be afraid of the unknown, Khivi. Baba says when you fear Akaal Purukh, all other fears are frightened away. And Akaal Purukh, who we mirror in our souls, is *nirbhao*, and *nirvair*: without fear and enmity."

"What happened to the pilgrims?"

"I explained to them what had happened to me, that I could no longer worship a few flames coming out of the rocks; when the Beloved is everywhere, what need is there to go to the far corners

---

51 Variously spelled: sahaj, saihaj, seheja. A state arrived at when one surrenders one's ego and lives spontaneously, naturally, fulfilling oneself without effort or will, in the flow of things.

of the earth to find Him? I quoted Baba's words to them: *To find truth, make a pilgrimage to the sacred shrine within your self, and inhabit it.* They said they would worship only Ma Durga and nothing and nobody else. I explained that all the forms and statues we worship of Kali are just small images for our small minds, reminders of the vast and unbound Beloved Being beyond time, beyond image. I wanted to expand their minds but they wanted to stay in their tiny little dark corners. They were very angry with me for jeopardizing their pilgrimage. A priest that runs away! They were appalled and frightened at their perceived consequences on me for stepping out of my family and community's faith. Their concerns sounded so hollow and superstitious to me. I saw what I had been in them, my life in an old, tight little skin, and didn't like it. I had been wearing blinders and veils that Guru Nanak has removed like cobwebs from my brain. The purpose of my pilgrimage has been fulfilled in Kartarpur. The pilgrims chose another priest from amongst them. All of me must serve one purpose now. I would rather be Guru Nanak's slave than lead a world full of such people!"

"But… you were also such a person. Have compassion."

Lehna looks at his wife, his eyes misting over with love, and says, "you are absolutely right, my love. Thank you for humbling me. You look worried, my Khivi."

"Every time I make dough I am reminded of how malleable the human brain can be, how easy to mold this way or that. Sickness, a dream, a desire can affect it."

"No, Khivi, this is not a trick my mind is playing with me. I have proof. The night I spent in Kartarpur I had a dream… many dreams, in fact. But let me tell you one. I am in Baba's courtyard and it is morning. A woman wearing a sari, the moon like a bouquet of jasmines in her long hair like a stream of night, is bent over something, near her, on the floor, is the sea… the huge roaring thing right there at her feet in the courtyard! She is taking a jar full of water, like liquid moonlight, and pouring it on something. I go closer and see that Baba is lying on his *manji,* his hair open and hanging down, like this," he demonstrates. "She is washing his hair, very lovingly, with a lot of devotion. She turns around, and it is Ma Durga! She smiles at me, then continues washing his hair." Lehna laughs long and hard. "Ma Durga whom we worship washes Nanak's hair, Khivi! It is a sign that she herself has led me to Nanak."

After a pause he resumes.

"I had many dreams, not quite dreams. I was taken through the hurtling stream of time, living moments of the future: I have thirteen turbans on my head and I am digging, digging; I am put on a skillet above a fire and hot sand is being poured on me."

"Oh," cried Khivi.

"I wade in a stream to cool myself, a rabab player sings to me, calming me; I am riding a horse into battle, and I have three beautiful wives."

"Oh!" cries Khivi, again.

"You have nothing to fear, my love!" He says, holding her close.

"In another my head is chopped off; but I must have been alive because someone stuck a knife into my belly, here; I am fighting in a battle and I am a woman! Don't look so worried, my Khivi! All is well, and better than well. I am being prepared to be fearless."

"So what are you going to do now?"

"Go to Kartarpur, live in the dera, be his servant, work in the fields. It is a magical place, Khivi, you will love it. People from all religions, Hindus, Muslims, Sufis, talk about their paths and study each other's. There is no bigotry, just openness to knowledge and wisdom from all traditions and sources. Baba has attracted many musicians who sing and teach raags[52] to people of all ages, from

52 Meaning "color" or "hue": a melodic mode in Indian classical music of five or more notes upon which various melodies are improvised.

little children to even old people! Baba reveres these musicians, even though they are from low castes. Theatre troupes visit the dera; arts and crafts are encouraged, and the place is teeming with scholars, poets, musicians, mystics, and warriors. Manual labor and physicality is given the highest regard. Martial arts are also taught! Baba believes the body is the house of the divine, and must be kept clean and healthy. And the *langar*![53] You must come with me, Khivi. Fresh vegetables and fruits are brought in daily from the fields and orchards. The women grow herbs and season the food so wonderfully."

"Really?" Khivi says, catching a bit of his excitement.

"And you will love the school for children!"

Khivi's eyes sparkle.

"I was thrilled when Baba talked about inventing a new script for Sikh scripture. A new alphabet! You know how interested I am in language! In another dream I saw all these letters swarming around me, like bees around a flower. It will be a script for the spoken language of Punjab, for the common people, unlike Sanskrit and Persian that nobody knows how to speak, read or write. When he saw my interest, he asked me to help him with it. I felt he had been waiting for me to arrive!"

"But how will you earn a living?"

Lehna looks at Khivi. He hasn't given it a thought.

"Things will work out, Khivi. Just wait and see. We need to trust in the power that makes all things happen."

"We need to be practical. We have three children."

"Yes, I know. But Akaal Purukh always opens another door when one closes."

"I don't know what to think, but I trust the glow on your face. I

---

53 A kitchen run by volunteers that feeds people, regardless of caste, religion, and social status.

have been teaching and giving cooking lessons for free. I will charge a small fee. I will turn one of the cow sheds into a small school."

"In the morning let's go shopping for some white cloth. Make me two sets of white clothes, Khivi, I'm going back to Kartarpur."

CHAPTER 6

Intimations

Buddha skips into Mardana's courtyard, Dharam Chand and his puppy, Shera, in tow, a bow and quiver slung on his shoulder, singing off key with gusto. His visits are always happy events and no one wants to miss out on those. Daulatan Masi hobbles in with a big smile, and sits down on a *peedee;*[54] Fatima sits at the edge of Mardana's bed, carding fleece; Mardana awakens from his doze, sits up, welcomes the six-year-old Dharam Chand into his arms, while his puppy, Motia, jumps off the bed and greets her playmate Shera rambunctiously.

"You haven't come for so long!" Mardana says angrily. "I have been waiting and waiting! What took you so long?"

"A lot has been happening at the dera, Mardana jee."

"Tell me! Don't neglect me because I am old! I want to hear everything. Everything, you hear?"

Aziza trips on her *burqua*[55] as she runs over the threshold into the courtyard.

"In *purdah* already! But she's only twelve years old!" Buddha says. "Baba says there should be no *burqua* for women."

"What do you know about anything?" Nasreen, who is washing

54 A small stool strung with colorful rope to sit on.

55 The long, black dress and veil that Muslim girls wear when they come of age. Also called an abaya in Arabic.

clothes and beating them with a bat in a corner of the courtyard, says aggressively.

Daulatan Masi begins quietly, delightedly, to babble incoherently.

"Walls. Brick yourself inside! Her song will bring him to him, the one who doesn't eat meat but eats it! She will be so happy and have children. Madder, yellow, blue, green! So many flowers blooming, blooming. Another jasmine! One, two, three, four, five six, seven, eight, nine, ten flowers! Ten? Eleven?"

"Mardana jee," Buddha says. "I found out something very important from Bebe Nanaki about what happened to Daulatan Masi.

Masi wasn't allowed to touch the infant Nanak, but one day, his tiny feet were sticking out of the blanket and unable to resist, she kissed them. Bebe Nanaki saw her do this, saw her fall backwards, stunned, then sit on the floor in a trance, her body stiff and lifeless; her hair wild and upright, as if pulled up by the gravity of the moon; her eyes wide and rolling in their sockets because they saw strange sights on her journey through time to the timeless domain."

"Why would kissing Baba Nanak's feet do this?" Aziza asks.

"Just the question I asked Bebe Nanaki, who said, '*Daulatan noon agam nigam dee sojhee hogaee.*'"

"What does it mean?" Aziza cries, impatient to hear and understand every word. She has grown up in Daulatan Masi's lap who is like a mother to her.

"Bebe Nanaki's explanation will tell you what it means. Masi had been forbidden to hold the infant Nanak because she wasn't ready to receive the gift of his touch. All at once, in a flash, all knowledge of here and there, past, present, future, all time, all space, everything, at once, poured into her, as if lightening had pierced through her skull and opened it to the immeasurable expanses of existence and experience that most of us are blind and deaf to. That kiss made her hurtle through inner and outer space, the entire history of her body from that first granule of life in the primordial One's palm, from which came the multitude of life, inanimate and animate, all animals and humans, the history of the earth, other worlds, stars, galaxies and universes in their orbits. It was a vision beyond ordinary, perceptual bounds, and Masi's mortal frame and brain couldn't handle the magnitude of her experience. She grew blind with the totality she saw, but in her blindness she sees much further than we can. Her words are prophecies we can't understand because of the limited capacity of our own brains."

In the long silence that follows, Aziza asks, "How many worlds are there? I thought there was just Kartarpur."

Mardana and Buddha have a good laugh.

"Baba says the number does not exist that can name them. The infinite One's world is boundless," Buddha explains.

Mardana smiles broadly. "Yes, the brain, our ego, is very limited, blind, arrogant. It thinks it knows everything! It is only in old age that the sphincter of my reason is loosening and I can approach a tiny little bit of that Mystery we come from and return to. I no longer doubt that our experience here in this life is just one little chapter of our histories."

Mardana pauses. His eyes with white membranes around the irises have a distant look.

"I dreamt a white horse came through our gullies, his forelegs muddied in the rain," Mardana resumes. "'Someone is knocking at our door,' Fatima says to me. She opens it, and in comes a white horse, unsaddled, without reins or carrying bags, its mien fluffy, like clouds. He looks at me, and in the globes of his dark eyes I see galaxies wheeling. The experience was both scary and exciting. In the dream, I get off my bed, amazed there was no pain in my legs and hips, I walk with strength and energy and in one leap, like a powerful, young man, I mount the horse. I think, 'I'm going on another long journey, I should ask Fatima to make some sweet fried bread for me, but then the horse speaks to me without speaking, and says, 'but you are invited to a feast!' It rises into the air, from right here in our courtyard, right by that *chulla,* into the air and we begin to fly together, he and I. And then I awoke."

"Daadujaan, you flew like the prophet Muhammad to paradise," Aziza says.

"Yes. Though it was a great dream and I was so happy in it, I frightened myself when I thought upon waking that it might mean I am going to die."

"But you promised you wouldn't!" Aziza insists.

"And I must keep my promise to you, my Zizu, Zizujaan," Mardana smiles, his eyes tearing up.

"I too have had a vision, Mardana jee. A waking vision, not a dream," Buddha says.

"Is there a difference?" Mardana laughs.

"There may be. Let me tell you the context. There's a huge drama going on in Baba's family."

"The usual one with his sons?" Mardana asks.

Buddha nods.

"It escalated some weeks ago into a physical battle in which many were wounded. Sri Chand saw the animals Lakhmi had killed in a hunt and went crazy, hitting and slapping his brother. Both parties got involved and it was a terrible fight. When Sri Chand and Lakhmi Das were battling, even I wanted to join in, break them up, but I was spellbound by a vision so powerful and vivid that I couldn't move. The scene before me was transformed – instead of Sri Chand's ragged though powerful army, and Lakhmi Chand's well-clad, luxury-loving followers clashing, I saw another battle, other people, other brave Sikh warriors, young men vying to die, on foot and on horses, brandishing swords shining brightly in sunlight, shooting barbed arrows hissing from their bows, killing and maiming imperial forces who were using weapons I couldn't recognize, thin tunnel like sticks from whose dark mouths few balls of fire, and deadly, fiery stones hurtling out of thick iron machines. It was not just a family skirmish, but a horrendous war in which many brave warriors from both sides fell, wounded and dying. The air was thick with battle cries, heart-rending moans, and groans of the wounded pleading for water. The earth was soaked in blood and piled high with corpses, dead and maimed horses, severed heads, arms, legs.

"It was so powerful, so real, Mardana jee, I saw it all with these eyes, and I was horrified at what I saw. I had no doubt I had foresight, that I was seeing a scene from the future. And I knew that I would be there, whether in the flesh or spirit, I could not tell.

"When the vision passed, I was very troubled. How could God allow such carnage? Each party evoked the help of its God; the battlefield was loud with Akaal Purukh, Waheguru, Allah, Ya Ali, Ya Ali! Is the Turk's God different from the Sikh's God? But Baba says there is only One, and whose side is He on? On both sides, on the side of evil as well as good? Or is there no such thing as evil and good, just different points of view? Even in the fight between Sri Chand and Lakhmi Das, I could see how both were right in their own way. It is wrong to kill animals, and yet, hasn't God made killing and eating a part of life? I caught a large fish once, and when I cut it open there was another fish inside it, and another fish inside that one. Is what we call evil and wrong also God's doing? It was frightening, and I was paralyzed by that fear, and still am, for I cannot choose which side to be on and my soul is in a tight knot."

Mardana is quiet for some time after Buddha's impassioned speech.

"One thing I have learned is that life cannot be understood through the mind," Mardana says, reflectively. "I have learnt from Baba that God is all there is. In the case of your vision, he is the

Turk, the Sikh, the horse, the battle, the battleground, the sword, the brave and the cowardly, the blood that is spilled, the warrior that is dead, dying, and the warrior in whose muscles He swells as strength."

"Then how can we take sides? Shall I just stand around, paralyzed?"

"But one must take sides," Mardana says. "It is our dharma to choose. We have a God-given sense of right and wrong and we must choose what our soul tells us is right. Heroes of all times have fought and died for real causes, justice, defense of the weak and meek, offense against evil, all-powerful, bigoted tyrants. They have been unafraid of the righteous act. Baba Nanak, too, has lived like a warrior. He has taken sides."

"Yes, even Krishna took sides,"[56] Buddha says, and after a long pause in which his body relaxes visibly. "Yes. You have put my soul at rest. The battle, whether inner or outer, never ceases. Conflict, the warp and weft of existence, is the universe's will, and I must not shun it, not sit on the fence, but jump with both feet into the fray, sword in hand, to kill and to die. Death is the greatest of our gifts, as Baba says, and we are not to be afraid of it. I can see now that Baba too must have had a vision similar to mine, and that is why children are being taught martial arts at the dera, together with music. Preparations must begin for what is to come. I have known for a while that I must practice my archery and learn to wield the sword. Conflict is the lathe on which we are shaped, the battlefield on which we are tested. And there is a mighty conflict to come."

"I am done with conflict," Mardana laughs. "I have no appetite for it anymore. I have lived my life, fought my battles; now I want my peace and rest. I am tired of divided roads, of choices, decision-

---

56 In the Hindu epic, Mahabharat, meaning the Great War, Krishna took the side of his cousins, the Pandavas.

making and want simply to graze in the vast field that my life has become, sleep under my guava tree, quietly, or with the sound of the rabab, like Zizu's playing, that enhances my silence."

"And oh yes, my vision of violence, blood, death, gore, was accompanied by the sweetest of music, of raags and *shabads* I have never heard before. It was at once terrifying and sweet."

"The beauty and the terror are all His. I can see that now at the end of my life. No matter what, music and Baba Nanak's warrior Sikhs will never be separated. I know that much about the future," Mardana says.

"The sight that impressed me most during the battle between Sri Chand and Bhai Lakhmi Das, Mardana jee, was Bhai Lehna calmly walking over to the dead birds lying on the ground, smoothing their feathers lovingly, looking carefully at them, and plucking a handful of the longest ones."

"Why?" Aziza asks.

"Oh, is Bhai Lehna back? I thought he had returned to Khadur," Mardana inquires.

"Oh yes, he was back, and has been sent away again. What a story that is."

"Tell me," Mardana relaxes on the pillows, prepared for a story.

"But first tell me why he was plucking the feathers!" Aziza says. "I asked first!"

"All in good time."

"Promise you won't forget."

"I promise."

CHAPTER 7

Saffron

"It was paddy-harvesting time when Bhai Lehna arrived," Buddha begins to recount. "Baba, together with other Sikhs, Sri Chand and Lakhmi Das, who were reluctantly helping Baba, had labored hard and long and were hungry. I returned to the dera to fetch lunch for them and when I walked into the courtyard of Baba's house, Lehna, who had just arrived from Khadur, wearing white clothes, was giving Bebe Nanaki a sack of pink salt from the mountains for the langar. He was eager to meet Baba and I told him I would take him to the fields after I had packed some lunch.

"When Bhai Lehna and I arrived at the field, an argument was in progress. Baba, who had just finished tying up the harvested paddy in three bundles, had asked his sons to carry them home, and they had refused, insisting that he pay laborers from the village to do it.

"Sri Chand said, 'I have done enough labor for one day. I have to meditate.'

"Lakhmi said, 'Here comes Buddha, tell him to carry them.'

"I wasn't about to pick them up, either. The bundles were heavy and oozing mud. Even as we argued, Lehna asked me to help him put the bundles on his head.

"'But your white clothes!' I exclaimed.

"'They're just clothes,' he said, bending down, picking up a bundle, and putting it on his head. He asked me to hand him the second one, which I did, and he put it on top of the first one on his head.

"Oh the look Sri Chand and Lakhmi Das gave him! There was instant hatred in them for Lehna. If they could have killed him with their gaze, they would have.

"We were all amazed because Bhai Lehna didn't bend down with the heavy weight of the two bundles, but stood straight and erect. He asked for the third one, too, and placing it on the second one, began to walk towards town gracefully, as if he was dancing beneath his burden; as if his burden was air!"

"Ah!" Mardana exclaims, and then again, "ah!" His face grows mushy with emotion as he shut his eyes. When he opens them again there are tears in them. "It reminds me of an incident when Baba and I were imprisoned by the emperor, Babar."

"Tell us," Buddha and Aziza say, simultaneously.

"First, you finish your story," Mardana says putting some food into Dharam Chand's mouth.

"By the time all of us reached the dera, Bhai Lehna was a sight, his white clothes all stained and dripping with mud! Nanaki and Sulakhni greeted us. While Nanaki laughed delightedly at the sight and clapped her hands loudly, Mata Sulakhni's mouth fell open in horror.

'Is this how you treat a guest?' she screamed at Baba.

'He's not a guest,' Baba said, quietly. 'He is here to stay.'

'But look at his new clothes stained with mud!'she screamed.

'It's not mud; it's saffron,' Baba said, quietly."

Buddha paused in his tale. Mardana and Aziza know from hearing so many of his stories that pauses always precede some significant observation.

"My vision of the battlefield is just one incident of something inexplicable that is happening to me. It began on the day I bowed before Baba as usual and he smiled at me very affectionately and touched me on my head. Since then I see things differently because *I* am different. Before that touch, I was living in a cave full of shadows and tight spaces. The very next day my archery jumped to another level. I used to think, 'I have to get better at it; I have to practice more and harder.' But that day it was as if the arrow shot itself, effortlessly, like a river flowing or the wind blowing."

"*Sehaj*," Mardana smiles. "You are in the flow of the river of life."

"Something else was moving through me, not me…"

"But also you," Mardana adds.

"Yes, also me. I experienced a way of being in flow and rhythm without effort. I mean effort must be, just like I must practice and become very good with the bow and arrow, and also with the sword, both of which Bhai Jodha is teaching me, then let it happen."

"I also want a sword! I also want a bow and arrow!" Aziza cries.

"Well, you can't have it!" Nasreen replies. "You are not a boy."

"Yes you can have it. I'll ask Bebe Nanaki," Buddha says.

"See? He will ruin her!" Nasreen shouts.

"I did not mean real ones, bhabijee," Buddha explains. "I meant the weapons of the mind without which all our physical weapons are like armor without a warrior. All of us have to use the sword of discrimination and the bow and arrow of the mind to hit our targets."

"I don't understand this rigmarole, nor do I need to," Nasreen replies tersely.

After another silence, Buddha resumes his story. "When Baba said, 'it's not mud; it's saffron,' I saw Bhai Lehna suffused with madder colored saffron. He was dripping with it, as if someone had squirted it on him playfully. Baba was laughing aloud, and Bhai Lehna, too, looking down at himself, burst into laughter. I think Mata Sulakhni saw it too, for I saw an expression on her face that I have never seen before. It was disbelief, confusion, awe, as if something had shattered her certainties.

"What is saffron?" Aziza asks.

"It is the color that Hindus bathe the idols of their gods in," Buddha explains.

"Is it the spice Daadi puts in the rice during Ramadan, that makes it yellow and orange?"

"Yes," Fatima replies. "It's very rare, precious and expensive. You know how saffron is dried? The flowers are picked and then put into burning charcoal. Saffron is a symbol for faith, which is often tested by fire. When we survive the fire we become as precious as saffron."

"And Bhai Lehna is passing that test. As gold is tried by the touchstone so is Baba Nanak trying Lehna. He serves Baba with body and soul, like a servant, carries and washes his clothes, shampoos his hair. We had a bitterly cold spell last month. We tried to dissuade Baba from going on his daily ritual of bathing in the Ravi River several hours before dawn, but he insisted on going."

"It is an old habit of his," Mardana explains.

"I was a bit concerned so I thought I too would accompany Baba and Bhai Lehna to make sure nothing untoward happens. Our breath was smoking out of our mouths, and the edges of the water had crystalized into ice. I had my blanket wrapped tightly around myself and was shivering violently. I couldn't even imagine touching the river let alone taking a dip in it. I have no desire to die early, though I always try to remember that I can go at any time. But Bhai Lehna stood on the shore as if it were springtime. A little later, he said, 'it isn't right for me not to follow my guru.' He stripped off his clothes and went into the river. I was really worried because at least Baba was used to it. When Lehna came out he was almost frozen to death. But Baba's embrace, and a fire I had made for them, restored him back to health.

Then the other night, at midnight, in that heavy rain we had, a part of the wall of Baba's room collapsed. He called out to his sons to do something, and they both said, "take another quilt and go to sleep, old man. We'll get masons in the morning to fix it." But Lehna got up right away and began to rebuild the wall. When he was done, Baba said to him, "it is crooked, throw it down!" Lehna obediently did so. Again Baba said "but the foundation must be moved back." Quietly, without complaint, Lehna started to build the wall for the second time. The sons said to him, "you're a fool, Lehna, for listening to a senile old man! Refuse him!" Mata Sulakhni also yelled at Baba for being unreasonable. But Baba wanted it torn down a second time. Baba was pleased by the third attempt, and we all got some rest. Baba did it another time, too, with his clothes; said he wanted them washed in the middle of the night. Bhai Lehna did so without complaint, as if it was the highest honor.

Baba's affection for Lehna jee, as for a son, is growing visibly just as Sri Chand and Lakhmi Das's bitter animosity towards him. I *adore* Bhai Lehna, too. The other day, determined to excel at archery, I was practicing very seriously. I had placed a hundred targets in the mango tree, in different locations, angles and heights. I felt full of power and strong as an ox. I was on my knees, reaching for the topmost one when Bhai Lehna came to me and said, "Oi Buddha jee, what are you aiming at?" I was very focused and didn't want to be disturbed. I turned around and my gaze was not friendly. Bhai Lehna was imitating my posture, bow drawn, brow concentrated, kneeling on the ground, aiming at the topmost branch, muscles tense, only he had no bow and arrow. He sang, spontaneously,

"If an arrow is shot at the sky, how can it reach there?
The sky above is unreachable-know this well, O archer!"

I stopped in my tracks. His words were arrows that tore through a veil in my head. My mind bloomed wide open, like a flower, and the whole mystery was present in that instant, all at once. I felt awake like I had never felt before. I understood, no, *experienced* something profound, though I cannot say what.

I was still amazed when Bhai Lehna told me to put my bow and arrow down by the root of the tree, and when I turned around, he lunged at me and wrestled me to the ground. I was unprepared and he had the advantage but soon I was into the game and it was wonderful, at once serious and playful, and very exhilarating. He is very strong, perhaps from being a dancer.

There is so much I admire about him. He's very emotional and it seems to me that he dances fluidly between his emotions, like a river, seamlessly, from thought to thought, emotion to emotion, action to action. He is like a child of the universe."

"But why was Bhai Lehna plucking the longest feathers? You haven't told us!" Aziza repeats. "And you still have to tell us the story about when you and Baba were imprisoned by the evil emperor, Babar, Daadu."

"I'm coming to it! I'm coming to it!" Buddha teases.

"You'll learn when you grow up, Zizu, that sometimes we have to take detours to stay on the path. Stories are like trees and rivers, winding and bending this way and that to get to where they need to go," Mardana explains.

"Tell me now!" Aziza orders, and Buddha resumes the thread of his narrative about Bhai Lehna plucking the feathers of dead birds in the middle of a raging battle.

CHAPTER 8

From the Mouth of the Guru

"I have to go back a little in the story first, and that may take some time. Baba has been mulling over the idea of a new alphabet for Punjabi for which, as you know, there is no script. The reason why he wants this is because few people, mainly priests who believe religious truths must not be passed on to common people, women and Sudars,[57] know and understand Sanskrit. This makes people dependent on priests to communicate with God while Baba believes that each of us can have direct access to God through our own hearts. Baba wants to invent something closer to the spoken language of Punjab that even women and low caste people can understand. He mentioned this idea to Bhai Lehna within a day or two of the latter's first arrival at Kartarpur, and Bhai Lehna and Baba have already created beautiful new numerals for Punjabi. Since his return from Khadur Bhai Lehna has been working on a script with total focus, inventing characters for the new alphabet for Sikh scriptures. I was there when Bhai Lehna brought the first letter of the alphabet, which he has named *oodaa*, to Baba. Baba looked at it and his face lit up with joy. It looks like this," Buddha says, reaching for Aziza's wooden slate leaning against the wall,

---

57 Low caste people.

and writing on it with *geru*[58]:ੳ. "In an inspired flourish Baba took the upper shackle of *oodaa* and opened it up and then he put the new Punjabi numeral 'one' before it, like this." As he draws, the upper arc of the second letter goes beyond the edge of the slate.

"You see how the oodaa is not closed, but open to space, pointing both down and up, towards the earth and the sky, its upper end making an arc in the air. Mine has gone off the slate to show you there is no end to the space in which it unwinds!"

"What does it mean?"

"I'll tell you in a minute. After Baba had done this, both Baba and Lehna went into a trance. I couldn't tell what it meant, but as I looked at it I found myself resonating like a rabab when Baba first touches it to make music. Later I got an explanation from Bhai Lehna.

The '1,' called *ik*, from the Hindi, *ek*, the numeral one, stands for the One supreme Energy of the universe: One, encompassing all the multiplicity of creation and all the contraries you can think of: chaos and order, black and white, secularity and spirituality. The second syllable is the holy sound, Om, or AUM, which the Vedas extol as being the first vibration that created the world. The last syllable, the 'M,' the way the Hindu *sanyasis* chant it, closing their mouths and taking the breath in, is indicative of their faith that the universe is entirely inner. This is why they 'leave' the

58 A dark paste made of clay to write with on a slate or as a paint for walls.

world and become recluses. Baba goes beyond the 'm' to that One indivisible, inner, outer, active principle of the universe. By adding 'kar,' which is the root for create, work, action, and which opens up the 'm' and takes it outward, shows his faith that the duality of inner and outer is One."

"Does the script have a name?" Mardana asks.

"Ah!" Buddha pauses. "Magical things are happening at the dera. They hadn't come up with a name for the script till Bhai Lehna had a dream. A few days after the *ik om kar* incident, Bhai Lehna came to Baba in the morning, his eyes sparkling with excitement, and said:

'I have had a very powerful dream, Guru Ji. I saw a being with fiery eyes drenched in a fine rain that was falling all around him like gossamer threads, enveloping him in a rich, warm, golden glow. The rain was full of healing nutrients for the earth. He was old, very old, toweringly tall, skinny, almost gaunt, with a grey beard, something like yours but whiter, thinner, longer, and on his head he had so many turbans – orange, blue, purple, green, all the colors of the rainbow. I couldn't count them, couldn't see the end of them as they ascended like a cone into invisibility. His palms were open towards the sky, like this, receiving the bountiful rain. Down by his feet was a little gnomish fellow, a lizard like being that was sitting on the rim of a well and guarding it closely. 'Mine,' said the gnome, 'mine, all mine.'

"The old man bent towards me, and his breath upon my face was like the sweetest of kisses. He whispered into my ear: '*Gur Mukhi.*' I didn't know what he meant.'

"After a stunned pause, Baba burst into laughter. 'Gurmukhi! Of course, Gurmukhi! He has given us the name for our alphabet, Lehna! What a perfect name! From the mouth of the Guru! For the ear of the one who is turned towards the Incomparable One!'

"They were both very contemplative, very inner, and then Nanak turned to the younger man and asked,

'But Bhai Lehna, who is this tall man with many turbans?'

"'I don't know, Baba Jee. I was hoping you would tell me.'

"'He is you, Lehna. And me. He belongs to us and we to him.'

"'He didn't appear to be like either of us.'

"'Appearance! Clothes that we shed when our time comes.'

"Baba is very pleased with the name and the script," Buddha continues his narrative. "Bhai Lehna is not only transcribing but also composing. He is also learning to play the rabab; Bebe Nanaki is teaching him. He has a lovely, youthful, almost feminine voice."

"Feathers?" Aziza asks.

"All right! All right! Bhai Lehna is copying Baba's *bani*,[59] and he was picking the longest feathers to make quills. Bhai Lehna has become Baba's scribe. Bebe Nanaki, who, together with Baba Nanak, has been making little *pothis* from a very young age, and transcribing Baba's words in them, has been teaching him calligraphy. Everything Bhai Lehna does, from cleaning the space where he sits, to cleaning the tools, he does in the spirit of intense devotion, reverence, worship. He sits cross-legged at his little desk for hours, his body, hands, fingers, mind, heart falling into a harmonious rhythm as he copies Baba's bani, sometimes reciting it aloud, sometimes going into a trance when on the feathers of his quill and the wings of Baba's words he flies into the Beloved's heart.

Once I looked over his shoulder and it seemed to me the words were dancing, each with the space next to it, and with each other, a dance between the black and the white, a perfect dance of beauty with truth. You can't tell where one begins and the other ends."

"But why was he picking the *longest* feathers?" Aziza asks.

"I'm learning a bit about quills, so I know why. He picked the

59 From Sanskrit, Vani, voice, sound, music, utterance. In the Sikh context it means the compositions of the Gurus and the holy saints and Sufis incorporated in the Sikh scripture, SGGS.

longest feathers, the ones that were not crushed and had a long spine under the plumes because the nib of the quill is blunted after about five pages, and it has to be cut further down the tube to make another nib. There has to be enough smooth space for the quill to be held, and if the feathers are beautiful they adorn the other end and dance as the scribe's hand dances. Once the main shaft of a feather has been hollowed it is thrust into hot, burning sand to make it hard, like a sword, which becomes unbreakable after it has been tempered in fire."

"The hot sand also makes the quill more brittle so the nib can be shaped," Mardana adds. "I was also Baba's scribe during our journeys, writing down the words as they poured out from him like water from a spring. My handwriting was adequate, but no matter how painstakingly I worked at it, it kept changing according to my moods," he laughs. "If I was calm it flowed out of me beautifully, the letters consistent and lovely, but if I was agitated, it didn't even come out in a straight line!"

"Once when Bhai Lehna was away from his desk, I saw Lakhmi walk over and spill ink on the paper on which Bhai Lehna had written. I screamed out loud, and Lakhmi caught hold of me and gave me such a beating I ached for days afterwards," Buddha says, starting to sob like a child.

How grown up and how childish he is at the same time, Mardana observes.

"I haven't told anyone but you. How much good work was ruined, how hard poor Lehna had to work to make up for it!"

"Strange that his sons should become what Baba has denounced all his life," Mardana reflects."And yet, not so strange. Children will rebel against parents. Even Baba rebelled against his father, as you know."

"And once I saw Sri Chand slap Bhai Lehna and it broke my heart!" Buddha says, wiping his tears.

"I think Sri Chand has the wrong idea about how to be *Udaasi*," Mardana comments, "One day on our travels we met a *sanyasi*[60] who asked Baba to define Udaas. Baba said, to make use of all things in this world, but not think they are yours; to live your life fully without being attached to any one, any thing, any desire, idea, and to keep the flame of Love alive in your heart is udaas."

"The other day some new musicians at the dera went to Baba and asked him, 'how shall we mortify our bodies to get nearer to God?' 'Sing!' cried Baba. 'Learn your raags, make it your daily practice, they will bring you and your listeners solace, deepen your faith and transport you to the very heart of Love!'"

"I love that story," Aziza cries.

"Baba preaches engagement with all aspects of life," Buddha says.

"What if you're a girl who is not allowed to do anything, go anywhere, become anything? Just live all locked up in purdah?

Buddha and Mardana are silent. Then Buddha sings, rather off key:

man ray garih hee maahi udaas.
gur kai sabad man jeeti-aa
gat mukatgharai meh paa-ay.[61]

"Buddha, if you really must sing, put a little effort into studying music," Mardana pleads.

"I didn't think I was that bad."

"You were."

"You were," echoes Aziza. "What does the song mean?"

"'*O mind, remain detached in the midst of your household. Through the Word of the Guru's Shabad,*[62] *the mind is conquered, and one attains the state of liberation in one's own home.*"

"You must write down that *shabad* for me. I will compose my

60 One who has renounced the world.

61 Explained below.

62 Divine utterances, holy sounds.

own music for it."

Buddha looks at Mardana, who nods his head.

"Yes, she is already composing, something I still haven't learned to do. I only sang Baba's compositions. Fatima! Fatima! Time for my halwa."

"I'll have some, too!" Buddha says, licking his lips.

"You don't want to eat this halwa. It has charas[63] in it," Aziza says.

"I will make some for us, too," Fatima volunteers.

"Yes, Daadi. Listening to good stories always makes me hungry."

"Some of Sri Chand's followers also have the dirty habit of smoking and drinking bhang, charas, and opium," Buddha says, turning up his nose.

"Ah, it's not a dirty habit, my friend. Don't close your mind to things you don't understand. In my youth I too smoked it. It was one of the pleasures of my life and still is, sometimes, when Fatima is kind enough to get some for me. My poor old lungs can't take smoking it, but Fatima cooks it for me in a delicious halwa! But I am careful not to eat too much of it. It gives me an appetite when I don't have one, which is most of the time; it makes my fading senses spring alive."

"Bhai Mardana jee, I didn't know you were so wild in your youth! But I will never smoke it. Akaal Purukh's name is a greater high, as Baba says."

"This herb that makes my life magical is also Akaal Purukh's gift! It helps me love Allah and his creation more! I am a poor creature who needs his little supports."

"I'll tell you what makes my inner and outer senses spring alive: being around Baba. He is the visible part of the Invisible, the very pulse and heart of life, the point where the universe lives and fulfills itself without any effort or will. In his presence one has the briefest

63 Hashish.

inklings of the invisible foundation of existence."

"Why, Buddha jee, you are talking like a poet!"

"I'm no poet but a puppet who speaks as he is spoken through."

Fatima hands small bowls of halwa to everyone.

"Daadu Jaan, tell us the story about when you and Baba were imprisoned by the emperor Babar."

"Before I do, can I ask Buddha a question that has been tickling my brain? Tell me, what happened after the battle between Sri Chand and Lakhmi Das? How is Baba taking the conflict in his family?"

CHAPTER 9

The Hot Whirlpool of Attachment

"When the battle between Sri Chand and Lakhmi Das was publically over, it moved into Baba's home. The family, including Nanaki, Jairam and myself, moved into the *haveli*.[64] Bebe Nanaki tended to Sri Chand, and Mata Sulakhni to Lakhmi Das, wiping their cuts and bruises and applying balm. Lakhmi Das looked very weary and depressed. All the things that had been simmering and bubbling inside everyone burst out in a war of words. It was quite a family drama with everyone participating, except me, the quiet witness, the shadow," Buddha narrates. He knows how hungry Mardana is for news of Baba so he enacts the different characters to bring the scene alive for him.

"It's all your fault!" Mata Sulakhni shouted, turning to Baba, shaking her finger at him, and addressing him with the not very respectful '*toon*.'[65] "You take no responsibility for your part in how things have turned out with your sons! You have been an absent father their whole life! Even now you care more for your congregation, your disciples and servants, like that Lehna, who you love more than your sons!"

"Lehna does important work. I can depend on him," Baba

64 From Persian: enclosed space.

65 There are many words for the second person singular pronoun, and 'toon' is the least respectful and also the most intimate, depending upon context and intonation.

said, as if to play down his love for him so as not to inflame the situation further." Buddha's voice as he relates Baba's words are calm, quiet, even.

"Baba has always avoided *kalesh*,"[66] Mardana adds, licking the ghee from his fingers.

"And here he was, in the thick of it." Mata Sulakhni lost all control. "Why don't you have your sons do your *important* work like scribbling your *immortal* words into books? Why don't you have them make your books and your quills and invent your alphabets?" Mata shouted.

"Because they are lazy and don't want to do it," Baba said, simply, honestly.

"I'm not lazy," Sri Chand said. "Just because I don't do things *you* think I should do doesn't make me lazy. I mediate for hours on end. I'm very diligent about my austerities."

"You also have a life to live," Baba said. "Plough the fields, plant, nurture and harvest the grains you eat."

'Life as *you* see it, father. My definition of life is different from yours.'

"We disobey you because you're deranged!" Lakhmi Das burst out.

"That's the sort of thing I'm talking about! You only say bad things about them, call them lazy, and then expect them to obey your mad orders. Build a wall in the middle of the night! Wash your clothes, also in the middle of the night! Why should they listen to you, who have given them lectures and orders instead of love?"

Mata Sulakhni was gesticulating expressively, like this, her hands and her whole body participating in the argument. Baba remained quiet and introspective as if Lakhmi Das's words had passed through him as if through air.

"I admit I'm lazy," Lakhmi Das said, groaning as Mata Sulakhni

66 Emotional turmoil, especially in the context of family.

put some ointment on his cuts. "I don't get up early in the morning and take a cold bath. I don't want to. I do the things I enjoy. I am what God made me."

"And yet he would like to succeed you as guru!" scoffed Sri Chand. "He thinks guruship is all about getting donations and living like a prince with his horses, dogs and hunting parties! He has no discipline and now he's admitted it! He doesn't deserve to be a guru."

"Neither do you," Baba Nanak said, quietly.

Sri Chand looked angrily at his father.

"I've told you to marry," Mata Sulakhni said, turning to Sri Chand. "How many times I have made matches for you, they come for the engagement bearing gifts and sweets and you don't show up!"

"I'm not interested in marriage," Sri Chand replied.

"If you don't marry, how will I have grandchildren?" Mata shouted.

"You already have one," Lakhmi reminded her.

"But he is sickly and weak. What if something happens to him?"

"He's not sickly and weak!" Lakhmi Chand said angrily, reaching for Dharam Chand, who was terrified by all the shouting, and hugging him.

"Even if you were interested in marriage, who will marry you?" Mata Sulakhni said to Sri Chand. "Look at your appearance! You look like a ghost in mid-day, followed by your drug-smoking beggars! But I say, marry, marry whoever will have you! You can marry and then abandon her like your father abandoned me. Without marriage, he will not make you the guru."

"Give it up, mother," Lakhmi Das scolded her. "Sri Chand is a killjoy. I just want to live my life the best I know how. I want to make up for the life that nobody in my family has lived. Not you, father, not Sri Chand who has followed in your footsteps, not..."

"Followed in my footsteps?" Baba asked, perplexed.

"It may not seem like it, but he has. He adored you, father."

"He's very right," Mardana interrupts Buddha excitedly, seeing the connections. "Sri Chand hung on his every word. He was only about five or six years old when Nanak and I left home for our journeys. Having no idea about who his father was, he idolized what he imagined his father to be. Before we went on our journeys, Baba did do some austerities and was very theatrical in the way he dressed. He drew everyone's attention, that was for sure! Everybody called Baba's journeys *Udaasis* – hence the name of Sri Chand's sect. He knew that Baba believed that everyone and everything, including animals, insects, stones in the universe are particles and cells in Nirankar's[67] Great body, and that is why Sri Chand's followers are from all races, castes and classes; that's why he's a vegetarian. He knew detachment was at the core of Baba's belief – why else would he leave home and family to wander the world? And that is why Sri Chand and his followers are celibate wanderers."

"Exactly!" cries Buddha, enlightened by Mardana's insights. "Lakhmi Das is very perceptive about all of this, as you will see as I continue the story.

'Sri Chand has followed in your footsteps,' Lakhmi Das continued. 'When we were growing up he believed all the rumors about you, that you were a *sanyasi*, that you didn't comb your hair, smeared ashes on your naked body, didn't eat meat like other wandering *sanyasis,* and he started to become the you he thought you were. But when he found out you weren't what he thought you were, it was too late. He was already set in his ways. I was there when some traveling Brahmins told us the story of the deer you ate at Kurukshetra, father; how a disciple had gone hunting and brought you a dead deer slung on his shoulder and you had skinned, roasted and eaten it! Sri Chand was so distraught he didn't eat for days! But I spoke to one of the Brahmins who had been converted

67 The Formless One.

by your arguments, and he sang for me the song you had composed. I don't remember it now, but I memorized it then and recited it to myself frequently. Something about how death is part of life, life feeds on death, and everything, including us, is a sacrifice to the Greater Life. It had something to do with how we are vessels of flesh, conceived and living with and in flesh. But Sri Chand's idol had fallen from the sky where he had placed it, and shattered all around him. He felt you had betrayed him, and for days he kept punching trees and walls. I told him to go hunt something and he would feel better, but he punched me so badly my jaw was swollen and I couldn't eat for days. But I was determined when you returned home to hunt and cook deer and other delicacies for you, father.'

Sri Chand looked at his younger brother," Buddha continues his recreation of the event, "and for the first time I saw some respect in his eyes for him; as if his words had illumined him in some way. I think he saw his brother not as the brute he thought he was but a thinking animal.

"Other than hunting I didn't and don't have any joy," Lakhmi Das continued. "And nothing's going to stop me from doing it. I wish I could get away from this endless family fight and hunt something juicy cooked in its own blood and feed it to this saintly brother of mine."

Sri Chand broke free from Bebe Nanaki and looked like he was going to start the battle all over again, but Bebe Nanaki sat him down and patted his hair and whispered, "listen, just listen."

"How can I listen when innocent, *baizubaan*[68] animals, mothers together with their young ones, are slaughtered mercilessly by this heartless and soulless creature with far less sense than animals? Everyone has noticed how there are fewer peacocks and deer since he has been killing them. He is an angry man. He drinks, smokes

68 Literally, without tongues, but here meant as 'speechless,' or unable to speak in our tongue.

opium, and takes pleasure in killing," Sri Chand shouted.

"I'm a sow's ear and you can't make a silk purse out of me,'" Lakhmi Das said. "I've been hunting since I was ten years old. I saw mother suffering from your absence, father, and I couldn't bear it. You have no idea how she suffered while you were away on your journeys to find your Akaal Purukh! She's right. You abandoned her!"

Mata Sulakhni broke down and sobbed and Bebe Nanaki put her arms around her.

"I want to live, for both of you," Lakhmi Das continued. "But I don't know what it means to live. You say it means loving the Beloved, father, but I don't know anything about that. I'm tired in my bones. Sometimes life isn't enough."

"What did he mean by that?" Mardana interrupts Buddha.

"He struck me as being very sad and very tired. His words triggered something deep and painful in Mata Sulakhni who revisited old wounds in between sobs. I was amazed at how the past is so deeply hidden yet so alive in us. What a thin membrane separates the past from the present – you only have to scratch the present, and the past becomes present in all its reality, in all its infinite layers existing simultaneously in some spaceless space in our hearts and minds. Mata Sulakhni lives in the present only in so far as it echoes the past. As her stories wove between the layers of time, not sequentially, but all connected to her perceived 'rejection' by Baba, I was struck by how and why humans persist in living inside their painful memories, recreating them over and over. There is something in us that sticks to pain like glue. She sat on her *peedee*, her grey hair covered by a shawl, one hand by her ear, the other gesticulating as she spoke about the past as if it were present.

'I should have seen the signs,' she said.'When my father sent you my horoscope before our marriage was finalized, you sent it back, saying 'I don't believe in astrology, I'm not superstitious."

"I wasn't rejecting you. I was ready to marry you anytime, whether our horoscopes matched or not," Baba said, gently.

"You called my father superstitious! Father had second thoughts about you. Then we heard your parents were thinking of marrying you to someone else. How shameful it was for me, all our neighbors whispering 'Mul Chand's daughter has been abandoned by the Bedi boy.' My mother was livid and hated you, and my father was angry beyond words. What a shame your marrying someone else would have been for me if you had backed out! Nobody else would have married me.'

'But I did marry you,' Baba said.

'Yes, and how brief was my joy!'

'All joys are brief, mother,' Lakhmi Das said.

'What a lovely *phulkari*[69] my mother and I made for my wedding. We wove the cloth, sewed it together, and then embroidered it. The whole village came to embroider it and I was so happy! With every stitch I prayed I would have a good life. But what did you do during our ceremony? What did you do? The whole village was watching! We had only gone around the fire four times, instead of seven,[70] the priest was invoking the sun and the moon, when you pulled me away unexpectedly and I stumbled and fell. Everyone attending the ceremony was stunned. You had broken our wedding! The shame of it! Before all the people! Because of this our marriage was only half a marriage. It wasn't long after you left on your 'important' journeys that have made you so famous.'

'After thirteen years,' Baba corrected her. But Mata Sulakhni wasn't listening. Time had collapsed in her mind, the interim between tragedies smudged on the tablet of her heart with dark,

69 Wedding shawl.

70 It is customary in a Hindu marriage ceremony for the couple to do seven perambulations around fire.

indelible ink.

'You didn't think when you left, what will happen to her? What will happen to the children? Will they live on the streets? Will they even have enough to eat?'

'I knew you would be well taken care of by my family.'

'Your family! What do you know about how they treated me? If my mother hadn't rescued me I would have been begging on the streets! Your father was so upset with you for not living the life he wanted for you that he took it out on the children and me! Your mother treated me like I was her slave! She made me do all the work while she herself sat on the *peedee* in white clothes, looking like a lady!'

'That's not true!' Nanaki interjected.

'What do you know? You were the beloved daughter, not the daughter-in-law! Things got so bad for me that I finally had to return to my parents' house after they had snatched away my oldest son for their barren daughter who had no children!'

'It was you who didn't want to take care of two children! I helped you out and helped myself, too. I was so happy to have him,' Nanaki said.

'She's right,' Sri Chand said to his biological mother. "I remember it because the memory is written with a knife in the flesh of my heart. I remember the moment you made the choice, mother, your gaze going from one to the other as we stood before you, fixing itself on Lakhmi with teary eyed love, picking him up and holding him close to you. *You* cast me away."

"Blame him," Mata Sulakhni said, pointing her finger at Guru Nanak, and then at Nanaki. "And blame her for bringing you up so badly and for making you who you are."

'I loved him. I am not responsible for his destiny. And I am hurt about the things you say about my mother. If she was what you make her out to be why would Vir Jee address so many *shabads* to her? She was a saint!' Nanaki said.

'A saint! A saint!' Mata screamed. 'I am surrounded by saints! I hate saints! I'm sick of being around saints!'

Mardana has a good laugh, and Buddha joins him.

"Mata just went on and on about how sick she was of saints," Buddha resumes. 'Everyone is a saint except me because I have feelings! How do you think I felt, not seeing your face for twelve whole years? I thought you were dead! Sometimes I heard reports from wanderers and fakirs like you that they had seen you dressed in strange costumes. I was visiting your parents in Talwandi. I was bent over the chulla to make sure the milk didn't boil over when I was startled at the sight of Mardana. I forgot all about the milk and it boiled over and your mother yelled at me. You weren't with Mardana. My heart stopped beating. I thought he had come to tell us robbers had killed you. I asked him and he didn't say anything because, I later found out, you had told him not to mention you. Mardana said he had come to visit his wife. Your servant had more sense than you!'

'Mardana is not my servant but my beloved companion,' Baba said."

"He said that?" Mardana says, sitting up straight and then slumping over and sobbing. Buddha pauses to let Mardana have his cry. Mardana wipes his tears with the edge of his shawl and says, "Go on."

"Yes, abandon your wife and have a *beloved companion*," Mata Sulakhni mimicked, not very kindly. 'Who was *my* companion? I was alone, completely alone!' Baba moved towards her but before he could put his arm around her, Lakhmi Chand put his arm around both her shoulders and pulled her to him, as if to say, 'leave her alone!'

'You had come back from one of your journeys because Mardana had said he would die if he didn't see his wife, parents and children again,' Mata Sulakhni continued with her memories."

"Yes, yes, I did say that!" Mardana says, looking at Fatima. "I was missing you so very much! I said to Baba, 'here play your own rabab, I am going home!' So Baba consented to returning to Talwandi on the condition that I not tell anyone that he had accompanied me back. He camped in the forest, and I was not to mention him if anyone asked. Oh what a story that was. Let me tell it!"

"But why didn't Baba want to meet his family?" Aziza asks.

"Yes, I want to know that, too," Fatima says.

"I don't really know," Mardana admits. "I rarely questioned him."

"I know the answer to that," Buddha says, "and I will tell it after Mardana jee tells his version."

CHAPTER 10

Mata Sulakhni's Story

"We turned our steps towards Talwandi because I insisted on it," Mardana picks up the thread. "When we reached the outskirts of the forest, Baba spread his blanket on the ground and told me to go into town. I couldn't for the life of me understand why he didn't want to visit his wife and family. I was so excited and in such a hurry to get home that I stumbled many times. I wanted to see Fatima again, to look into her eyes, to touch her; I wanted to see my son and daughters, to eat a meal cooked by Fatima, and just sit around in the courtyard surrounded by love! But Fatima wasn't very nice to me on my return at all!"

"What did you expect? You were gone for so long without thinking about your family. Mata Sulakhni is absolutely right!"

"I thought about my family all the time! Ask Baba! I was like a parrot repeating, 'home, home, home!' And we made up, didn't we? Remember?" Mardana looks at Fatima, as if sharing a secret all their own.

Fatima blushes and turns away.

"So, to get back to the story, I ran all the way home," Mardana continues. "I had hoped nobody would see me, but a few villagers saw me hurrying home and started whispering, 'Mardana is back! Mardana is back! But where is Nanak?' They feared he was dead. I was in a very awkward position. I had to lie and say he was in another town. But I got caught in that lie by my desire to take Baba a good meal, and as I was hurrying out at dusk, I was seen again, and the rumors started all over again."

"Let me pick up Mata Sulakhni's story from here," Buddha interposes. "She said to Baba, 'you were camped outside Talwandi, you didn't want to see me. I was nothing to you! But I heard everyone whispering, and your father, mother and sister wouldn't hear Mardana's pleading that you didn't want to see anyone. They got ready to go with food and clothes but they wouldn't let me come! I sat at home with my burning heart turning to cinders. The maid, who went with them, carrying all the gifts for you on her head, told me everything when they returned, without you! She told me how your father had tried to tempt you to return home: 'I will build you a new home!' He said. 'I will get you a new wife because I know Sulakhni is a shrew and has a big tongue!' 'And what was my reply to my father?' Baba turned to Mata Sulakhni. I said 'I have exchanged hearts with those to whom my body is attached. God arranges marriages. He joins them forever, for this bond between man and wife is the battleground where we learn love.' But if you want to know why I didn't come to see you, Sulakhni, it was because I was afraid I would get attached to you and the children all over again and I didn't want to because my pilgrimage was not over, because I hadn't yet learned how to be detached in my attachments.'

'Pilgrimage, shmilgrimage! Go to hell!' Mata Sulakhni, who wasn't really listening to Baba, shouted.'

'Mother, we have heard this story many, many times,' Sri Chand said, curtly. I could see at that moment why Sri Chand never wanted to marry! He had had enough of family *kalesh*!" Buddha said. "Mata Sulakhni beat her breast: 'What do you know? It is inscribed in the pulp of my heart. These memories are alive in my *kaaljaa*,[71] and when I burn on the pyre it will cry out loudly so the whole world will hear my story.'

'Time to put the past to rest, mother,' Sri Chand said again impatiently.

'Shut up, let her talk,' Lakhmi Das said.

'If my life was any better now, I would forget. But even now he is a *lohai da thun*.[72] Even now he prefers Lehna to his own sons and me.'

'What's so special about Lehna? He is a good servant, that's all,' Sri Chand said.

'Only he doesn't get paid. We should pay him to make his status clear,' Lakhmi added.

'Just because Lehna is mad like you, you worship each other!' Mata said bitterly.

'Lehna is a gem,' Baba said, quietly, resolutely, as if he had made up his mind to finally speak his heart.

'And your own sons, your flesh and blood, are not?'

'What is blood to me? The same blood flows in all,' Baba replied.

'And what is your wife to you? Get some other flesh and blood which is no different from the mother of your sons!'

'That I will never do. We are joined forever.'

'I hope not!' Sulakhni shouted. 'I want a better husband than you in my next life!'

Baba smiled broadly, lovingly, really amused by his wife.

'But I will want you even in my next life,' Baba said, quietly.

'Send Lehna away now, then,' Mata Sulakhni said. I could tell she was pleased by Baba's words.

'That I won't do. He is indispensable to me.'

'Why don't you guide your sons like you guide him? How can they learn anything unless you guide them?'

'Nobody guided me,' Baba said. 'Lehna needs no guidance. Akaal

---

71 Literally, the liver. Used interchangeably with 'heart.'

72 An iron udder.

Purukh has already taken him in hand.'

'I demand you send Lehna away now!' Mata said. 'I am a wife! And a wife has a right to expect things from a husband. Who else is she going to expect from?'

'You would be happier if you lived life without expectations,' Baba said.

'Then why do you expect things from your sons?' Mata Sulakhni asked.

'I did. I don't anymore,' Baba replied.

'Then why are you unhappy with them?'

'I am not. I accept them for what they are.'

Mata Sulakhni calmed down visibly. In that space I could see in her face the hope that things may yet be right.

'Then one of them will succeed you as guru?'

'I don't want to succeed him,' Lakhmi Das said.

'Sri Chand, then?' Sulakhni said, not very happy about Lakhmi's refusal, but resigned.

'No, that will not happen.'

'I am not good enough for him. I never have been,' Sri Chand said, sounding like a child. 'The servant will succeed you?'

Baba was quiet. Then he said, 'Neither of you has the discipline to submit where submission is called for. Obedience is sometimes entirely essential. When your boat is in trouble, you have to enforce some rules and regulations.'

'You quarreled with your father, too,' Mata Sulakhni said. 'He also had dreams for you that you didn't fulfill.'

Baba was very quiet.

'He's not saying it, but he's not denying that Lehna will succeed to the *guddi*,'[73] Sri Chand said angrily.

'Is that true? I'm asking you, is that true?' Mata Sulakhni shrieked her question.

---

73 Literally, cushion, but here symbolizing the seat of spiritual authority.

'Of course it's true!' Lakhmi Das smiled bitterly.

The family broke into such a noise, everyone speaking at once, shouting, weeping, and attacking Baba. He quietly picked up his rabab and walked out into the night."

"Why is there so much conflict in the world?" Mardana cries, sitting up in bed. It was as if he was feeling Nanak's pain, and he couldn't bear it. "The human, the human, how can anyone circumvent the human?"

"Baba says, duality and conflict are God's will. The only way to transcend it is to embrace it as *hukam*."[74]

"I take Mata Sulakhni's side," Fatima says.

"I can see how Baba's need to seek his Beloved on every continent, every people and event, conflicted so severely with his wife's needs," Mardana reflects. "I too was destined to be his servant, his accompanist and companion, and how hard that was for you, my dearest Fatima. One person's destiny conflicts with another's, and tragedy results. But I also think it is destiny that brings people together in the first place. Saints like Baba need women like Mata Sulakhni to balance and temper their divinity. I have heard of a Greek philosopher, Socrates or something. He was married to a shrew who used to empty pots of piss on his head!"

"Their difficult domestic situations enlighten them!"

Aziza asks, "And then what happened after Baba took his rabab and walked out of the door after the family fight?"

"Why we had almost forgotten that story!" Mardana says. "Thank God for young minds that don't forget these strands! My memory is becoming a sieve. Yes, tell us, Buddha jee," Mardana says.

---

74 A very rich word in Sikh philosophy, meaning "Divine Law," "Cosmic Order."

CHAPTER 11

My Stranger Soul

"The moon was almost full, and Baba, the rabab strung on his shoulder, walked out the door while Mata Sulakhni, Sri Chand and Lakhmi Das were still quarrelling, and followed the dirt road out of the village towards the fields. I could tell from his stride, a little hurried, that he wanted to put some distance between himself and his family. He was wading knee deep in the burning pool of attachment. He had learned to stay above the human condition but it was all around and in him, palpable and present in all its stubborn insistence, unavoidable, like death.

I followed him at a distance. When he got to the grove of mango trees by the well, he leaned the rabab against a trunk and sat down by it, his head buried in his hands. But he didn't sit like this for long. Soon he slid down and stretched out on the earth, as if deriving strength from it. He has always thought of the Earth as his mother and glorified it in his songs. His arms clasped beneath his head, he looked up at the stars. After a while he sat up, his spine straight, his legs crossed in the lotus position, and meditated for a long time; so long, it almost tired my patience and I thought about returning home. But my love and curiosity got the better of me and I stayed, and how glad I am now that I did, to witness what you have witness so often in your life, Bhai Mardana jee: the birth of a *shabad*!

When Baba Nanak was done meditating," Buddha resumes, "he reached for his rabab and played a chord. Shutting his eyes he played some long, slow notes in raag *aasaa* as if listening to them, letting them work their mystical magic on him."

Inside her room Aziza tunes her rabab, begins to play the chords and hum the raag.

"Haltingly at first, then gaining fluidity, without hesitation and pause, certain and sure in its direction, like a stream, an impassioned melody accompanied by words began to pour into and out of him, ringing in the night air, his breath and voice spiraling from, into, beyond his heart to the stars above, and back again.

'*Merai jeearaiaaa, paradesia, kit phavai janjaalai raam*,'" Buddha sings in his raspy voice. Aziza picks up the refrain and sings in a voice whose depth of feeling stuns her listeners into silence. Together, haltingly, learning the words as they go along, with Mardana joining in with his aging, quavering voice, they sing the refrain, addressing themselves to their lives, to the creatures in them that suffer so easily and inevitably: '*You, my life, my soul, stranger from another country, another world, why entangle yourself in the web of this dream? Turn away from the noose of attachments towards the True One abiding in your heart.*"

The silence that follows the singing is broken by a single sob from Aziza, accompanied by the words, "And then?"

"I don't remember the rest of the words."

"Get them for me tomorrow! Promise!"

"By the time he arrived at the last lines Baba had transcended all his turmoil and had returned to peace once more. He sat in silence for a while, then picked up his rabab and returned on the path back home, myself following surreptitiously in his shadow."

"Most of us get stuck in the marshes of attachment, sinking deeper and deeper," Mardana reflects. "But Baba is the true Sikh, the true Gurmukh who has trained himself to turn in his suffering to words and song, healing, magical, heart-widening, heart-melting song, bridge over an abyss connecting us instantly to the One, who soothes and calms us back to peace."

"Yes, he had found, again, in his heart, where his Beloved lived, the deep, cool, pool of sweet water in which his burning soul bathed."

"It is a spring called *Salsabil*, the fountain of Paradise in the heart," Aziza says. 'Daadi told me about it."

"What a lovely name, Salsabil," Buddha says.

"And then?"

"When Baba was returning home, his steps were certain, slow, determined. I ran through the fields, backtracked, and pretended to meet him on the road. I could tell from the way he smiled at me that he knew I followed him everywhere, like a shadow, watching the drama of his life. But he *said* nothing, and I, who have always felt a little guilty about my shameless, if not destined, curiosity, was reassured that I had his forgiveness, if not approval. He put his arm around my shoulder, laughed, his eyes twinkling in the night like stars, and said:

'No one can avoid attachment and *kalesh*, my child. It is the shadow of flesh, given to all! How it bakes and boils us in fire and slices our hearts with its razor sharp knife! But you, my Buddha, my sweet young old man, you will be the Witness. You will learn to look at the lives of people around you and see how they are all caught in the web of His dramas, without even knowing it! They are as fish in the Fisherman's Net because they do not know this Perspective, this Reality seen from His perch, which alone can free us of our entanglements. We are helpless on our own. The hand that picks us out of the net and throws us back into the ocean of His heart to live and breathe freely belongs to the High One. He alone drowns, or saves us. But beware of thinking you are above it all! Beware! You *will* lose your perspective. But ah, how wonderful losing our perspective is when we arrive at it again! How wonderfully sweet this union after each separation! It is enough to make you want to court separation, sing it!'

Becoming serious, he said, 'Buddha, when you grow up and have a wife, listen to her for she speaks much sense. Sulakhni is right. How difficult it is to obey God's will when you have your own ideas about how the world and people in it should be.'

'But Lakhmi Chand was rude to you!' I said.

'I deserved it. My father wanted me to be somebody I was not, and now I am pushing my own desires on my sons. God has made a colorful world in which no two people are alike. I wanted them to be like me! How foolish I have been! And what a terrible husband! I must make it up to her.'

'But Mata Sulakhni told you to go to *kumbee narak*, the darkest part of hell!'

Baba laughed loudly. When he quietened down, he recited a line from a long poem he has been composing, called the Poem of the Alphabet, where he takes each character of Gurmukhi that he and Bhai Lehna have invented and weaves a stanza around it. About the letter 'D' he says, '*Do not blame anyone but yourself. I have suffered for my own actions and behavior; I do not blame anyone else.*'

We walked in silence for a while. As we entered the village, we met Bhai Lehna jee, standing by the village well, carrying a lantern, waiting.

'Ah, Lehna,' Baba said, standing before him and looking at his face, his eyes. 'It is time for you to return to Khadur.'

Bhai Lehna, so used to obeying his master's every little whim and wish, quavered with confusion and gathering tears, like a child. As if sensing his thoughts, Baba said, putting his hands on his shoulders and looking him in the eye.

"No, you've done nothing wrong, Lehna. It is time for us to be separated. For a while," he added, seeing the anguish on Lehna's face.

'But who will serve you when I am gone? Who will give you a glass of water when you are thirsty? Who will fetch your shoes and wash your clothes?'

'I will,' I said, knowing what was afoot in Baba's family, though I think Bhai Lehna must have known about Baba's sons' feelings towards him.

'Let me stay with you,' Lehna cried, and fell at Baba's feet. 'Don't send me away! I'll bear all suffering if I can be in your presence daily! But I can't bear the thought of separation."

"There is presence even in absence, my Lehna," Baba said, lifting him up.

"But let me stay and serve you, Baba!'

'I am with you, wherever you are,' Baba replied, 'Go, put some distance between yourself and Kartarpur, my son, and I will visit you there. You have but to think of me, and I shall arrive."

"Then you'll have to arrive all the time," Lehna said.

Baba smiled, and said, "You are needed in Khadur. It is Akaal Purukh's will.'

Bhai Lehna bowed before Baba Nanak, and said, 'if you send me away, I will go; if you call me, I will come. I will obey your *hukam* in every way, my Master.'

"The Beloved alone is our Master, Lehna. Say these words to Him in your prayers and you will always stay on the path which will be joyous in all circumstances."

We walked in silence to the dera where Bhai Lehna went to his quarters and Baba went inside his house. I didn't want to leave him, so I stood at the door, listening and peeping. Mata Sulakhni sat alone on the *peedee,* still clutching her head. Baba pulled up another *peedee* and sat by her, and put his arm around her shoulders. She pushed him away, but he only got closer.

'I have never abandoned you and never will. We will be together for lifetimes, Sulakhni. I know you'd like someone else, but you've got me, and that will have to do.'

I could tell Mata Sulakhni was pleased by his words but she still pretended to be angry and upset.

'And do you know why I didn't come to see you that time when I stayed in the forest outside Talwandi while Mardana visited his wife and family?'

'I don't care. I don't want to know!' Mata Sulakhni sulked.

'I couldn't trust myself to see you then leave again. Though I had overcome the temptation of bewitching beauties I encountered in my journeys, I knew I couldn't overcome you. To have you in our bed, to have our children and my parents around us, to eat your delicious food: I would have been ensnared. I would never have been able to return to the Beloved, for my anchoring in him was weak. I wasn't ready to be attached without attachment.'

'Your Beloved! My *sautan*![75] You are all alike! Like Gautama Buddha[76] who left his wife and never returned.'

'But I came back. See, I am here, with you. I believe in marriage. I trust the human need to need. You have taught me love, Sulakhni, you have taught me to love in absence. I am sorry I have been such a difficult husband.'"

Fatima let out a sob.

"Come here, come sit by me," Mardana says, wiping away his own tears. Fatima comes and sits beside her husband. He extends his arm and holds her hand. She withdraws it at first. Such demonstrations of affection before others were absent in that milieu. But upon Mardana's urgent insistence, she lets her hand lie in his grasp, and even entangles her fingers with his. Thus the old couple sits in their courtyard, tears in their eyes for the way their life had been, for what has been is ever present in the human heart that knows no time.

---

75 A rival in love.

76 The father of Buddhism who left his wife and never returned home.

"Mata Sulakhni, too, broke down and wept," Buddha continues. "Baba drew her to him, stroking her back and hair. It was a very sweet scene.

'That is how the first part of our lives had to be, my love. Let it go. Let it go willingly, welcomingly, and you will be able to experience the untold wealth that is given to us now,' Baba said to Mata Sulakhni.

In the days that followed, I could tell Baba had made a choice to make up to his wife. He understood her perspective and felt compassion. She had woken him up to the abyss between his words and actions. I caught glimpses of many scenes of affection between them. Instead of sending me with his lunch while he worked in or supervised the work in the fields, Mata Sulakhni takes it most days; they sit and eat together by the well in the shade of the trees; they spend time with Dharam, telling him stories and laughing at his words. Baba tried to make up with his sons, too, but without much success. I could tell that what mattered to Baba was that his heart was clear and unencumbered, not the outcome. Though his sons were pleased with what they perceived to be their father's rejection of Bhai Lehna, they would never be fully content till they were named his heirs. And I knew by the scene at the well, when Baba called Bhai Lehna 'son,' that *he,* not them is his spiritual son and heir. I know this without a doubt now."

Mardana sits up, stumbles off his bed, bends and kisses the ground, and lies thus for a while. When he gets up and returns to his bed, everyone looks at him questioningly.

With tears in his eyes he says, quietly. "I kiss the earth on which Nanak was born and from which he will never pass away."

The shadows have lengthened but storytelling is not over. Buddha wants to fill Mardana in about everything, so he begins anew.

[illegible] Shaktiman [illegible] down and wept. Fondly, [illegible] her [illegible] back and [illegible]. It was a very sweet scene.

'These [illegible] of our lives had to be [illegible]. Let [illegible] will try, we [illegible], and you will be able to [illegible] the mutual [illegible],' Babu said to Mr. Shaktiman.

In the days that followed, I could tell Babu had made a choice to make up for his [illegible]. He had understood her perspective and [illegible] compassion. She had woken him up to the [illegible] between words and [illegible] glimpses of many scenes [illegible] between them [illegible] with his father while he worked in [illegible] the fields. [illegible] that takes it most [illegible] days [illegible] the [illegible] and [illegible] at [illegible] He [illegible] to make up with his son, [illegible] without [illegible] that [illegible] to have [illegible] that [illegible] Though [illegible] that they perceived to be their father's [illegible] would [illegible] they [illegible] his [illegible]

[illegible]

[illegible] about everything [illegible]

CHAPTER 12

A Drama Staged in a Dream

"I forgot to tell you the most important thing!" Buddha, says, lifting his head up and to the side, nose in the air, a hand on his hip and the other held out, as if resting on a sword. "A troupe of players is in town, performing the stories of Radha and Krishna[77] and Raja Bharatrihari.[78] We all went to see them, including Baba, who had been composing *shabads* about the drama of human life, and then the actors arrived, as if his songs had summoned them."

"I also want to go and see the plays!" Aziza says, clapping her hands.

"They are going to play all week."

"Aziza is in *purdah* now and won't be going anywhere with you," Nasreen says through clenched teeth.

"I *am* going to see the play!" Aziza says defiantly. "You can't stop me!"

Her mother walks over to her and slaps her hard with her wet and soapy hand.

Daulatan Masi screams as if she has been hit, and begins to wail and moan softly.

---

77 Krishna is the arch lover in Indian mythology and Radha is his consort.

78 A king and poet of the sixth century A.D. who renounced his kingdom to become an ascetic. His story is told further in the chapter.

"Don't!" cries Mardana. "How often have I told you not to hit her?"

Aziza sobs and runs to Fatima, hoping she would defend her. But though Fatima suspends carding for a moment, and seems to want to take Aziza in her arms, she neither hugs her nor says anything. After both an external and internal struggle, Fatima, with many prayers for her well-being, has given up control over her granddaughter's destiny and surrendered her to the Power that has brought her into being.

Aziza runs into the *kothari* and Buddha runs after her.

"Where are you going," Nasreen says, standing like a pillar before Buddha.

"I hate you! I hate all of you!" Aziza cries from inside.

"That's no way to talk to your mother!" Mardana says, not very convincingly.

"She's not my mother but an evil witch! And Daadi Jaan is an evil witch, too," screams Aziza, sticking her head out of the door.

"Better kill yourself than behave this way!" Nasreen shouts.

"I won't kill myself! I will go to see the plays with Buddha and Daadu," Aziza yells.

"Let her go," Mardana says, almost under his breath. "What harm can it do?"

"See how she's been spoilt? And it's all because of... him!" Nasreen points at Buddha. "I demand you stop his coming to our house now!"

"Then where will I get my news?" Mardana whines.

"I *will* go, nobody can stop me! And you can't stop him from coming to see me. He is my friend!" Aziza shouts defiantly.

Her mother bolts and locks the door of the *kothari* from the outside. Aziza bangs on it for a while, then begins to play the *rabab* in a fast and furious *Bhairav.*[79] Buddha listens sadly for a while, then looks at Mardana and smiles:

"Ma Durga doing the dance of destruction!"

"She's getting very good, better than her father," Mardana admits. "Shehzada is quite good with the *rabab*, but his technical virtuosity is not tempered with feeling but impatience. His ego strives for mastery and power over the instrument. I know because I was like that. But in Baba's service he will learn, like I learned. But Zizu, even at this age, has feelings. She has heart. You cannot have music without heart."

"Are you teaching her?" Buddha enquires.

"Only after making her promise that she will never, ever perform in public," Mardana whispers.

"But how can you do that?" Buddha almost shrieks.

"I must. I had to. I was made to."

In the long silence that follows, punctuated by Daulatan Masi's wails, they watch the puppies playing with each other and with Dharam, quite oblivious to the tragedy that is unfolding around them.

"Baba and Bebe Nanaki are teaching Amro to play the *rabab* and sing. I myself have given up the *rabab*; I'm no good at it. I love my bow and arrow. You want to see me shoot a guava for you?" Buddha asks.

"Yes, yes," Mardana replies excitedly. "See that yellowing one on top? I can't reach it and the parrots will get. But don't shoot the guava or there'll be nothing left for me to eat!"

Buddha shoots an arrow and brings it down with a small stem and two leaves still attached to it. Mardana looks at Buddha in awe and adoration as he holds out his hand and takes the guava.

"I want one, too, a green and crunchy one," Aziza shouts. Buddha

---

79 A raag associated with Lord Shiva, the God of Destruction. Durga, also associated with destruction, is one aspect of his consort.

shoots another one.

"Daadi, give me my guava."

Fatima opens the lock and hands it to her granddaughter through a crack.

"When you mentioned Bharatrihari, I was reminded of an incident when Baba and I traveled to Ujjain," Mardana reminisces.

"Tell me!" Buddha says, eagerly, sitting at Mardana's feet, reaching for and beginning to massage his feet. Mardana is diffident at first, but then relaxes and begins to enjoy it.

"We were in the land of Malwa.[80] The river, Shipra, which means the Fast Moving, meandered so lethargically, leisurely, one could mistake it for being still were it not for the equally gentle breeze that rippled its surface. Life there was a slow, silent unwinding like the river in its own time. The cows grazed in the sun the day long, and slept in the shade. The cattle, like the people, were also mild-eyed, as if they too had chomped at the abundant, sacred bhang[81] bushes of Mahakal.[82] I lay about in the sun, happy as can be, but suddenly unseasonal rains made us seek shelter in a cave. Soon other sadhus also took shelter there. One of them asked us, 'do you know whose cave this is?' We didn't, so he began to tell us about Bharatrihari, the great yogi who was once a king but had renounced his kingdom to become a wandering ascetic."

"I can't hear you, Daadu," Aziza yells. "I want to hear the story. Tell me who he was. Speak louder." Mardana changes the angle of his *manji* towards the room and begins to speak a little louder.

"I still can't hear you! You are getting too old!"

"Shall I tell it? Then you can fill in the incident with Baba."

"Yes, that's a relief. It takes too much energy."

With her daughter safely bolted inside the room, Nasreen leaves

80 A region in west-central northern India occupying a plateau of volcanic origin.

81 Marijuana.

82 Another epithet of Shiva. Bhang is associated with Shiva.

the courtyard to do other chores, and Buddha is emboldened to be uninhibited in his narration.

"Bharatrihari was a famous king – a poet, a philosopher, a linguist who lived many centuries ago. He had many wives," Buddha begins in a loud voice. "But his favorite was Pingala, who he loved and believed she truly loved him, too. In the first scenes they are in each other's amorous embraces. Bharatrihari says, lifting a crystal goblet of wine to her, 'you, my beloved, are the *ras*,[83] the juice, the essence and soul of my being. This love between a man and a woman is what life is all about.' In the second scene, the king is holding court with his courtiers and the common people when a Brahmin enters the stage with a gift for Bharatrihari. It is wrapped carefully in golden silk. Bharatrihari unwraps it, and sees it is a fruit, one he has never seen before. The Brahmin explains: 'it is the fruit that bestows immortality, sire. Somebody gave it to me and I thought, who is more deserving of it than our great king, Bharatrihari?' In the following scene, another scene of loving embraces, the king gives the fruit to Pingala. 'Survive me, beloved,' he says. 'Then I will be free of my fear of losing you. Let me die happily in your arms!' Pingala takes it."

"Yes, yes, this is the story Baba and I heard from the sadhu, but not as well as you tell it," Mardana said.

"It is not me, but the actors, Mardana jee. I have a deep respect for them. Through play, pretense, make believe with costumes, curtains and make up, they bring history, characters, stories to life and convey deep truths. Let me skip several scenes and come to another one. The king is holding court again, and a *tawaif*, a prostitute, dressed in the costume of her trade, her hairy legs showing..."

Aziza bursts into laughter.

83 Literally, juice, taste, but here meaning 'essence.'

"You know, of course, that men, or *hijraas*[84] play the roles of women, and this actor had forgotten to shave his legs. She came in, wriggling her butt and jangling her bangles, and said 'my lord, my king, I have received a wonderful gift that is unworthy of the likes of me, miserable and soiled as I am. I am weary of my life, my king, and do not wish to prolong it. So I have brought the gift for you.'

I have to add that the actor spoke so movingly – I have only summarized her speech – that the audience forgot all about her hairy legs and wept at the plight of prostitutes. For an instant they forgot their prejudices and self-righteousness, and their hearts bloomed in compassion. Who knows, a bit of the feeling will be carried over into their lives?"

"What was the gift?" Aziza asks.

"The audience gasped in surprise when the king unwrapped the gift. It was the fruit, the same fruit that the Brahmin had given Bharatrihari and he to Pingala!"

"Didn't Pingala eat it?" Aziza asks.

"That is the story. The king is dumbfounded. He asks the prostitute, 'where did you get this?' 'It was given to me by Chandu, your officer, lord,' she replies. Chandu is summoned and questioned about where he got the fruit of immortality. Chandu is very hesitant to tell and has to be tortured to confess: 'the queen, Pingala, gave it to me!' He went on to describe how much she loved him, how and where they had their passionate meetings, how one day she brought him the fruit and said, 'survive me, beloved. Then I will be free of my fear of losing you. Let me die happily in your arms!'

"The same words the king had said," Aziza cries. "But why did Chandu give it to the prostitute?"

"That is the point! Human passion is such a crazy thing that nobody loves the person who loves them! Chandu loved the prostitute the way the king loved Pingala, and Pingala, Chandu."

---

84 Transgenders and eunuchs.

"That is not the interpretation Baba gave us as we sat huddled in the cave," Mardana adds. "He said the need to love is greater than the need to be loved. And that is why the world goes crazy trying to fulfill this need. Only the One Beloved is worthy of our passionate need to love, for he alone reciprocates it a thousand fold."

A long pause follows Mardana's words. Buddha bows his head and kisses Mardana's foot.

"Don't ever die, Mardana jee!" he pleads. "So much wisdom, so many memories of Baba will die with you."

"No, don't die, Daadu. Promise you won't die!" Aziza pleads.

Mardana laughs. "I promise," he says, and laughs louder.

"I have told you and Zizu so many stories. I think I am empty now."

"And then what happened?" Aziza prompts.

"What happens after this revelation is the real story," Buddha says, pacing the courtyard. "Bharatrihari's world shatters. The crystal goblet containing the heady wine of human love and passion falls from his hand and shatters all about him. In its shards he sees his reflection fragmented into a hundred pieces. He sees the world and human love for the illusion it is. He takes off his crown, his shining robes, his jewelry, his shoes, wears a loin cloth, smears his body with ashes, and barefoot, begging bowl in hand, walks off the stage and retires to a cave by the shores of the Shipra to find another *ras*, the *amrit*[85] of the gods."

"The very cave that Baba and I took shelter in!" Mardana exclaims.

"But he takes a moment to recite a poem before he makes his exit:

'The clear bright flame of a man's discernment dies
When a girl clouds it with her lamp-black eyes.'"

"And does he find this *amrit*?" Aziza asks eagerly.

Buddha and Mardana both burst into laughter.

---

85 Ambrosia. Ras literally means 'juice,' but can also mean 'essence' or 'ecstasy.'

"The sadhus we talked to believed he had found it in renunciation," Mardana says.

"But in truth he had only exchanged one illusion for another," Buddha continues. "In one scene he is walking on the street and sees juicy *jalaibees*[86] being made in a shop. The *halwai*[87] is squeezing them out into hot oil in a large pot, and then sieving them into another pot full of hot, sweet syrup. Bharatrihari, used to eating berries and roots, craves some. Extending his begging bowl, he asks the *halwai*, 'please give me a few.' The *halwai* laughs. 'This yogi[88] wants *jalaibees*!' he shouts to the audience. Everyone laughs. A yogi is supposed to have renounced 'life,' but the king is blinded by his desire for the sweets and asks again. 'If you want some, work for them. Do the dishes,' the *halwai* answers. The king does so, gets the *jalaibees*, and as he begins to eat them, he realizes: 'even though I have slept on the earth, eaten dried crusts of bread, mediated hours on end, desire has not left me.'"

"Sri Chand's followers are all Bharatriharis!" Mardana laughs. "But they will want *jalaibees* soon!"

"They do enjoy *kadaa parshaad*, though they pretend it is something they *have* to eat."

"I could have some right now!" Mardana says. "Fatima! Fatima!"

"I heard you," Fatima says, laying aside her spinning and going to the area of the courtyard surrounded by small mud walls plastered with cow dung, which serves as the outdoor kitchen in good weather. She takes a few of lumps of brown sugar from an earthenware jar and puts them in a pot with water to boil into a syrup while she roasts a bowl full of coarse wheat flour in a generous portion of ghee till the whole house is perfused with the aroma. Fatima pours the hot syrup into the flour and ghee till it bubbles and

86 An Indian sweet.

87 The man who makes sweets.

88 One who renounces the world.

the liquid congeals into a delicious lump that she breaks up with her ladle. She serves it to them in *katoris*,[89] and invites Nasreen to stop and eat some, too. She takes a *katori* to Aziza, opens the door, places it inside and shuts and locks the door again.

"Don't feed me like a dog! I don't want it! I'm not going to eat it!"

"So Bharatrihari goes back to his kingdom, wears his crown and his robes once more," Buddha distracts Aziza with the story."But once again something happens to disillusion him, and back he goes to the cave. A hundred times he does this, the actor changing costumes in rapid succession before the audience: crown and robes, then loin cloth, begging bowl, ashes, back and forth, back and forth from cave to throne. Even after the curtain falls you can see his shadow going from one to the other, the implication being that Bharatrihari has been doing this for a thousand years, without getting any wiser, without finding the *amrit* he is looking for."

"So where is this *amrit*? Is it nowhere to be found? Is it a lie?" Aziza cries.

"The story isn't over, Zizu," Mardana reassures his granddaughter. "As we sat in the cave, we all felt the presence of Bharatrihari's troubled spirit, torn even in death between the sensual and the spiritual world, between being a yogi and a king, between sensuality and renunciation, sexuality and celibacy. Baba said to me, '*rabab chaid*, Mardanaiya.'[90] I tuned the *rabab* and as I began to play raag *aasaa*,[91] as he had told me to, a silence fell in the cave and a stillness descended. The peace was palpable. Buddha jee, get me my *rabab*," Mardana says.

Buddha fetches it. Locked inside the room, Aziza too begins to play raag *aasaa*. "Let me explain the *shabad* Baba sang, so that when I sing it, you will understand it, Zizu," Mardana says, tuning

89 Small bowls.

90 Awaken the rabab. 'Mardanaiya' is an affectionate variation of his name.

91 One of the many raags in Indian classical music.

his *rabab* and clearing his phlegmy throat. "In this *shabad* Baba addresses himself to Bharatrihari as if he were present. We all felt his spirit quiet down, as if it were listening intently, as Baba sang his intoxicating song. Guru Nanak gives him the recipe for the *ras* that never exhausts itself: '*Make wisdom your molasses; add the herbs of meditation; heat it on the fire of faith; add the ambrosia of the Beloved's name, and drink it in the Cup of Love. Its taste on your tongue will make you forget the wine of the world and take you into the cave of the Self; you can be a yogi while sitting on a throne.*'"

Mardana begins to sing in a quavering voice and as he proceeds, everyone joins in, including Masi, babbling off key. It is far from a perfect performance; Buddha's raspy and labored singing, Mardana's aging and out of practice voice, the accompaniment of a child still learning her lessons, makes for a rather scratchy outpouring. But there is love, and a longing to drink in the best, the very best that life has to offer by way of spiritual sustenance. For at least the duration of the song, they unite as one as they quaff the same, soothing nectar.

Mardana's family is still in the warm glow of the spontaneous singing when Daulatan Masi begins quietly, delightedly, to babble incoherently. She laughs then falls sadly silent. "The other one, my one, my dear, sweet one, bricked inside a wall you will fly everywhere. My bird, no one will hear your song. A flower no one will see, smell. Darkness, darkness, seeds sprouting in the rain of tears, rain on your cheeks, you will learn, light you will learn, you will learn, my one, my sweet dark one so full of light, darkness will take you to light and love love love love love love love. Love love love love love love love love." She keeps repeating the last word till it becomes inaudible even as her lips keep miming the word.

In the silence that follows Aziza fears story telling will be over unless she prolongs it.

"Tell the story about when the Emperor Babar put you and Baba in Prison, Daadu Jaan. You began it without completing it."

"When Baba and I were put into prison by Babar's soldiers," Mardana begins, but is interrupted immediately by his granddaughter.

"But why were you put into prison? Don't be lazy, Daadu, I won't let you sleep before you tell us the whole story."

CHAPTER 13

The Terror and the Beauty

Mardana clears his throat, and begins.

"Baba and I were returning from one of our travels, I forget which one, there were oh so very many! Baba was tireless, physically strong, full of vitality. He wanted to see God's whole world, all the people in their different colored skins, their cultures, customs, religions; he wanted to hear the rhythms of different languages, music, melody, song. And he wanted to bring all he met the message, through his words and music, that 'we are one, we are one in, and of, the One! We are all made of the same Light. Remember it! Love it. Turn to it in your sorrows, as to the Sun that dispels darkness and shadows."

Mardana was silent. His brimming eyes contained themselves after a little spillover as his adoration turned to anger.

"What a far cry from Baba is Babar, the Butcher! Our emperors shame Islam!"

Another silence followed in which he recouped his strength, compromised by the outburst, and began in lowers tones.

"Before we found ourselves in the middle of the slaughter that Babar had unleashed in India, we rested in one of the loveliest of places by a lake. Lotuses bloomed, white swans with red beaks glided in the calm waters followed by their little hatchlings, some chicks riding the backs of their mothers. And when they flew with their strong wings up into the air, trumpeting and whooping, we were filled with awe. It was such a heavenly scene that we stayed there for quite some time, singing, sleeping, wandering, looking, admiring, praising. Baba composed many *shabads* there. You know, of course, that the swan is a symbol of the soul and of the enlightened being, the *parmahansa,* the Supreme Swan.

But you can't take your symbols too seriously. One day a hunter with a bow and arrow shot one of them. I was very upset and wanted to kill the hunter, but when he made a fire, cooked it, and offered it to me, I ate it, enjoying it tremendously!"

Mardana has a good laugh before proceeding.

"One day a fox got one, too, and that was really heart-rending because it was a mother nesting with her little ones. And on looking back at the event I realized it was a harbinger of what was to come.

Baba was like one possessed, as if the veil of time was torn away and he could look into the future. He had visions of terror, of rivers of blood; his compositions were full of images of violence and descending darkness: 'bodies will be shred like cloth; women will apply blood in the partings of their hair;'[92] they will smear themselves with the saffron of blood."

I knew that his visions always came true and something terrible was going to happen. I wanted to stay longer by the lake but Baba wanted to travel towards Saiyidpur to meet with Bhai Lalo, his long time friend, the carpenter at whose house we had stayed many times before. When we reached his house, Bhai Lalo complained about the Pathans,[93] how they terrorized the people of the town, taking what they wanted from their homes, eating their grain and raping their women. Baba said to him, 'what you have experienced

---

92 Traditional women apply a red powder in the parting of their hair as a symbol of marriage.

93 A tribe from Afghanistan and Northern Pakistan, also called Pashtuns. The men tend to be warriors.

is nothing compared with what is coming. Take your family and go to the pool where the swans nest and you will be spared. Everyone in this town will be killed.'

Then Baba composed a *shabad* addressed to Bhai Lalo, about how Babar, bringing a bridle procession of sin was coming from Kabul to demand wealth and power as his bride; how the devil would read the marriage service and Hindus and Muslims alike would rend the skies with their wails.

Bhai Lalo, after cooking us a meal, left with his family and I wondered why Baba had saved him and not us. I worried a lot about what was going to happen, and it didn't take long for it to begin.

We stayed the night at Bhai Lalo's house, and it was an unholy night, loud with cries and screaming. The next day I peeped out of the window and saw soldiers in red uniforms and armor on horses with lances, skewering people, dogs, children, women. The dark, violent shadow of the Moghuls had surfaced from the deep, dark roots of hell, and was walking the streets in broad daylight. It went on for days, the whole town was destroyed, and a stench of rotting corpses filled the air.

We stayed holed up for a couple of days, and when things quietened down a bit, we ventured out. We were not prepared for what we saw: heaps of corpses of men, women and children with flies buzzing on them; a child, still clutching her rag doll with black hair made of wool still clutched in her hand. Limbs, heads, torsos, rotting guts, but no, I will not describe it all before we sleep. I still have nightmares about it. Besides, that is not the point of the story.

But I remember one detail very well. Walking through the blood-stained, corpse-littered street I was surprised to find that I was very hungry! At first I scolded myself, thinking that I was unfeeling but realized that I liked the feeling of hunger. It meant I was alive! Another detail I remember was how shaken Baba was. Usually he just moves through the terror and the beauty, dispassionately watching and experiencing the drama, but he was sobbing with grief at the sight of so much carnage. Singing was his daily practice and he stopped singing altogether and when he finally did, he sang an angry song addressed to his Beloved. Oh yes, Baba's relationship with his Beloved included quarrels and rebukes.

'Don't you feel pity and pain at the sight of this carnage? Doesn't your heart bleed at the sounds of wails and lamentations?' He was very angry with God."

"For how long was he angry with God?" Aziza asked.

"I don't remember."

"Remember, Daadu, you must! I want to know! Did he have to work on not staying angry with God?"

"Don't measure yourself against Baba, Zizu. We ordinary human beings must work on it. Who can presume to know what goes on in him? But I know from knowing his *shabads* intimately that it couldn't have been for too long. Nanak breathed God like fish water. God was inside and outside of him. *Outside you, I burst and die!* He says in one of his *shabads*. Slowly as the days went by in Babar's charnel house, a change came over him. It was as if he was watching God's dark Leela.[94] God's supreme detachment became Nanak's detachment and he looked at the scenes before him with wonder and awe at the ways of creation and destruction. He made up with his Beloved, I know, because he sang, '*Nanak sings the praises of the lord in the city of corpses. True is the lord, true his decisions.*'

I didn't want Baba to sing. I was afraid it would attract the attention of the soldiers. But Baba had to sing when he was compelled to. I refused to play the *rabab*, wouldn't let him touch it, but Baba sang in his deep, beautiful, strong voice suffused with feeling, glorying in life, in all of it, including senseless slaughter. I couldn't understand him. The human in me couldn't relate to the god in him, and I was confused and upset that he was endangering

94 Play; magical creative power of the creator; Creation.

our lives by his singing.

My worst fear came to pass. We heard the hooves of horses and saw Babar's soldiers in the distance. We hid behind a heap of corpses and I pretended to be dead but we couldn't fool their hawks' eyes. Seeing our fakir's garbs and the *rabab* on my shoulder, they arrested instead of killing us. One of the soldiers was Mir Khan, the superintendent of Babar's army. He was a very fierce-looking man, with red eyes in a pale face, his starched moustaches extending two inches beyond his cheeks. Babar had given orders to his solders not to kill holy men but convert them to Islam. Being the survivor that I am, I eagerly told Mir Khan that I was a Muslim. Baba, however, said he had no more religion than wind and fire.

They imprisoned us. I admit I was disgusted with myself for claiming to be a Muslim to save my skin. I fumed inwardly at what power hungry and twisted men had made of Islam, what Babar had been doing in India and what is still going on. His generals forced people to convert to Islam. Those that did were given gifts of land and property seized from Hindu families. Babar called himself a *Ghazi*, a title given to Muslims who kill non-Muslims. *Ghazis* are ensured heaven with *houri,* young virgins in the next life, together with rivers of wine and honey."

"Then I am also ashamed to be a Muslim, Daadu," Aziza adds her voice from her prison."Like the moon, wind, water, trees, I will not have a religion, but pick and choose the things I like from many religions and reject anything that imprisons my spirit. And then what happened, Daadu Jaan?"

"When they heard Baba sing in the prison – by some miracle of Baba's making they let us keep the *rabab* – they doubled their efforts to convert him, but Baba continued to refuse them. They tried to persuade me to leave the 'infidel,' but I refused."

"I am proud of you, Daadu."

"But my rebellion did not have a good outcome. I was sent to the stables, to clean dung. Those Arabian horses sure know how to make dung! There was always heaps of it."

"I love the smell of horse dung," Aziza exclaims.

"So do I!" Buddha adds.

"Well you would have been in horse dung heaven there!" Mardana chuckles."And they gave me the worst horse in the stable to groom and train. His name was *Dhanak*, which means 'wild and un-trainable.' He looked fierce, just like Mir Khan. When I groomed it he gave me a couple of good kicks. Just as I was doing his muzzle he snorted so loudly in my ear that I couldn't hear for several days. He bit me many times. I still have bite-shaped scars!

Baba was sent to carry bricks from an ancient Hindu temple they had razed to the ground to build a mosque to Allah in its place. Fools! My own labors disturbed me less than the thought of Baba's rigorous punishment. I had many sleepless nights over it. My mental state was very disturbed during that time.

Once I ran into Baba and he said to me, 'Mardana, give your burdens to God and he will turn them into air.' I didn't quite understand what he meant even though in my prayers I tried and struggled to surrender my burdens. I didn't succeed and hated Dhanak even more. I wanted to kill him, actually, and even thought about ways to do it, but I knew that the punishment for that would be death.

One day I was asked to take the horse from the stable to another building in the prison compound. I managed to bring him out of the stable but when he saw he wasn't going towards the field where the horses play, he just sat down on his haunches. Though I pulled and yanked at his reins, Dhanak refused to budge. Mir Khan had said if I didn't get Dhanak to his destination by lunch, I wouldn't get food for two days. As it is we got such meager meals that I was a skeleton and I was certain two days without food would kill me. I had to do it, but that beast looked at me insolently and just sat there.

Who do I see coming towards me but Nanak, carrying a *tasla*[95] full of bricks on his head. He saw me straining and struggling with the horse and shouted to me:

'Forget about the horse, Mardana! Go get your *rabab* and play it!'

I thought Baba had gone mad.

'Play the *rabab*? Can't you see that both my hands are busy? Can't you see how important it is to get this horse to his destination?'

'Trust, Mardana. Let go the bridle and play the *rabab*.'

His words opened something in me, like a locked gate. No, like a tight bud that begins to unfurl into the light, and I thought, *why not, Mardana? Go, obey your guru, and fetch your rabab! Play one last time before you die.*

I let go the horse and went to my corner in the barn where I slept on straw, and lovingly picked up my *rabab*. I didn't care that all the progress I had made with Dhanak was wasted, that he had returned to his stall and stood there like a stubborn mule. I ran out of the barn with the *rabab*. The *shabad* that came to me as soon as I tuned and touched the strings was: *keeta loriai kam so har pai aakheeai, kaaraj dai savaar satgur sach sakheeai. Give whatever work you want to accomplish to your Merciful Beloved. He will resolve all your affairs.*

Baba was ahead of me by the time I came out of the barn and I followed him, playing the *rabab* and singing in the sun, happy as I could be. The music, the words lifted me out and up and I felt full of hope and joy. But just then I stopped in mid song when I noticed something really strange. Baba's *tasla* full of stones and bricks on his head was floating four or five inches above Baba's head, as if it was carrying itself as Baba hummed and sang along with me."

"Like Bhai Lehna and the muddy bundles!" Buddha exclaims.

"Yes. Your story reminded me of this incident. Mir Khan, who was coming towards me with his whip, stopped in his tracks and saw

95 A large metal bowl for carrying stones and bricks.

what I was seeing. His red eyes popped out of his head. He wanted to get angry at Baba, but what could he say? He was speechless. He turned to me in his anger and rage, and I was certain I had had it, for there were only a few minutes to lunch time and here I was, with Dhanak back in the barn, and me with my *rabab*, singing. One look at Baba and his tasla was enough to reconcile me to any punishment that awaited me. It was the first bit of joy I had had in a long time. But Mir Khan's expression changed from rage to amazement as he looked at something behind me. When I turned around to see what he was looking at, there was Dhanak, following me meekly, like a lamb, his reins dragging in the mud!"

"Music tamed him!" Aziza laughs and claps her hands, delightedly.

"Baba was right," Mardana adds. "Give your burdens to the Beloved and he turns them into air!"

Buddha is silent a long time before he speaks. "Bhai Lehna lives in this *Sehaj* all the time. There is another little story I forgot to tell you. The other day Baba walked into the pond outside Kartarpur to take a bath and his *lota*[96] slipped into the water. He asked his sons to retrieve it but they balked at the thought of diving into the pond. Lakhmi Das offered to buy him a new one and Sri Chand said he would fetch someone to retrieve it. But Bhai Lehna touched the pond and the *lota* rose to the surface, right into his hand.

There is a way to live in which the universe works for and with you. Everything gets done without your doing it. It is as if you have caught a current of air, like a bird gliding in the air without flapping its wings, effortlessly. Even humans can catch this wave that keeps us so totally in the moment, and ride it without effort and thought."

"How do you find it?" Aziza asks.

"By constantly surrendering, as Baba says," Buddha replies. "It is our egos that keep us from finding the paths that rivers and

---

96 A metal jar for water.

streams find. The arrow shoots itself. The ego thinks, unless *I* do it, it won't get done. But how deluded the ego is!"

"It struggles and pulls and strains at the reins of the horse instead of singing!" Mardana laughs.

"How can you live without effort?" Aziza wonders aloud.

"By living like a river. It does not force anything and it does not hold back. There is a space where our Mother Father Earth carries us, together with our burdens, like infants in the womb," Buddha philosophizes.

"I don't understand why we should burden God with our burdens instead of carrying them ourselves," Aziza replies.

Buddha laughs. "God created one hundred thousand universes without a grain of effort."

"Baba says in the *Japji*, God wrote a Word and a hundred thousand rivers began to flow. The whole universe is God's utterance," Mardana adds.

"He takes our burdens and gives them to the Energy that is Life fulfilling itself naturally, spontaneously, like a flower."

"I am spontaneously falling asleep," Mardana says, yawning loudly and sliding under the covers.

"But Daadu you haven't told us how you got out of prison!"

"Let Daadu rest. It is late," Fatima reprimands.

"Tell me briefly. Then I promise I will let you sleep. I'm getting sleepy too, but I want to know or I won't be able to sleep, imagining you still in prison, whipped by Mir Khan."

"Mir Khan, instead of converting us, was himself converted to Baba! He told the emperor what he had seen and experienced and how Nanak's singing in prison comforted the prisoners. Babar told him to bring us to him. Baba was not kind with Babar and told him to take a tour of the streets to see what his orders to his soldiers had accomplished. Baba fearlessly sang a *shabad* reminding Babar of his own death; how the victorious of today will be defeated tomorrow.

Where are those kings of yesteryear, he asked? Where are their stables with wild horses, the bugles, the clarions, the palaces, the armies in red uniforms, the signs and symbols of wealth and power?

The emperor grew furious and gripped the end of his throne and half got up. Baba signaled to me to start the *rabab*. The strains calmed Babar, and I could see as our *shabad* progressed that he was charmed by it. Just for an instant the tyrant saw the truth of life. His heart was humbled and he said to Baba: 'ask something of me! You are free to go, of course, but ask for something else. A chariot, a trunk full of gold, a kingdom.'

'There is only one kingdom I acknowledge, the kingdom of the Emperor of Emperors. But if you want to give me something, release all the prisoners!' Baba said.

The emperor did so. His compassion and change of heart was temporary and momentary, for like a pig's tail, he refused to be straightened and continued with his carnage later."

Mardana's voice was slurring with sleep.

"One last little question, Daadu. What did Baba think about temples being converted into mosques?"

"Baba doesn't care one jot for temples or mosques. He knows they can't contain God. The spirit cannot be contained in any house, whether of bricks or the flesh. May I sleep now?"

"But why did he make a gurdwara?" Aziza asks.

"It is the place we go to, to get Prasad for our minds and hearts through music and kirtan. We actually don't have to go anywhere to get it since it is already inside us, accessible through prayer, praise and song. But some people need places to go to get it. We can get it from a mosque or a temple, too, if we go there humbly, leaving our egos behind with our shoes[97] and go in with our hearts totally surrendered to the One Power," Buddha explicates. "But if they

97 It is customary in Eastern religions to take off your shoes before entering a place of worship.

are only hotbeds of corruption with priests and mullahs exercising power over the populace, and lining their own pockets, then they are all to be razed to the ground."

Fatima, having moved to her bed, stretches out on it. Buddha gets up.

"I'll return to the dera."

"Be sure and return soon," Mardana says. Though he wants to offer him a bed, he knows his daughter in law would object.

"Boys can roam the streets at night while girls have to be locked into rooms," Aziza says after Buddha has left. "But I'm glad you locked me up, Ami! Do you hear me, Ami? Wake up and hear the voice of your daughter," Aziza shouts from inside the room. "I'm sure you wouldn't have locked me up if you knew how much fun I would have tonight listening to the stories. *And* I didn't have to do the dishes!"

CHAPTER 14

In Khadur

As instructed by Baba Nanak, Bhai Lehna returns to his hometown, Khadur. The rumor that Bhai Lehna is Guru Nanak's successor precedes his return, a rumor that he himself does nothing to encourage or dismiss. He wants more than anything else to be his Master's servant, obey him in every respect, live in his bright shadow, and follow the path in his footsteps to the Divine.

As bees are attracted to a particularly fragrant flower from which they can gather the nectar to make their own honey, the people of Khadur and the outlying villages throng to see Bhai Lehna, touch his feet, love and adore him. But when Takht Mal, the chief of the city, touches his feet, Bhai Lehna steps back in trepidation. He is used to bowing before Takht Mal and the gesture feels awkward to him. Bhai Lehna assures him that he is but Nanak's servant, and all honors are owed to his guru alone. But Takht Mal is not to be deterred. He allocates vast resources to be given to Bhai Lehna to do with as he pleased. Takht Mal hopes Bhai Lehna will build himself a better home, buy some horses, land, and cows, but Bhai Lehna opens a langar instead and puts his wife, Khivi, in charge of it. Farmers bring sacks of wheat, flour, corn, lentils, rice, brown sugar; cowherds bring milk, buttermilk, butter and ghee. Khivi, now called Mata Khivi, is happy. To feed people, take care of those in need, has always been her dream.

Bhai Lehna remains behind the scenes, missing his master, longing to behold Nanak. His one desire is to connect to his guru through meditation and reflection. When people plead with him for spiritual advice, he sings Guru Nanak's words. His voice has matured in the intervening years to a rich and soulful depth, and his skill with the *rabab* leaves nothing to be desired. Kirtan,[98] attended by many, resounds far and wide in the mornings and evenings at the new dera in Khadur. The traditions that have sprung up in Kartarpur around Guru Nanak are carried on in Khadur. Takht Mal, a frequent visitor, sits quietly in the courtyard, looking at Bhai Lehna with adoration. Bhai Lehna's message is a perpetuation of his master's message: the cultivation of love for the Divine and fellow creatures, utterance, recitation and remembrance of His Name, and the many rewards, material, psychological and spiritual to be gained thereof.

Amro, who is thrilled to have her father back after many years in which she has seen little of him, accompanies him in his singing. Her mother, Mata Khivi, has nurtured her daughter's talent by hiring an instructor of classical Indian music. Amro learns the raags, her scales, but her passion for singing is her greatest instructor. People think of her as Saraswati, the Goddess of music herself. Along with Akal Purakh, Amro continues to worship Ma Durga and the other goddesses, remembering when she tends to think of them as literal beings that they are feminine manifestations, images, and names for unnamable energies. To her ample repertoire of Baba's *shabads* she has added some of her father's compositions. The house resounds with melody as she sings: *khasmai kai darbar, dhaadee vasia. Sacha khasam kalaan kamal vigsaia: Minstrels live in the Beloved's Mansion, their lotus hearts blooming with adoration and ecstasy.*

Amro is also skillful with the bow and arrow through Bhai Jodha's instruction. Dasu and Datu, without the discipline for either the

98 Sung text from the Sikh holy book, the SGGS.

rabab or archery, still squabble with each other and Amro, throwing tantrums whenever they don't get their way. But they are eager for, and take pride in the adulation that is paid to them as Bhai Lehna's sons.

But Bhai Lehna himself is uncomfortable with being the center of attention and feels an intense need to withdraw. He wants solitude in which to commune with the Beloved, his highest and most exalted desire. Bhai Lehna is stricken with grief over his separation from his beloved Master. It is as if he has lost a limb. Mata Khivi, always attuned to her husband's needs, suggests he retire in secret to the cottage of Nihali, whose name means 'one who is full of wonder and awe.' She is a family friend, a frequent visitor at the dera, a recluse who has never married and devoted herself to prayer and the solitary life. She lives at the edge of town and makes her living by collecting dung, making patties and selling them for fuel. She also owns a cow that she grazes and tends, selling milk and ghee. Engaged in the humblest of professions, she is rumored to have become an enlightened spirit. Only those who have love in their hearts for the Divine recognize this; for the others she was just a low-caste menial.

Leaving Amro in charge of the morning and evening Kirtan sessions, Bhai Lehna visits Nihali in secret early one morning while it is still dark. She, long-sighted woman, has been expecting him. She has prepared her hut with a bed in one corner, a *daree* in another, with a heap of coarse grass near it. Having been a dancer to Durga in his earlier life, and being a disciple of Guru Nanak who emphasizes physical activity, Bhai Lehna does yoga on the daree and weaves the grasses into strings to make manjis, *moodaas,*[99] and peedees, a practice he had begun in Kartarpur. He wants to keep his hands busy while his consciousness stays focused on his guru and his God.

---

99 Seats made of dry grass and bamboo.

Bhai Lehna does not want to be disturbed so he asks Nihali to lock the room from the outside. He wants only three bowls of milk a day as sustenance. Baba Nanak's *shabads*, one copy of which he has brought with him, are his constant companions. He finds solace in Baba's words and music. He enters a period of ferment in his cocoon of rest and stillness to be ready for his destiny when it should find him. He continues to miss his master and his longing is like a physical pain. He finds relief only in meeting him in the Beloved, in whom all beings reside. As soon as he connects to the Divine, Nanak is present.

CHAPTER 15

Flight

"She has escaped! She has run away with that boy, that prostitute!"

Nasreen's midnight screams waken all the sleeping members of the household and they rush to the *kothari* where Aziza had been locked up.

The window frame, embedded in the mud wall of the room has been yanked out with a lot of force, and a jagged, gaping hole stands in its place.

"Buddha would never do such a thing! It is clearly done from the inside," Mardana insists. As they stand there, shocked and incredulous that a young girl could have such brute strength, Aziza's face appears in the gap in the wall. She sees the assembly and fearlessly climbs back into the room.

"I flew away mother, I escaped my prison. I went to see the play," she says, calmly. "You should come with me. It is very entertaining and instructive."

"She is possessed by a jinn," Nasreen shouts, grabbing her by her shoulders, shaking her violently, then slapping her again and again while Aziza stands and takes the abuse without flinching, though tears begin to stream out of Mardana's eyes.

"Radha leaves her house, her husband, her family, and goes out in the middle of the night, lured by Krishna's flute,"[100] Aziza says

100 Radha is a married woman in love with the Hindu God, Krishna.

in between the slaps. "She is not afraid."

"She is becoming a heathen, a Hindu! Saido! Saido! Saido!" her mother cries with each slap on Aziza's face. "Kill yourself! Why don't you kill yourself, Saido?"

"Why are you calling me Saido? I am Aziza, Aziza, Aziza."

"That's enough!" Shehzada, Aziza's father, at home for a change instead of spending his nights with his musician friends, pulls Nasreen away from his daughter.

"First make her swear on Allah she won't leave this house ever again. She can leave with a husband or in a coffin, if she likes, but not otherwise," Nasreen insists, turning to her husband.

"That's what all the mothers and mother-in-laws say to their daughters and daughters-in-law when they leave their home in the middle of the night to meet and play with Krishna in the forest," Aziza responds.

"Swear it!" Cries Nasreen.

"Go ahead, swear it," Shehzada says, weary with the unending conflict in his home.

"I won't," Aziza says defiantly.

"Make her swear it!" Nasreen screams, turning to Fatima.

"Can she come with me to my hut and to graze the sheep?" Fatima asks, referring to a little shack she had made for herself at the boundary between habitation and wilderness. "Give her this much freedom."

"No! You will let her escape again!"Nasreen shouts.

"Yes, she can go with you, Amma Jaan," Shehzada responds.

"No!" Cries Nasreen.

"I have some say in this matter and I say she can!" Shehzada shouts back.

"But promise me she will never, ever see the face of that boy Buddha again!" Nasreen turns to Fatima.

Fatima hesitates for a moment.

"Promise!" she shouts again.

"Don't, Daadi Jaan! Don't! He is my friend! He teaches me so much with his stories! Please don't!"

"I promise," Fatima says, quietly.

"Daadi! Daadi! What have you done?" Aziza sobs, tears steaming down her less than clean cheeks, streaking them.

"And I won't leave her in this room. She will escape again!"

"Come, child. Come sleep with me," Fatima says, trying to take Aziza's hand.

"I hate you," Aziza spits, yanking her hand away.

"Then I'll lock you in the *kothari* without a window!" Nasreen threatens.

Aziza sticks out her tongue at her mother, and reluctantly follows her grandmother to her room. She lies down in Fatima's bed but turns her back to her grandmother.

The next morning, after their meal, Fatima says to Aziza:

"Come, we're taking the sheep to graze."

Aziza slings her *rabab* over her shoulder and the two step over the threshold. The sheep follow them, bleating and leaping, and Motia, too, springs up in anticipation of the outdoors. Both females are wearing their *burquas*, but while the older woman leaves her wrinkled face uncovered, the younger one has to cover hers.

"Why do you get to uncover your face and I have to look through these webbed eye holes?" Aziza asks, angrily.

"You'll have to wait till you are as old as I am to uncover it," Fatima replies.

Sullenly Aziza follows her grandmother down the streets of Kartarpur, kicking stones and pouting. They walk in silence past the village, past the houses huddled together, past the outlying fields, past a stretch of uncultivated land with fields of wild shrub and grasses where the sheep begin to graze, to a small mud hut that stands at the edge of the jungle.

A tiny patch of cultivated land, fenced with brambles, surrounds the hut. Herbs, culinary and medicinal, in different shades of green, together with whorls of lance shaped leaves with clusters of the small yellowish flowers of madder grow in neat beds of soil. The patch looks tended with love and care.

The rickety front door with a little verandah in front of it, has a large iron lock, but instead of opening it, Fatima goes to the window, opens it from the outside with a hidden lever, and the two climb in. It is dark inside with just a few streaks of light streaming in through chinks in the windows and door. Fatima takes a long stick from the corner and slides a slate off the roof. Light floods the room. Aziza, who has never been here before, looks around. A makeshift bed with a less than clean *daree* spread on it lies in one corner; a small chulla with kindling and cow patties stacked beside it, together with a rusty lantern, lie in another. Three different sized looms stand on the mud floor with three colorful weavings in different stages of completion. A basket full of balls of wool and a spinning wheel rolled upon them, lie beside them. From the rafters hang skeins of thread dyed in different colors. A small addition to this room houses large vats for dying and other implements of the trade.

"What is this place? I don't like it," Aziza says, sullenly, removing her burqa and flinging it on the bed.

Fatima is silent. Aziza swings around and screams: "I hate you, Daadi, I hate you!"

Fatima says nothing.

"Why don't you tell Ami to let me live my life? Why don't you defend me against that witch? You are a coward!"

"Yes, I am. Your Daadu and I are getting older, Zizu," Fatima says after a pause.

"What does that have to do with anything?"

"Who will take care of us when we are old but your mother? We can't make your Ami our enemy."

"I will take care of you. Let mother go to hell."

"Zizu, that's no way to talk about your mother."

"Why did you say I would never see Buddha again? I am very angry with you, Daadi. Why? Why? Why? The only person who loves me is Daadu and he alone is my family and my home. I hate all women!" Aziza kicks her grandmother, her sentences broken up by sobbing, her tears staining her grimy cheeks.

"I love you more than you will ever, ever know, my dearest, my darling," Fatima speaks quietly. But Aziza is in no mood to hear anything but the noises in her own head. Fatima stands there, allowing herself to be beaten, almost as if finding relief in it.

Aziza turns around and kicks a loom. "I hate your looms, too!"

"Don't kick the loom. It may save you one day as it did me."

"I don't want to be saved, I want to die!"

"You will be grateful for life one day, Aziza. Baba Nanak says it is a rare gift and must not be squandered away."

"I don't care what Baba Nanak says! I don't believe in anyone or anything. You promised I would never be allowed to see Buddha again and I know you always keep your promises. And what if I want to marry him?"

A long silence follows Aziza's outburst. Then Fatima speaks in a harsh, determined voice.

"That will never be. The sooner you get rid of the idea, the better you will be."

"Why?"

"We have to wait for a better world than ours for it to happen. It will take centuries, but one day our sisters and our daughters will be free."

"I want to be free *now*!"

"You will have to discover another way to do it. This much I know from loving Baba Nanak's words, that the Beloved can change a cage into a mansion if you bow before His Will."

"Baba is in a cage, too? A *man?*"

"We are all in cages, Zizu. Our lives are limited, by our family, our society, country, world. We are bound by how the universe has made us. But Baba's cage is Love. In this cage he is as free as any mortal can be. He says: *soohat pinjar paraym kai bolai bolanhaar. Sach chugai amrit pee-ai udai ta aykaa vaar: 'In the cage of divine love, the parrot sings. It pecks at the Truth, and drinks ambrosial nectar; it flies away, only once.'*

"Does it fly away and never return?" Aziza asks, confused.

"It only flies away when it dies. And then it flies right into the Beloved's heart."

"Well, I don't want to be in any cage."

"I was as angry as you once. While your Daadu was away on his many journeys with Baba I felt very alone, unhappy, and angry. Why was I not allowed to play the *rabab*? Why was I not allowed to accompany Baba and your Daadu on their journeys? I wanted to travel too, to see the far corners of the world. Why was I cursed to be a woman? For many years I hated your Daadu for being away, I hated Baba, I hated the *rabab*. But my anger brought me no peace. It made me unhappier. It was peace I wanted all along, not this or that circumstance.

Then one day I had a dream," Fatima continues. "Baba came to our house and I ran away from him, but in whichever direction I ran, he was there. I stopped running and picked up a broom to hit him but the broom flew out of my hand and hit me hard on my back. Baba came to me and put his hand on my head. I was very surprised at what I did next. I fell on the floor and kissed his feet. Something happened to me despite my own will, as if something had simply decided, through its illimitable mercy, to bless me.

The next day I allowed myself to enter and embrace my loneliness. It unfolded like a flower and kept unfolding as if there was no end to it. I accepted my destiny, I said "yes" to it. You see,

Zizu, Baba is absolutely right when he says we have to eat what we are given to eat."

"Even if we are given poison? Even if we are given a *cage?*" Aziza asks, spitting out the last word.

"Even if. We must all find space within the life we have been given to create joy. After I accepted that I was going to be alone till your Daadu returned, *if* he returned home at all, I changed. I fell in love with my aloneness. And within that aloneness I found a companion, the loom.

It was practical too, for while your Daadu was away I sold *loees* and *darees* to support the family. I found I loved weaving in solitude so much that I couldn't live without it. I loved it to the exclusion of all else. The sound of the shuttle moving through the warp, the battens and comb pounding the weft, the rhythm of the heddles empties your mind, which becomes silent, unwrinkled by thought. I would wait, almost impatiently, for the children to fall asleep so I could return to it. I even found myself wishing I didn't have a family so I could spend all my time with my looms," Fatima laughs. "Weaving and singing, wonderful as they are, are very jealous lovers. They both take time away from your family life. I dreamed about having a place of my own where nobody could disturb me and I could think all my thoughts and feel all my feelings in peace. But that was not possible then so I had to find a way of building an inner castle, invisible to everyone else, where I could retreat. It was here that I could begin my journey to myself. I almost used to wish your Daadu wouldn't come home from his journeys and interrupt my solitude and weaving!"

"Daadi, you wished Daadu dead?"

"Yes, sometimes!" Fatima laughs again. "But then something happened – it was after I had another dream of Baba. He was in a field, and he plucked and gave me a sheaf of wheat – and I began to long in my heart for my husband to return – my anger and contentment with my life turned to longing; my fear turned to hope. Soon after this your daadu returned and I was so very happy to have him back! I knew my dark desire was only preparing me for the worst and had nothing to do with my love of him."

Aziza listens quietly to Fatima's story, feeling privileged to hear what no one else had heard.

"So when we moved to Kartarpur and all the family was together, I asked Baba for a little piece of land that would be all my own. He himself allocated this to me. It is not much, but see, the whole jungle facing away from the town is mine. I made this hut with my own hands, with a little help from your father, your daadu, and some of his disciples from the dera. It is the castle where I live with the other members of my family, all of whom are myself. I am never alone here. We will come here together, you and I. It will be our secret. You will help me fix the room and add another room. We will make a loom together and you will bring your *rabab* here, too, to sing as loudly as you please."

Silence follows her words.

"I have seen a great solitude growing in you, Aziza, and you will find yourself, I know. I was beginning to feel very sad and upset about what was happening to you, but then I had a flash of insight – you will suffer, but you will be fine; you will be ground down, like madder is ground, to yield its colors."

"But how will I hear Buddha's stories?" Aziza bursts out.

"I never promised you wouldn't be allowed to *hear* him again," Fatima says, cryptically.

"What do you mean? How can I hear him if I can't see him?"

"Through this," Fatima says, picking up a spade and beating the wall with its thick wooden handle. She beat it repeatedly till a hole appeared in the mud, dung, and straw structure. A small circle of light came through and cast a sphere of light on the opposite wall.

"This is where I will put my ear!" Aziza skips excitedly to the hole.

"Yes, yes, yes, Daadi jaan, this will be our secret! And you would have kept your promise! But why is the hole so low to the ground?"

"So Buddha can sit while he tells you his stories," Fatima says, taking one of a pair of old *moodaas* from the hut and putting it in the verandah.

Aziza takes the other moodaa and places it by the hole inside the hut, very pleased with the arrangement.

"But Daadi," she stops and faces her grandmother. "Who is Saido? And why does Ami call me by that name?"

"Your father's uncle was married to your mother's first cousin, Saido. Having grown up in a family of *rabab*is, she played the *rabab*, and loved it, like you love it. Saido's father loved her and encouraged her to play. Saido and your mother were very close, like sisters, and loved each other very much. But when Saido got married, her in laws wouldn't let her play or sing. They locked her up in a room without the *rabab*. She tore her burqua and hanged herself with it."

Aziza is quiet a long while.

"I will never marry, Daadi. My heart will belong only to Krishna. Only he can return my passion."

"Then what will you do?"

"I will herd sheep; I will play my *rabab* even though no one will ever hear me. I will come here and play it. And you will teach me how to weave and grow herbs."

"You might change your mind as you grow older. It is very difficult to live alone."

"And it isn't difficult to live with others who tell you what to be, and what to do? You think it was easy for Saido? No, I swear by Allah I will never marry. And I also swear by Allah that I will never kill myself."

"You have to be a survivor, Zizu, not like those Hindu women who burn themselves on their husband's pyres. You are a survivor.

I know you will be well, no matter what happens."

It is a charged moment. Fatima has tears in her eyes as she opens her arms wide and Aziza goes into them.

"I love you, Daadi Jaan. And though I hate Ami, I love her too. She doesn't have an easy life. Abba is away all the time and all she does is work, work, work. She lives in the cage of her own fears and prejudices. Let's all of us go to see a play while the players are here. But I won't go unless you persuade Ami to come along. We will take Daadu, too."

"Yes, let's."

"What is this?" Aziza says, spying something under some skeins thrown on the bed, pulling it out and spreading it on the bed. It is a shawl with a very subtle pattern in beige and red, the texture and the weave thrilling the eye. "I love it. Give it to me!"

"It is not for you, Zizu. I have been making it for Baba for a long time, with a lot of attention and love, reciting the thousand names of God while I thread the warp, with each packing in of the weft with the reed. He uses the image of madder in so many of his *shabads* and I always think of him as I tend my madder plants and dye my wools, remembering to dip my soul in the unfading dye of Remembrance of the One whose color never fades. You will learn to make one like it too and have it."

"How can you give away something so very beautiful?" Aziza hugs the shawl to her heart.

"You, too, will learn that the pleasure of possessing something comes nowhere near the bliss of making it. The labor and joy of making it, the whole process from goat and sheep to fleece and yarn, the dyeing, the stringing of the loom, the weaving, the beating – that alone is mine. But when I take it off the loom, it is done, over, and it belongs not to me but the Universe that gifted me the making of it. The *shabad* that came again and again to my mind as I was weaving this for Baba was Kabir's, song:

koree ko kaahoo maram na jaanaa.
sabh jag aan tanaa-i-o taanaa.

"I know it! Daadu has sung it often!" Aziza says, reaching for her *rabab* and beginning to play raag aasaa, one of her favorite raags, playfully. Grandmother and granddaughter clear some space on the daree, and begin to sing together:

No one knows the secret of the Cosmic Weaver. He has woven the fabric of the universe, which the Vedas and Puranas[101] say, is only a fringe of his tapestry. The Earth and the sky are his warp and weft on which he weaves the sun, moon and stars. Working with my feet and hands I am awed by the skill of the Weaver who has come to live in my heart. Says Kabir, when the loom of my body breaks, the Weaver shall blend my thread with His thread.

---

101 Ancient Indian holy texts.

CHAPTER 16

The Blessing of the Curse

"Are you dying Daadu Jaan?" Aziza asks, peering into her grandfather's face and opening his eye as he lies with his eyes closed on his bed.

"Yes," he replies feebly.

Aziza's face contorts before she bursts into uncontrolled weeping, fat tears rolling from the pools of her large, dark eyes.

In a weak voice, Mardana recites a couplet of Baba Nanak's:

"'*Ho-ay puraanaa kaparh paatai soo-ee dhaagaa gandhai.*

Maahu pakh kihu chalai naahee gharhee muhat kichh handhai.'

'*The cloth has become old and torn,*' he explains. '*Mended with needle and thread it will not last for a month, or even a week. As it is, it barely lasts for an hour, or even a moment.*'"

"You are my home, Daadu! Please don't die!"

"No person can be your home, darling."

"But why not?"

"Because people die. Nothing except God can be our permanent home."

"But you *are* my home! I will be homeless when you die! What will happen to me? I had a dream last night that I am in a jungle and it is cold and raining and my feet keep sinking in the mud. Then I come to our door and keep knocking but nobody lets me in. You were dead and no body let me in! Please don't die, Daadu jaan!"

"I don't want to die, Zizu. I want to stay alive, for you, for Motia, for Daadi and for her delicious halwa; for Baba who I adore so much I can't bear to be parted from him; for Buddha, too. I want to see the great and far spreading tree he will become; I want to live to see our mango trees in bloom and eat the fruit. But my leaving was ordained from the moment I was conceived."

"No, Daadu, No! I won't have it."

"Here, have some of this halwa and then I will tell you something important," he says, putting some in her hands. She puts it in her mouth and eats it, sobbing all the while.

"Now wasn't that delicious?"

"What have you done? What have you done?" Nasreen screams. Fatima too, comes into the scene to see what has happened. "He has given his halwa with charas in it to my daughter!"

"Oh, I forgot. I'm sorry! I'll never do it again," Mardana says, looking at them sheepishly.

Aziza climbs into bed with her grandfather and cuddles up to him.

Nasreen tries to drag her out of bed. "You will have to drink soapy water now and throw it up."

"Let her be," Mardana says, holding her tightly. "I promise by Allah that I will never do it again."

Nasreen returns to her chores still grumbling while Fatima sits on a peedee with her spindle and fleece.

"Baba has always said, 'If you surrender to the Beloved, enter him, become a part of Him, you never die, for He is outside of Time, Akaal. Everything that was, is and will be is contained within him. In Him we will always be together. Let me tell you a story, Zizu," Mardana clears his throat, coughing up a gob of phlegm. "Baba and I were returning from Baghdad."

"I don't want to hear a story. I want you to go on living!"

"I will go on living. The God in me never dies."

"Is there a God in me, too? A girl?"

"In everyone. Do you want to hear the story?"

"There's no new story! You have told me all your stories!"

"But you didn't listen to this one when I told it to you before. Otherwise, you would never feel bad about being homeless."

"What is it called?"

"The Blessing of the Curse."

"I know it by heart. You were returning from Baghdad to India in one of your many journeys with Baba Nanak. After the boat had dropped you on the shores of India, you walked and walked for many days and your feet were sore."

She sits up in bed and begins to tell the story, embellishing it with details from her own life and experience, enacting it, waving her arms about and miming her words, like an actor. Her gaze turns to her grandfather, and seeing his ragged old sunken face with death written all over it, she breaks down in tears again, hugs him, and sobs. Mardana holds her, rocks her, and whispers, "It is okay. Everything is okay, my darling. There is nothing to fear. There, there. Be brave, and know that everything God does is good, that in His heart there is never any separation. When his summons comes, we must go, readily. Come, tell me the story, for I have forgotten many parts of it, and long to hear it again. Help me; remind me of it again."

Aziza wipes her tears. Her grandfather's words have reassured her and she feels expansive.

"Evening was spread out like one of Daadi's dark blue shawls, embroidered with stars. But you, Daadu, couldn't see the beauty because you were so very hungry. You were tired of your long exile from home. See, I remember the word, 'exile.' You said, 'Baba, I cannot walk anymore. You have forgotten that I am ten years older than you.'"

"My bones are more brittle, my muscles old and aching,"

Mardana picks up the dialogue. "This, Baba, is my final trip with you. When I get home to my wife and children…"

"'…and Aziza,' " Aziza adds.

"'…and my Aziza, though she isn't born yet in the story but who is sitting on my bed right now. Once I reach home I will find my roots and never, ever leave again.' Baba laughed, repeating my words, 'never, ever leave again.'" Mardana tries to laugh like Baba laughed but breaks out in a fit of coughing.

"Rest, Daadu, I will tell it. Baba laughed, and you were angry with him, and repeated that you were very hungry. 'In that case, Mardana, you must see if you can find food at once,' he said.

Just then you saw a village on the side of a hill.

'Come on, come on,' you said to Baba.

'No, Bhai, I will sit under this tree and meditate. You go, and may God fulfill your hungers,' Baba said.

'The sun was shining brightly on the green wheat fields in the distance and your spirits soared like a bird. The sight of the village tucked cozily on the side of the hill was like a blessing. And it looked like a prosperous village, too! No patched roofs, no hovels. Even the cows and sheep grazing on the hillside looked well fed and fat. As you got closer you imagined eating all your favorite foods…"

"*Pakoras* with chai, hot *paranthas* stuffed with potatoes, onions, peppers, and biryani with a lot of meat in it," Fatima adds.

"…followed by *halwa* with almonds and bhang," Aziza picks up.

"…and raisins and slivers of crunchy coconut! Oh, my poor teeth hurt just thinking about it!"

"The dirt road gave way to a cobbled path and as you stepped on it, you were hit on your forehead with a stone with such force that you fell backwards," Aziza says, rubbing her grandfather's forehead. "You were in a daze and before you could even get up you heard someone say,

'Go away! We don't want any strangers here.'

You looked up and saw a woman's scowling face at a window. By her side stood a young boy aiming another stone at you from a slingshot, and shouting, 'Go back to your own home.'

'I don't have a home,' you pleaded. 'Please give me something to eat.'

'Eat this,' said the boy, releasing yet another stone from his slingshot that hit you on your shoulder. The boy's mother laughed, and shut the window.

'I'll try someone else. Surely there is someone in this village that will help me,' you thought, not discouraged by this rude reception. You knocked on a door. Knock, knock, knock. A man opened the door and said, harshly, 'What do you want?'

'I am a hungry minstrel of God," you said.

'Why don't you earn your own living as we do? This village doesn't believe in God. We like to keep our hard earned money and food to ourselves. Now get away from here at once before someone breaks your leg!' he said to you, slamming the door in your face.

You decided to walk a little further into the village to take another chance. You saw a woman walking towards you with a basket on her head and a dog at her heels. 'There is food in the basket! Surely there is food in it!' You thought.

'I'm a pilgrim,' you said as you neared her. 'I don't have any money, but I could play the *rabab* for you and sing a song composed by Baba Nanak, if you would please give us something to eat.'

'A song for food! You must think I'm a fool!' The woman said to you.

'It's no ordinary song. The words will enlighten your dark mind and illumine your path through the jungle of your days,' you said.

'You think my mind is dark and needs a light, you idiot? Here, Shera, go get him, Shera!" she called her dog, who began to growl and bear his teeth – gr… gr… bow, bow. You ran all the way out of the village with the dog at your heels. You didn't stop till you reached Baba Nanak, still meditating under the tree.

'It's a rude, ungenerous village, Baba,' you said. 'They pelted me with stones and set loose a dog on me!"

"'We have to eat what we are given, Mardana,' Baba said, turning the palm of his hand up.

'Eat stones? Eat hunger?' you said. 'You will have to bury me here, far from home. I'll never ever see my family again. I don't have a home anymore! Baba, are you listening to me, I don't have a home!'

The charas has gone to work; in the depth of feeling the oil of the herb has aroused in her, the words are wrung out of Aziza with a heartfelt cry. Tears glimmer in her eyes as she realizes for the first time the relevance of the story to her own predicament. She wipes her tears and resumes.

"Baba said, 'Trust, Aziza, trust!'"

"Aziza?" Fatima looks up.

"I mean, Mardana. 'Trust, Mardana, trust. All will be well.' Baba turned towards the village, held up his hand in blessing, and said: '*Basdai raho*: may you remain settled in your homes. May your roots go deep into the soil, and your homes remain secure against invasions. May suffering not touch you.'

'What?' you said. 'Baba, have you lost your mind? Why else would you bless these ungenerous, unkind, rude idiots with the boon I would have liked in my life? May I have stayed in my own home and not wandered all over the earth exiled from my dear, loved ones! May my roots have gone deep into the soil where my wife, children, and granddaughter, live.'

Baba was silent as he got up and began to walk again. After another long journey through wilderness the two of you came to another village. You were certain the villagers would also give you stones instead of bread. 'Oh Allah, please, please,' you prayed in a fit of despair. 'I will eat whatever you give me, even if it's just a stale *roti*. But please make them give me *something*. A little old *daal*[102] with it would be great, and a little ghee… oh heaven! Dare I hope? Allah, Allah, I have reached the end of my tether, and unless you feed me a little something this will be the end of this old dog.'

"This will be the end of this old dog," Mardana echoes.

"You crossed a little bridge over a stream, walked by a pond in which the buffalos soaked, past a large banyan tree in which green parrots with red beaks preened and squawked as they fed their tiny little fledglings. A child in rags skipped up to you and bowed.

'Baba Jee, Baba Jee. Mother, mother, two holy men have come!' she said, and led you through an open door into a courtyard where buffalos were eating from a trough.

'*Dhan bhaag! Dhan Bhaag*!'[103] said a woman, coming out from inside a room, and touching Baba Nanak's feet. 'Blessed be the day that brought you to our home. Kaka,'[104] she called a young boy. 'Kaka! Go tell your father we have holy company, and tell him to bring mustard greens from the fields.'

Kaka ran off to fetch his father, and in the streets he sang, '*Sadh sangat! Sadh Sangat*! Holy company! Holy company! Come be in the presence of saints.'

Even though you received such a warm welcome, you despaired: how long was it going to be before the mustard greens were harvested and cooked? The woman lay down two manjis and spread clean sheets on them. Then she put a pot of water on the fire so you could wash up. Your eyes followed her as she picked up a wooden ladle and moved to an alcove where a blackened earthenware pot, like ours, was simmering above a low fire. Your stomach stirred with hope. You knew milk was being pasteurized in the pot. There was probably a thick layer of cream on top, too. The woman stirred the contents of the pot, beating in the cream. Then she ladled a thick

---

102 Curried lentils.

103 Good fortune! Good fortune!

104 Kaka is a generic name for young boys in Punjabi.

liquid into two tall brass glasses worn half-white with wear, filling them to the brim. As if reading your desire, she added honey from a jar, a little ghee, too, spiced the drink with cloves, cardamom, and ginger, and offered the glasses to Baba and you. You grasped the glass a little too eagerly, and chugged its contents down. You smacked your lips, wiped your mouth with the back of your hand, and burped loudly, like this," and here Aziza lets out a loud burp that sets Fatima and Mardana laughing.

"The young boy's cries of '*Sadh Sangat*!'" Aziza resumes when the laughter dies down, "summoned people in the village who poured into the courtyard bearing soap and oil to wash and massage the feet of the weary travelers, and ingredients to prepare for a feast: ghee and brown sugar, rice and milk, fruit and nuts. Even the dogs came and licked your feet, hands and cheeks and wagged their tails while the children climbed into your laps," Aziza adds as Motia comes into the courtyard, jumps up on Mardana's bed, and licks his face.

"Then Baba Nanak retired to meditate and rest, and you, your body singing in contentment and anticipation, told them all they wanted to know: where you had been, where you were coming from, and where you were going.

"Soon, they gave you a *thaali* with a thick and crispy *makki de roti*[105] with a heap of *saag*[106] on it. The hostess had put two glasses of cream in the *saag*, like daadi does, and half a small bucket of milk, so it was de… li… cious!"

"In a hole in the saag was a large gob of fast melting ghee, which had already flowed to the edges of the mustard, over the roti, on to the platter, and into the yellow *daal* beside the lumps of paneer,"[107] Fatima adds.

"You and Baba stayed for a few more days and then went on

---

105 A pancake like flat bread made of corn.

106 A Punjabi dish made with mustard leaves, ghee and cream.

107 Homemade cottage cheese.

your way. The whole village came to see you off till the bridge, and with tears in their eyes, bid you both goodbye. A few miles away, Baba stopped on top of a hill, from where you could see the village spread out beneath you. He held out his hand in a gesture of blessing, and said: '*Ujad jaao*!'

You stopped dead in your tracks, Daadu Jaan, your tongue paralyzed by the storm of confusion in your brain. How could Baba wish upon this wonderful village and its generous inhabitants that they be destroyed? Uprooted? Exiled? Become homeless? Why did he want them to suffer? You could not contain yourself and broke out: 'Baba, you *are* mad? They welcomed us, hosted us, fed us. The other village, the one full of greedy, ungenerous, selfish people you blessed. They will live safely and securely in their homes with their children and grandchildren and lead a fat life rooted in *one* place. With your curse the good people will become exiles, like me! Why must they loose hearth, home, family, clan to wander the earth alone and friendless?'"

Aziza's words of despair are followed by a long silence following which she resumes in a voice that is calmer and deeper than before.

"'Because suffering purifies those whose faces are turned towards God, Mardana,' Baba said to you and me. 'Suffering is holy, and the cure for the ills of the world. Suffering, if we are open to the message and the gift it brings, teaches us to root ourselves in God, who is everywhere; to take shelter at the Beloved's feet in our very hearts. *Rabab chaid*, Mardania,' Baba said to you."

Aziza moves towards her *rabab*, and brings it by the bed. "You sat on the grass under the stars, and held the bow in your hand, like this, and ran it over the strings," Aziza's speech harmonizes with the sound of the soulful stings.

She begins her long and heartfelt *alaap*[108] in which Fatima puts

108 Sung at the beginning of a raag, an improvised, slow, arrhythmic exposition of the raag in Indian classical music.

aside her spinning, and Mardana, touched beyond words at the story that his granddaughter brought alive before him, sits up in a rare display of energy and says in a whisper loud enough to be heard, "I remember the thought that flowed into my soul before we began to sing: *I follow Baba because he makes me think in ways I do not dream of thinking and because he gives my soul wings.* It is good to remember that I will be losing a home to arrive Home."

Both Fatima and Aziza are moved by his words, which remind them that Mardana is on his deathbed; that there is a lot of suffering in store for them.

"Then Baba began to sing a long paean to suffering," Aziza returns to the song Baba and her grandfather had sung at the end of the story. Mardana and Fatima join their granddaughter as she sings accompanied with the slow, resonating notes of the *rabab*: *Dukh daaru sukh rog phayaa: suffering is the tonic, and peace the disease.*

Part II

Into the Great Heart

CHAPTER 17

Dialogue in Kartarpur

Time, the river that is always coming towards us, moving away, and remaining, flowed inexorably on in Kartarpur, changed its course, often subtly, sometimes violently and suddenly. Years passed, as they always do, in the blink of an eye. People grew up, married, moved away, died even as new birth carried ceaselessly on. During the course of many monsoons and dry spells, the river Ravi, in its ceaseless journey and thrust to lose its identity in the sea, carried away the debris of houses, trees, corpses… without being burdened or sorrowed by any of it. The seasons, too, spun out with the turning of the earth, like a spindle or a lathe, recurred, stayed, moved inevitably on, and just as inevitably, returned. It all happened imperceptibly, beyond the comprehension of eyes, like the rhythm of the day, from the first ray of light to its blooming into noon, its decline and muting into the glow of dusk, then disappearance into the folds of darkness, the stars, the planets and the moon wheeling silently, ever silently, into day again.

It is yet another spring in Kartarpur. The forests around the habitation are alive with color and life. The wild acacias and *Gulmohar*[109] bloom in shades of pinks, purples, yellows, and blues; fragrant lotuses and hyacinths flower in the ponds and marshes;

---

109 An ornamental tree, the Royal Poinciana or Flamboyant. Also called Flame tree.

peacocks with their thousand eyed feathers, cuckoos, doves, larks, thrushes, hawks call and cry, bees buzz and hum gathering nectar, and in the abundant grass thick and lush with winter rains, the young of monkeys, tigers and deer, snakes and rabbits, and all the varied life on Earth, water, and air cavorts and hunts with new life.

It is Trinjan[110] day in Kartarpur in the spring of 1612, and excitement is in the air. It is only held once a month, the day of the full moon. Though the women are eager to meet more frequently, it is impossible for them to make time from their household routines. They are grateful to have it at all, considering the resistance the idea had received from the men.

Their opposition carried on for years before Baba, with the help of Nanaki and Sulakhni, negotiated an agreement during one particular meeting between the women and men who thought of it as a 'waste of time.' This meeting, which took place in the spring of 1611, needs to be described before we go on to Trinjan day.

In an evening session of music, Baba sang many *shabads* of the equality of men and women to soften the men to receive his message. *Naaree purakh sabaa-ee lo-ay*, he sang: 'the same Light shines in women and men;' *naar na purakh kahhu ko-oo kaisay:* neither male nor female, how shall I describe this Being?' he sang of his Beloved.

After singing, Baba Nanak went straight to the point: the Trinjan was a necessary institution; women learned from each other the important art of spinning without which the men would have no clothes and walk around naked like the animals – an image that provoked much joking and laughter before some men expressed their serious concern that the Trinjan was only an excuse for the women to get together and gossip about their men.

The women – unveiled, because that was a precondition for

---

110 Trinjan is the name of the hall where the women and girls meet to spin, embroider, weave. Used here as an adjective to describe the event.

meetings – protested loudly, simultaneously, and Baba gently told them they would have their say, but they had to hear the men out.

Who knows what schemes they may come up with in their Trinjans to further torture their spouses, the males continued. As an example they cited the play they had seen in Kartarpur in which the women collectively decided to blackmail the men by not sleeping with them till each got what she wanted: baubles, trinkets, the right to visit parents at least once a year, and to own property. The women had watched the play too (on Baba's insistence), and who knows what ideas it had put in their heads?

"Women are so unreasonable," a man shouted. "You can't communicate with them."

"They refuse to be obedient!" said another.

"You are the ones that are unreasonable," the women cried.

"Man and woman together is God's *hukum*. We can't do without each other. " Bebe Nanaki said. She was dressed in her usual white *salwar kameez*,[111] white silk *dupatta*[112] delicately embroidered with flowers in shades of violet, purple and indigo covering her white hair, the color of the moon, pulled back into a long braid behind her back. Her clothes were simple demonstrations of care towards cleanliness and beauty. Her body, at once frail and strong, neither too thin nor plump, was the body of a person who made it a practice to know itself, its hungers and needs for indulgence and abstinence, and the limits and benefits of each.

"The more the pity," some men cried.

"Our only choice lies in making our relationships as good as they can be. Relationships are the workshops in which we learn love for each other and God. Baba says, 'Without women there would be no one at all,' Nanaki quotes her brother's words. 'We are all

---

111 The traditional dress of Punjabi women, the pleated, lose pants and long shirts, respectively.

112 The veil that covers their breasts and sometimes, hair.

here because of them.'"

"But where would they be without us?" The men shouted.

"Union of both is central to our existence. Baba says, '*jah daykhaa tah rav rahay siv saktee kaa mayl: Wherever I look, I see the Lord pervading in the union of Shiva and Shakti,*[113] *of consciousness and matter.*' We need each other, so learn to get along. And women," Nanaki said before the men got too voluble again, "become soft, gentle, concede and..."

The men were most pleased by this while the women grumbled about having to concede all the time.

"...speak your mind and heart, and learn to say 'no' politely but strongly to your men," Nanaki completes her sentence.

This did not go over too well with the men but the women listened and applauded.

"If you want love and companionship you will have to learn to give up power and accomplish things with love," Nanaki said. "More can be achieved through love than pride and ego."

"Power works, too. You have to keep a stick behind them, as with cattle," Shai Tani, an outspoken woman in the community, said. The men burst into an uproar.

Shai Tani had come to Kartarpur from another village with a young child and an infant. When women asked her what her name was, she had said, 'Shai Tani.' The women were taken aback because 'shaitan' was the Arabic word for Satan, and her name could be interpreted as 'female Satan,' though 'shaitan' was often also used for children who were disobedient and naughty. A large part of the community had wanted to turn her away, but Bebe Nanaki had said the community must turn no one away and Shai Tani must be taken in. Baba Nanak had concurred and sung a *shabad: sabh ghat mayray ha-o sabhnaa andar jisahi khu-aa-ee tis ka-un kahai.* 'God

---

113 God and goddess of the Indian mythological pantheon, symbols of the male and female principles of existence.

says, all hearts are mine, and I am in all hearts. Who can explain this to one who is confused?'

Shai Tani had become the 'un-feminine' town clown and bawd. Bebe Nanaki had taken her under her wing, employed her against public opinion with the support of her brother and her husband, Jairam, and, not merely for altruistic reasons but because she saw how Shai Tani's thought-provoking character and behavior constantly challenged her ego and prejudices, edited, amended and balanced her own idealistic and mystical view of the world.

Men and women periodically got very loud about getting rid of Shai Tani. Bebe Nanaki told them, 'Shai Tani, in speaking thoughts repressed by most for the sake of politeness, expresses something in all of us; in accepting her, we are accepting all of ourselves.' Bebe Nanaki went to some length to explain to them what she meant by this: that the world as we see it is us; that it is up to us to make our world and ourselves either expansive and vast or restricted and small; that we all have dark areas in our minds and hearts: finding them and accepting them made us whole, the way God was whole and vast; that everything that exists, including what we call 'evil' or 'sin,' the polluted and the pure, the criminal and the saint – exists in God's Great Heart.

Ultimately Nanaki had to accept that not all who heard her understood her. She knew only that she knew very little of God's purposes in making some people obdurate and ignorant; that compassion had to be extended to them, too; that battles sometimes must be fought, and fought courageously. Nanaki periodically got into battle mode and took on the task of waging the war to keep Shai Tani in the dera despite repeated demands to expel her.

"If you use power," Bebe Nanaki turned to Shai Tani, "you run the risk of becoming a bitter shrew."

"Shrews are made, not born," Shai Tani retorted. "It is their life and circumstances that make them that way."

Nanaki was silent. She thought about Mata Sulakhni, who was her image of the shrew; she thought about Shai Tani, whose history was revealed as time went by. She had been raped in the village she came from and became pregnant from the rape; her husband had abandoned her and his child because she had become 'impure.'

Shai Tani's words made Nanaki pause and aroused compassion in her heart for both Shai Tani and her sister-in-law.

"Though it is true that adverse circumstances force us to change," Nanaki said in her soft and gentle voice, "we can have some control by not letting them change us for the worst."

"Please tell us a little more about power and love," a woman asked.

"You can either have ego, the seat of power, or love. It is not easy to learn love. It takes work, vigilance, awareness, attention, and self-examination but it is the best prize life can offer us."

Nanaki was thinking less about her relationship with Jairam than the relationship of her parents. Power did not enter her relationship with Jairam; both of them always only wanted love and peace and were willing to work for it. Perhaps they had simply been gifted it by the Merciful, Generous One. But her parents' relationship had been very conflicted while Nanaki was a child. Her father, Mehta Kallu, practical, controlling, limited in his vision, almost averse to spirituality, had a temper and always had to have his way with everything. Her mother, Mata Tripta, tried to resist him but it only made matters worse. When Nanaki was growing up she remembered terrible fights in the house between the two of them. But a change came upon her mother when she became pregnant for the second time, with Nanak. Mata Tripta became very inward, facing the universe inside her, all her energies focused upon the new life growing in her womb. She was calm, non-reactive, peaceful and full of love, even for her husband. It was as if her ego became just one little point in the vast spaces of her being, something to be acknowledged, paid attention to, watched, contained, but not be mastered by. Nanaki recalled that things changed in the house and remained calm till Nanak grew up and refused to do his father's bidding, refused to become a businessman, and the household became a battle zone once again.

"Tell us more about how we can control the outcome of our circumstances," someone asked Bebe Nanaki.

"Always ask yourself: do my circumstances have anything to do with me? Am I to blame for what happens to me?" Bebe Nanaki replied.

"How can you say that?" Shai Tani burst out. "Was I to blame? I was only taking a shit in the early morning when the pig, the bastard pounced on me! Was that my fault?"

"Sometimes the Universe sends us experiences out of the blue, its true. Shai Tani, you could have rejected the child born of this horrible event, but you didn't; many women in your circumstances kill the child, especially if it a girl, as yours is: you didn't; you could have become like other women who become so timid, afraid, almost deranged with their trauma: you didn't. Instead, you opted for strength, honesty, openness. Is that not taking control of your circumstances? You took care of your children. It is a very heroic thing to do."

There was mixed reaction to Bebe Nanaki's words. Shai Tani burst into tears, something no one had ever seen her do before; some sympathetic women put their arms around her; some men sniggered at the word 'heroic,' and some allowed Bebe's words to change their minds and hearts.

"In difficult moments," Nanaki continued her thought after an appropriate time had elapsed, "when the universe seems to be conspiring against you, ask yourself, 'am I reacting with my ego or is there a better perspective to view the circumstances, one that will change both my world and me for the better? It is by asking yourself this essential question that you embark on what Baba calls the 'Pilgrimage to Yourself.'"

To several present her sentences seemed like abstractions that had nothing to do with reality; to some it contained the highest sense; others, simple folk who lived the only way they knew how, didn't understand her. But all listened, not because she talked forcefully or oratorically but because they trusted her and sensed she was speaking from her heart and from knowledge. She embodied her message. Her relationship with Jairam was legendary. Every woman wished she had a Jairam. They had seen him by the well, collecting water for their house and washing clothes and sheets; Jairam even cooked! Some visitors, who quickly spread the news, had seen him scrub the utensils with ash and even sweep the floors of the courtyard! He made no distinction between 'male' and 'female' roles, supported, honored and loved his wife unconditionally, and she, him. All the men wished they had a Nanaki, so loving, attentive, and solicitous of her husband. She accompanied him to the fields and helped him to prepare the soil, sow, seed, weed, harvest, and cut fodder for the animals.

Women wrote and sang songs about them: how Jairam, at the age of eighteen, mounted on a horse and surveying the land for Daulatan Khan Lodi,[114] had seen the child Nanaki at 11 as she stood with her friends at the village well in Talwandi, and had fallen in love with the light in her; how he had asked for her hand in marriage and it had been granted; how he visited her frequently at her parents' house and they would sit on the swing together, eating and talking, becoming best of friends; how they did not marry till she was seventeen.

"I don't understand what you mean by 'pilgrimage to yourself,'" Shai Tani said, wiping her tears.

Nanaki shut her eyes and was silent. It seemed to her audience

---

114 A governor or ruler under the Mughal Empire.

that she had traveled, in an instant, to some space deep within herself. When she spoke, slowly, thoughtfully, her voice was soft and distant.

CHAPTER 18

Pilgrimage to Yourself

"Within and beyond the whirling, sorrowing, conflicting, noisy circumstances of our lives, at the very center of it," Bebe Nanaki began, "is a holy place which is calm, unruffled, steady, and beyond birth and death. This place, within us, is the truest temple of all, the home of The Beloved, the only place worth making a pilgrimage to. All geographic pilgrimages to manmade places of worship are trivial and meaningless compared with it."

Bebe Nanaki's words and voice transported many to the sacred temple within them. A long silence followed, and then someone asked.

"How do we begin?"

"By listening. Our souls are constantly calling us to embark on this long, often arduous journey. Though some, like Baba, like all enlightened beings, are fortunate and destined to embark upon it before birth, all of us, without exception, have the longing and capacity for it. We can begin with a commitment to making this journey, knowing that it takes us to our true goal and purpose without which we are as fallen leaves tossing and tumbling about in the storms of life."

"And then?" someone asked.

"Observe the workings of our ego that obscures this sacred space and keeps us from discovering the truth of who and what we truly are; notice how it takes control of our thoughts and feelings, separates us from everyone else, makes us doubt ourselves, others, and the everywhere present Power that forms and informs us. We need to be vigilant to the workings of the ego, observe our thoughts and feelings, examine and evaluate them like a jeweler separating the worthless from the invaluable; be aware of our unconscious reactions to circumstances, people, events; become conscious of the pitfalls that can destroy our health, sanity and life; steer, with the aid of our guru's words and message, towards kindness, compassion, trust, faith, expansion, and love; surrender to our Highest Self, which is another name for the Beloved, and let it guide us Home."

"How can the Beloved make a home in sinful beings like us?" Shai Tani asked.

Bebe Nanaki looked at her brother. So attuned were they to each other's souls that Baba reached for his *rabab*, and Bebe Nanaki for hers. Without any verbal communication, they tuned their instruments to Sri Raag, a raag at once serious and playful, dramatic and sincere, strong and innocent. Bebe Nanaki explained in melodious words that harmonized with the chords of the raag that the *shabad* they were about to sing was written by Saint Ravidas,[115] the 'untouchable' saint of the fifteenth century.

"Ravidas says, '*You are me, and I am You. The difference between us is like the difference between gold and a gold bracelet, the ocean and a wave.*' Ravidas anticipates your question, Shai Tani, and says playfully to the Beloved, '*If I weren't sinful, how would you have earned the title of 'Redeemer of sinners?'*'"

Baba began the *alaap* with the first note, *sa*, coming from a deep place inside him, like the center of the earth, and spiraling up through time and space to a place beyond; it was a sound that had a deep silence within it, that stilled and moved each open heart

---

115 An 'untouchable' saint of the 15th century. Of his compositions, 41 have been incorporated into the Sikh holy text, the SGGS.

that heard it; a fundamental note so rich and deep it contained all the other notes, and echoed the primeval sound that birthed the cosmos with its vibration.

tohee mohee mohee tohee antar kaisaa.

kanak katik jal tarang jaisaa.

The silence that usually followed their singing in which the sense of the words were absorbed and savored, was interrupted in due time by Shai Tani, who brought it all back on track.

"But we want our Trinjan!"

"We won't have it," the men cried, reacting to Shai Tani. "We won't build one."

"Who will make you lovely, warm *loees* if the skills are not passed on to the future generations?"Baba asked.

Some men reiterated that the Trinjan would take time away from their wives' duties at home. Who would cook their meals and do the dishes? Who would feed the animals? Who would light the lamps and lanterns?

"If you make your own meals once a month, clean the utensils, feed the animals, you will learn a new skill, connect with the female inside yourself and have compassion for the heavy burdens your women carry," Nanaki suggested.

There were loud protestations by the men that their burdens were far heavier than the women's.

Mata Sulakhni, who was also present, said, "Do you have the burden of bearing children?"

The men quietened down and Mata Sulakhni talked at length about the travails of carrying, delivering, and rearing young. She couldn't help but shoot a barb at the end of her talk by saying that if men left their homes to go wandering all over the world, a woman had to do it all. And here she went into many details that held her captive audience silent.

"What did you mean when you said we can 'connect with the

female' inside us?" A newly married man asked Bebe Nanaki.

"Baba says, *purakh meh naar naar meh purkhaa boojhhu barahm gi-aane. Understand, O lover of wisdom,*" Nanaki translated, "'*the female is in the male, and the male is in the female.*'"

Nanaki could tell by the expressions on their faces that this would require further explication.

"Each of us contains characteristics of the other sex which we need to get in touch with if we want to be whole. Another human being can't make us whole; we have to learn to be whole within ourselves."

"If Akaal Purukh graces us," Baba Nanak added.

"If Akaal Purukh graces us," Nanaki echoed her brother's words, humbled by them. *Nanaki, how could you have forgotten something so important?* She chastised herself.

"Or if the Guru sends you a guru, like Nanaki," Baba Nanak said, smiling at Nanaki.

"Be our guru! Be our guru!" the women shouted.

"I have been forgetful in talking about the most important thing," Nanaki admitted to the audience. "We cannot embark upon the Pilgrimage to Ourselves without a prayer to that Power who makes all things possible and right. Our own efforts will get us nowhere. Everything comes down to remembering and loving the Beloved. '*He alone is the Life of the World, the Fulfiller of all Desire,*' as Baba says. He alone is our Guru, the One who dispels our darkness. Without Him we are helpless, blind, foolish, confused."

"Teach us how to have good relationships with our spouses!" Someone requested.

Nanaki spoke some more in her gentle, melodious voice. Above all it was the sound of her voice, form of the formless, which conveyed sense to their brains in its indelible script. Indescribable in its gentleness, love, concern, kindness and compassion, it flowed into their ear canals like a salubrious current of invisible air, a vibration from source to source, touching their souls, lulling, moving and awakening them to realities and possibilities they hadn't suspected before; a way of thinking, believing, being, behaving that fulfilled to the highest their purpose for being alive.

It was this that finally convinced the men to build a Trinjan for the women. They realized in the process that they too needed a building where they could teach their sons carpentry, woodworking and masonry; where they could meet socially and play *chawpat*, *shatranj*, and other games, laugh and joke about women. Since this meeting took place when Bhai Lehna was still at Kartarpur, listening to and absorbing the dialogue at the dera, he suggested wrestling and *kabaddi*,[116] too, and the men loved the idea.

116 An Indian sport which involves a bit of wrestling.

CHAPTER 19

Trinjan

So, it is finally Trinjan day in Kartarpur that spring of 1612. The women, having done double time the day before, cooking meals and *rotis* for the men, troop in one by one, mothers with their children, infants, girls, women of all ages, projects in hand. Some carry musical instruments like *dholaks*[117] and *chimtas*[118] since music and singing is an integral part of their gathering. They are invariably on time, knowing that the day has limited hours and they want to take full advantage of their desire to teach, learn, and socialize with friends and acquaintances. They bring lunches with them, simple fare of *rotis*, onions, and chutneys of green or red chilies, easy to prepare and carry. Some come with pieces of cloth, thread, needles to learn embroidery; some bring spindles and fleece, wool to card or spin on the communal spinning wheels, grasses for basket weaving, or skeins of wool to make into balls. Others come with projects that are already underway, to get advice from others, or just work on them in the company of friends and neighbors.

The atmosphere is alive, electric, filled with chatter from all ages. After the initial greetings, they settle into their tasks, the elders sitting on *peedees* and string cots, and the younger ones on the floor on *darees*. Fatima takes charge of the spinning and weaving and

117 Double-headed drums.

118 Long tongs, with cymbals, for keeping time.

Bebe Nanaki the embroidery. Girls and women gather into clusters, ask questions, show each other their projects, gossip, give and take suggestions. The first half of the day is devoted to individual tasks while the other half is taken up by collective work, like making quilts for the *dharamsala*[119] in the dera; today they will embroider a *phulkari*, a wedding shawl for Bissy, who is to be married in a few months.

Fatima goes from student to student, looking at their work and offering suggestions: "'this color goes better with this one, see?' 'You'll have to dye this wool again, it hasn't taken the color well; card some more white with this black, it is too dark; your warp has to be tighter; beat the weft down strongly; the warp is showing, it must always be invisible; moisten this end with your spittle, like this, so it will stick to the spindle; make a thin but strong filament to begin spinning; twirl it like this, at this angle between the wool and the stick, a little faster, so you can get a continuous strand.'"

After Fatima has put each to her task, she goes to a spinning wheel and begins to spin some white yarn she has brought with her.

What shall I make with this? Fatima wonders, looking at the whiteness of the fine spun yarn. *Not a shawl or loee, we have enough of them. A sheet? A winding sheet?*

She stops spinning. *What am I thinking? For whom?* The first person she thinks about is her husband, Mardana, but instantly buries the thought. It is altogether too disturbing. And yet… hasn't she prepared for such an event? Isn't the resourceful, far-thinking mind always inventing scenarios of the future to prepare the soul for all eventualities? Hasn't she thought she would, in that fateful eventuality, have more time to weave and take Aziza under her wing, teach her how to weave?

No, she thinks, *this thought is born of fear*. *If the image of a shroud*

119 A free boarding place for travelers or anyone who needed a temporary home. Free meals were also served from the langar.

is a harbinger of death, it is Daulatan Masi who is already older than any human should be. Fatima settles into a state of comfort again with an image of Daulatan Masi huddled in a corner wrapped in a quilt even though the weather has warmed considerably, a smell emanating from her. *I don't like cleaning up her excrement. I will miss her but her death will also be a relief.* She plans to burn the quilt, clean the space, and put a *manji* in it for herself for the summer, for it is the coolest corner of the courtyard. Being a self-reflective woman she pauses and wonders at the workings of her mind: how easily it reconciles itself to, and even benefits from, death.

Her gaze falls on Bebe Nanaki, her students clustered around her, jostling with each other for her attention. Her skin, almost translucent, is thinning with age. Wisps of white hair shining golden in the sunlight, give her an angelic air.

How full of light she is! Fatima thinks. *Is it possible she is without shadows?*

Fatima tunes into the conversation around Bebe Nanaki.

"I like my stiches big and inelegant," Shai Tani says. "I saw a woman in the market wearing a *ghaagraa*[120] made of patches of different colors, prints, sizes, shapes sewn together with *topaas*[121] of different colored thread, without any thought, it seemed, but with unmistakable, unplanned beauty. I loved it and I'm trying to recreate it in this blanket."

"The mind is made to look for pattern and harmony and even if she hadn't planned it consciously, I'm sure there was an unconscious picking and choosing of colors," another woman says.

"No, you could tell she just used what she had," Shai Tani replies. "It covered her, kept her warm, and that was all that mattered."

"This woman must have been a gypsy," someone comments.

"Yes, she was, in fact!" Shai Tani responds."She was peddling

---

120 A long skirt.

121 Large, inelegant stitches.

beads and wild herbs. I must have been a gypsy in my past life and that is why I had the experiences I did in this life so I could become a gypsy again! I have been thinking about what you said about my life, Bebe Nanaki, and I think that somewhere it was all for the best."

"That's what makes you special, Shai Tani," Bebe Nanaki says. "That you can see a pattern even in chaos."

"Maybe, maybe our lives are like that patchwork *ghaagra* and everything fits together even though we can't see how, being too focused on a particular, irregular piece!" Shai Tani exclaims. "To tell the truth, I wasn't happy with my married life. I felt I was in a very tight cage without even bars to look out from – just a small metal cage without any windows. My husband treated me like dung. He would visit whores and beat me up after drinking. My mother-in-law and sister-in-law were bitches and witches, harping at me constantly for not bringing any dowry. The pig, the rapist, set me free!" Shai Tani bursts out, as if with new insight."I should thank him! Not only was I set free but I have a child who I love. I am happier and freer than I have ever been! Perhaps bad things happen so good things can come from them?"

A long silence follows her words, each woman going inward to revisit the worst event of her life to see if something good came of it.

"What about *my* stiches?" Aziza asks, breaking the silence, showing her handiwork to Bebe Nanaki.

"*Topaas*!" replies a woman.

"I like them," Shai Tani says. "You will make a good gypsy."

"Don't put ideas in her head!" Nasreen says angrily.

"My thread always gets knotted!" Aziza cries. "I don't do anything to it, just leave it lying straight when I have to go do something else, but when I come back there's always a knot in it."

"When you pick up the needle again after a lapse, check to see if there is a knot. If there is, see it, and relax around it."

"Don't go into a panic, saying there's a knot, there's a knot!" a woman advises.

"I hate knots and don't have the patience for them," another woman complains.

"Without knots there would be no life," Nanaki says.

"No embroidery, no sewing, no looming, no clothes, no ropes, no water from wells," Fatima says.

"Life is a knot in the formless ocean of consciousness," Nanaki explains. "When it opens, you die. Baba says in one of his *shabads* on death, '*the knot of life is open; arise, your allotted time has come.*'"

"But I still don't like knots!" Aziza confesses.

"And I don't like the knot I get in my heart when I have a fight with my husband. I am learning to untie it by communicating with him as soon as it appears," a woman adds.

"You have to make sure they don't happen *before* they happen," Nanaki advises.

"How can that be? I am not Daulatan Masi. I am not a prophet!" Aziza exclaims. "There, I've got another nasty one! I also don't like it when the wool won't stick to my spindle or when my thread breaks."

"A good weaver pays equal attention to each step of the process, is patient in learning how to avoid delays, knows that delays and mistakes are inevitable, and corrects them in the same spirit in which she weaves in rhythm. This way, you can keep in the flow all the time, like the river which does not stop when it encounters a boulder but slides around it."

"I'll show you another miraculous way of approaching them," Shai Tani says, reaching for a scissor. "Just cut the motherfucker off!"

The Trinjan is filled with laughter. Nanaki, too, laughs. "Why, that's always an option! Sometimes there is no other way!"

Aziza takes her cloth to a corner and begins to practice what she has learned.

Her students each doing her thing, Bebe Nanaki allows herself to go within and reflect as she picks up her own project of embroidering blue lotuses on a *dupatta*. Cutting a thread she feels the surfacing of an emotion that had been arising within her frequently.

This sense of something dark on the horizon… is it Vir jee?

The *dupatta* Nanaki is embroidering falls from her hands. She picks it up, dusts it, acknowledging that she can barely breathe.

Calm down, Nanaki! She admonishes herself, taking some long breaths. *The Beloved sends sorrows but also strength to bear them. Never to hear him singing, never to hear the voice that makes my heart lose its boundaries, its thin skin expanding to include the whole universe.*

No, Nanaki, no, it is something else, not your worst fear. He is five years younger than you, Nanaki. You will survive him. But what if…? I couldn't, no. But, Nanaki, this darkness could be something else. It could be someone else, yes. It could be you! There, that thought feels good. I will die before him. This is oh so bearable.

Bebe Nanaki picks up the *dupatta*, threads her needle and resumes embroidering the lotus.

What is she up to now? Mata Sulakhni wonders, looking at her sister-in-law with whom she has an uneasy relationship. *Probably had one of her crazy 'visions' again. Who knows, she may just be making them up in her head?*

Recalling an incident long ago, Sulakhni feels an old anger and jealousy grips her heart.

They were both in the kitchen, Nanaki making *rotis* while she herself was feeding the boys. Suddenly, tears began streaming from Nanaki's eyes as she stood up, and bowed repeatedly before nobody, before air. Sulakhni had turned away, as if from someone having a fit. For days Nanaki had been radiant and Sulakhni finally asked her what had happened.

"One must not speak of such things," Nanaki had said.

"Tell me!" Sulakhni had shouted at her.

After some hesitation Nanaki had said, "I was sitting by the chulla, making *rotis* for myself after you and the children had eaten. I am not a very good roti maker, as you know, but these rotis were turning out perfect: round, fluffy, browned, yet soft, just the way Vir likes them. Watching the rotis billowing out to a puff I had this sudden, intense longing to feed Vir. And when I looked up, there he was, wearing a chola, his feet covered with dust, his hand out to receive the rotis. I put some ghee on them and watched him eat with relish before disappearing."

"He came from a thousand miles away to eat your rotis? Are you mad?" Sulakhni had said to her.

"Maybe," Nanaki had laughed. "But I wouldn't trade my madness for all the sanity in the world!"

"He came to his sister, but not his wife? Why did he marry me when his love was his sister and his Beloved?"

"Bhabi, you are his earthly wife, without a doubt. He told us before he left that if we truly remembered him, sincerely, with love and longing, he would come, no matter where he is."

And I didn't truly remember him with longing, Mata Sulakhni thinks, sitting in the Trinjan with the older women on a *manji*, the memory still smarting. *I was busy with the children. What does she know about the pain of bearing, birthing and rearing them? She bypassed it all, and still had the pleasure of having a child in her life by taking Sri Chand away from me. Let it go, Sulakhni, pluck out this thorn from your heart. It doesn't serve you anymore. You have Lakhmi, who heals you with his love. Dear boy. He will take care of you in your old age.*

CHAPTER 20

Blue Lotus in the Sky

Nanaki threads her needle with blue and begins to embroider another lotus, piling stitch upon stitch to make its textured gyres. She looks up and sees Sulakhni looking at her. Their eyes meet, briefly, then turn away.

What do I know about the mystery of a match such as theirs? Nanaki thinks, turning her gaze towards the lotus, and admiring her handiwork. *He loves her, I know he does. He is fixed to her as surely as he is fixed to the Beloved.* 'Grow more in love for your wife daily,' *he said somewhere. In all his travels he must have been attracted to other women, but didn't act upon his desires.* 'As fire is extinguished by water, desire becomes the slave of the Lord's slaves,' he sang.

He probably married her thinking and hoping his marriage would be like Jaidev's![122] Nanaki thinks, twirling the thread around the needle and recalling the story Nanak had told her about the saint: how Jaidev wandered from place to place, sleeping under the open skies, writing and singing the Great One's praises; how detachment from the entangling world was his sole aim: he would not spend two nights under the same tree lest he grow attached to it. But it all changed one day when a crazy Brahmin insisted vehemently and aggressively that Jaidev marry his daughter. "It is the Merciful

122 A poet, saint, dramatist and essayist of the 12th century, known for his Gita Govind. Two of his hymns are incorporated into the SGGS.

One's unshakable will," the Brahmin had cried. Jaidev at first balked, almost ran away from him, but in a flash of insight saw a divine purpose in the Brahmin's craziness, and consented.

It turned out to be a very happy marriage, after all. Lovers of the Beloved, true companions traveling together from place to place, singing Jaidev's impassioned songs.

When father made a match for him, Vir probably thought: the universe is giving me a bride, like Jaidev's. He wanted so much for Sulakhni to be his partner and companion; they would both go singing together into the world. He was probably very disappointed. But he accepted Akaal Purukh's *hukum. But how incompatible some couples can be, like them, like mother and father! Mother had to become a saint to cope with father's anger and rage. Sometimes I wonder if Vir didn't leave home because of his wife's nagging. No, Nanaki, no, this is not the way to think! It is small of you. And yet I have this smallness, too. Take away my smallness, Dissolver of Darkness, if it is your Will. If not, let me see purpose in it. What? It makes you human, Nanaki, yes, gives weight and heft to your existence, makes you real, humbles and teaches you compassion for people who cannot transcend their smallness. Thank you, Beloved, for my smallness!*

Nanaki looks at the children in a corner of the Trinjan and pauses in mid-stitch to watch them frolicking and playing, her heart expanding in widening circles of delight and joy.

They are all mine! Nanaki thinks, tracing in her memory the arc of her magnanimous love for all God's creatures.

I was just a female when I was young, full of the dark, primeval need to procreate: my womb appropriated my mind, screaming its craving to fulfill the purpose for which it was made; the aching emptiness in the breast, the heart, the womb; the bellowing, and then the mute, screaming agony of the cow's eyes after her calf died; pregnant women avoided me, afraid of my infertile shadow. I was 'a little boat, unsteady on a stormy sea at night, on the verge of capsizing with every gust of wind.'[123] *How I begged you, Giver, Depriver, for a child, when all I should have asked for was strength to bear my fruitful emptiness. I turned my back on You, a dense, leaden knot in my heart. Without You, I had only my own anguish, and no way out of it. But Vir reminded me: 'Your not conceiving is hukum, Nanaki. What you cannot change is the Beloved's Will. Accept it. It will become sweet.' Then he sat down with the rabab, and sang, 'saglay dookh amrit kar peevai baahurh dookh na paa-idaa: drink joyously from the chalice of suffering and you'll never be sorrowful again.' I gave my womb to you, my Husband, my Lover and you birthed joy in it. How full my empty womb has become, teeming over with riches of Your bestowing.*

What silly things people advised me to do to get pregnant! She chuckles to herself, remembering: *heat water over the burning pyre of a young bachelor – never a female; who wanted them? Wash your hair with it; cook rice on the pyre, eat it, and the soul of the young man will enter your womb as a boy; bathe naked at the crossroads under the full moon, sacrifice a goat, and recite charms. How Vir laughed at these superstitions! How against them he is!*

She recalls the story Mardana had told her about their trip to Hardwar. The Brahmins were standing in the shallows of the Ganges before beginning the ritual of washing away their sins in the river, and offering holy libations to their ancestors. They pressed Baba to return to his Hindu roots, its practices of sacrifices, burnt offerings, worship of cremation grounds. Baba had not replied. An 'untouchable' had stepped into the river and all the priests attacked him for polluting them and polluting the river. Men, facing east, offered handfuls of water to quench the thirst of their ancestors who they believed lived in the land of the rising sun. Baba had faced the west and splashed water vigorously in that direction instead.

'Why are you throwing water towards the west instead of the

123 From one of Guru Nanak's shabads.

rising sun?' They asked him.

In turn, Nanak had asked, 'why are you throwing it towards the east?'

"We are offering libations to our ancestors in the hereafter,' they replied.

'How far is the land of the hereafter?' Guru Nanak asked them.

'Billions of miles away, you fool!'

Baba had resumed throwing water towards the west. Pressed for a reason for his bizarre behavior, he had replied,

'I had sown a field in Talwandi before I started my travels and did not leave anyone in charge. I am watering the young sprouts,' he replied.

The Brahmins had laughed. 'You are a fool. How can your water reach thousands of miles away?'

Baba had replied, 'if my water can't reach Talwandi, how can your water reach your ancestors in the after life?'

What a character he is, at once rational and mystical! How many strange things he did while growing up: quitting school because he said there was nothing more to learn from the teacher. 'Burn worldly knowledge, grind its ashes into ink, make your intellect the paper, divine love your pen, then write, writer, what the Guru, the Arch Writer, writes through you,' he sang when he was asked why he had left school. How he behaved at the investiture of the holy thread, so important for Hindu boys to 'become' men.

She relives the incident, surprising herself that though she doesn't remember her own childhood, she recalls in vivid detail her memories of Nanak: the relatives and community had come from far and wide; goats had been slaughtered for the feast that was to follow the ceremony. As Hardial, the priest, began to put the *janeu*[124] around him, Nanak held his hand, and asked, 'what does this thread mean? Why should I wear it?'

124 Holy thread of the Hindus.

'Without wearing it you will be a *sudar*.[125] You can't be great in this world and happy in the next without it. This ritual has come down to us from the time of the Vedas. You are not a Hindu without it, but an outcast, a person without a religion. Your thoughts, words and deeds will be pure after wearing it, and you will become strong, wealthy and wise. '

'Are your thoughts pure because you wear it?' Nanak had asked.

Hardial had spluttered: 'I am a priest. Of course they are!'

'If you have a special thread that will harness my mind, tether me to my home inside my self, bind me to the Guru of all gurus with love, then put it on me,' Nanak said, taking the thread from Hardial, pulling and snapping it. Everyone gasped. It was a bad omen!

How ungrateful I had been. My heart was the womb and the cradle in which he was born, my child, guru, friend, guide. In holding him I held the Universe in my arms; his gurgling laughter at birth, curdling light into a million dancing particles.

She looks at the lotus she has just completed.

The purpose of life is not to procreate but conceive consciousness; the lotus is its symbol; its stalk rising straight and tall from the mud and watery ooze that feeds and sustains it, blooming on the pads of its leaves, unfurling its petals into the blue air, exuding loveliness! Vir is the lotus, his roots connected to the whole universe. He will continue to bloom even after death!

A woman walks into the Trinjan with a basket full of damp wool, and says loudly, "I'm late because I was finishing the dying, yet again, so I could get your opinion on the color, Bibi Fatima." As she holds up a skein, the women gasp at the vibrancy of the color, a deep madder red bordering on orange with hints of brown. Nanaki takes one look at it, shuts her eyes, and falls into a trance.

Aziza, who adores Bebe Nanaki, knows what is coming, drops

125 Low caste.

her embroidery on the floor, picks up Nanaki's *rabab*, and moves towards her. The other women, gathering around Bebe Nanaki sitting on her *manji*, squat on the floor beside her. As she opens her eyes, Aziza hands her the *rabab*. Taking it, Nanaki runs the bow across the strings. Aziza fetches her own, sits on the floor by Bebe Nanaki, her bow in the air, waiting to hear what notes Bebe Nanaki would play in her *alaap*.[126]

Aziza recognizes it as the *alaap* of *raag tilang*, a folky, soulful raag, and begins to play the chords, noticing how Bebe Nanaki plays and sings her notes, lingering on each, stretching, bending, expanding, unwinding it till it sounds like the many moods and modes of a deep river in its meandering journey, from the source to the audience's ears and from thence to the Beloved's invisible ears, and the very core and pulp of the blood red Heart of His Soul.

Instinctively the women shut their eyes to go within to that space where the highest and best in human nature communes and co-mingles with its Self, the Divine. The *alaap* has made the muscles of their hearts malleable and receptive to feeling.

ih tan maa-i-aa paahi-aa pi-aaray
leet-rhaa lab rangaa-ay.
mayrai kant na bhaavai cholrhaa pi-aaray
ki-o dhan sayjai jaa-ay.

Even those who barely know how to sing, even Mata Sulakhni, and most surprisingly of all, even Nasreen, joins in as they sing the familiar words of Guru Nanak to the Great Dyer of the world. The words are familiar; many *kirtanias*[127] have sung them before at the kirtan sessions at the Gurdwara. But Bebe Nanaki's melody is entirely new. Though even the male kirtanias tuned into the feminine in themselves while singing these words, Bebe Nanaki's

---

126 Sung at the beginning of a raag, an improvised, slow, nonrhythmic exposition of the raag in Indian classical music.

127 Kirtan singers.

voice is the very flesh and spirit of receptive femininity. Her voice exudes an anguished longing so intense it conjures up the Invisible Beloved, palpably pulsing and present in His absence.

The cloth of my body, dyed in the fading colors of Maya, is not pleasing to You. How shall I come to our marriage bed? Make my body your dyeing vat, my Dyer, dissolve the madder of Your name in it, then see my irresistible color! You'll be so pleased with your handiwork You'll never, ever leave again.

CHAPTER 21

The Golden Needle

It is lunchtime – always a joyous event – at the Trinjan. Everyone brings out small bundles of lunches wrapped in cloth, unroll rotis, uncover small earthenware jars of crushed onions and chutneys. A woman, whose husband had killed several *boddards*[128] the week before when he went hunting with Lakhmi Das, has brought some peahen pickle she shares with everyone. There is a collective outcry of delight as women lick their fingers and cry, 'give us the recipe!'

"I tried to make peacock pickle but it wasn't anything like this," a woman says.

"Because females are tastier than males," the pickle maker responds to much laughter.

"But males are more beautiful with their thousand-eyed feathers fanned."

"My hens look so ordinary while the cocks are so majestic," one comments.

"Human males are beautiful, too!" Bissy, the bride to be, says.

"Your man is handsome!" a young girl smiles.

"*And* rich!" says another.

"I love this *boddar* pickle," Bissy says, licking her fingers.

"We shouldn't kill the *boddards*," a vegetarian scolds. "The birds will die out without the females. Why do we eat such beautiful

128 Peahen. Drabber looking compared to the peacock.

creatures, anyway? It is such a brutal thing to do!"

"I have a pet peacock couple that comes to my *chabaara*[129] daily. They eat corn from my hand," another relates. "I wish I didn't eat them, but I am tied to my tongue. When I return from the fields after a day of heavy labor, and my husband has brought home a kill, I eat it."

There is a lull in the conversation, each woman examining her own relationship to the brutal fact of eating fellow creatures.

"You once said that everything that exists, exists in God's Great Heart, even evil and smallness, greed and lust, Bebe Nanaki. Then why should anyone be good if we all end up in the same place anyway?" A woman addresses herself to Nanaki.

"Perhaps it's not a question of ending up anywhere but being here now. The present is everything. And here, in this Now, there is so very much to be gained by being good. The path of kindness and compassion is its own reward. Though there is suffering in every path, with goodness suffering takes wings and poison becomes nectar. This is the path that leads to God's Heart – you fly into it instead of creeping along. On the other path, you perish before you get there. You don't even glimpse paradise, you live and perish in Hell."

"Which is also in God's Heart?"

"Yes," replies Nanaki. "Yes. If it weren't so, how could sinners be redeemed?"

Bissy turns to Bebe Nanaki and confesses innocently, "Bebe jee, Baba is always warning us against Maya but I have to admit I love it in all its forms! Clothes, jewelry, a nice big clean house, servants, soft beds and silken sheets, I love it all! I love these gold

---

129 The rooftop of a village home is connected with the roofs of other homes with a small wall between them. A great deal of social interaction, including love trysts, takes place on the chabaara.

jhumkas[130] with tiny coral beads my in-laws gave me for *thaaka.*[131] I want more, with different colored stones."

"And that is why the All Knowing has blessed you with a rich man," Bebe Nanaki laughs.

"I find I am also a little greedy. When I see something beautiful I want it!"

"I wanted the gypsy woman's skirt!" Shai Tani admits. "I loved it so much!"

"And I love pretty stones that the river brings, and smooth pieces of wood, soft wool and of course, *rababs*!" Aziza adds.

"The other day I recited Baba's Japji in the hope that I will stop wanting things, but came to the conclusion that my wanting was also the Great Giver's hukum," Bissy concludes.

The women laugh.

"There's nothing wrong with loving lovely things," Bebe Nanaki says gently. "God made the beautiful material world to be loved. All forms of Maya, whether natural or manmade are reminders of the beauty of the Creator. I love flowers, trees, sunrise and sunset, the river as it winds its way to the sea, birds in flight, and lovely silken dupattas!"

"My father used to say that humans go astray because of the senses," a woman says. "Does Baba also believe that?"

Nanaki laughs.

"How wonderful the senses are! On his travels Baba met a Brahmin who kept his eyes closed so he wouldn't get any pleasure from them. He said that with his eyes closed he saw the secrets of the world. Baba took his *lota* and hid it behind him. Not being able to find it, the Brahmin got very agitated. Baba said, 'if you know the secrets of the world how come you don't know your lota

130 Dangling earrings.

131 A pre-engagement ceremony where the boy and girl are promised to each other.

is right behind you?'"

"Now that I have Bebe Nanaki's approval, I will enjoy it all!" Bissy exults.

"You will enjoy it more if you are not attached to your enjoyment, Bissy. Nothing is ours. Be ready to sacrifice it all when the Beloved's hand reaches out for it. Separated from Akaal Purukh, Maya is just trash and a trap. Let me tell you a story as we work on Bissy's *plulkari* about a woman who had forgotten the Beloved in her pursuit of Maya and how Baba awakened her."

"But before you tell it can I ask a question, Bebe Nanaki?" Aziza asks, diffidently.

"Of course you can," Bebe Nanaki says, opening wide her arms. Aziza goes into them and allows herself to be hugged. "Ask, child."

"What does Baba mean by the '*anahad*'[132] *shabad*? I understand and love sound, music, words, that which my ears can hear, but what is the Unheard?"

"Ah!" Bebe Nanaki says, shutting her eyes. She is quiet a long time and silence reins in the hall.

"Can you hear this silence? You can hear Anahad if you listen carefully, between the notes, between *sa* and *re*, the pause between them, the silence that makes all sound possible. It is the pause between two words without which there would be no communication. Take another example: the Anahad, which means unlimited, without end, is the invisible fabric of this world upon which everything that exists is woven, embroidered. It is the primal, invisible base and fundamental of all that is visible and heard."

"Sufis call the primal sound *saute surmad*, the tone that fills the cosmos," Nasreen adds. Aziza's head swivels around in amazement at her mother.

"Ami, how do you know this?"

"I know a lot of things you don't think I know," Nasreen replies.

---

132 Unheard sound. Explained in detail below.

Aziza feels awe at her mother. She asks, "Have you heard it, Ami?"

"Sometimes. Between the clattering of pots and pans," Nasreen replies.

"Have you heard it, Bebe Nanaki?" Aziza asks.

"You don't just hear it but become it when you fine tune your body by listening to it, the way you listen to the notes of the *rabab* when you tune it. Ah, then, you become the instrument that resonates unheard harmonies. I know you will experience it, little one, if you continue on the path of singing, making it your daily practice, the very heart of your day."

Lunch is over and they all move to the communal task of embroidering Bissy's *phulkari* that is spread out on darees, eager to hear Bebe Nanaki's story. The cotton cloth had been spun, sewn together, and dyed a dull madder red in earlier Trinjan meetings, and the intricate geometric pattern interspersed with flowers traced upon it. The central flower and much of the adjoining pattern is so well and densely embroidered that the foundation does not show. The women pick their colors of red, yellow, white and orange silken floss and gather around the phulkari, each working on her own little corner.

"What is the story called?" Aziza asks Bebe Nanaki.

"The Golden Needle."

"I know it!" Aziza cries. "Daadu told it to me! Daadi Jaan knows it too, but Ami doesn't."

"Where do I have time for stories?" Nasreen replies sadly. Aziza's heart goes out to her mother.

"In his travels with Bhai Mardana jee, Baba came to a town where Duni Chand lived with his wife, Savitri. Though Duni Chand has made it into the pages of history, his wife hasn't, but let me bring her in. Duni Chand had a reputation for being one of those unusual men who was good, honest, *and* wealthy, a rare combination. His wife, the source of his wealth, embroidered shawls."

"In purples, violets, blues and indigos," Aziza adds. "And they were not topaas, but fine, fine stiches like Bebe Nanaki's."

"Yes, very fine, elegant work with well crafted needles and silk threads on the finest of woven wools, with not a stitch out of place, everything aligned to the design, beautiful in conception, execution and symmetry," Bebe Nanaki describes. "She employed a hundred Kashmiri embroiderers, and her customers were the royalty of the country, rich merchants and businessmen. Duni Chand and his wife were good people who welcomed wandering holy men, minstrels, and housed them in a building they had made especially for them in their rambling compound. Their home was a luxurious palace. When Baba and Mardana ji arrived at the gate… "

"Let's describe the palace some more!" Bissy says. "The palace was surrounded by Moghul gardens that Savitri had personally designed with the help of the best architects and renowned gardeners. Fountains, miniature rivers of paradise, geometric designs, flowering bushes and trees with different colored flowers and trellises upon trellises of roses, fruit trees, and mulberries. But their extensive property was surrounded by sprawling hovels of beggars, poor people, naked, hungry children, and starving cows and dogs," Nanaki adds.

"Kids with snotty noses, no shoes, torn shirts, or no shirts, their ribs showing, hungry dogs sniffing empty streets," Aziza embellishes.

"When Baba and Mardana jee arrived at their gate, Duni Chand himself received them. He was most kind. Baba and Mardana jee were fed well, pampered with baths, massages, beds with clean sheets and all the comfort we can imagine. Weary from their travels, they stayed for several days. Every morning and evening they sang and Duni Chand, but not Savitri, attended. She was too busy with her business. They had heard she was very beautiful and very proud of her beauty and skill. They saw paintings of her on the wall, all bedecked in silken clothes and jewels. Though Duni Chand attended Baba and Bhai Mardana's kirtan, they got the feeling that he was lukewarm in his devotions, that he did it more out of a sense of duty than love. His passion lay in business, in accumulating and managing his wealth. Proud of his estate, he gave them a tour of his home, gardens, stables to show off his Kabuli horses and European buggies made of silver.

On the way to the building that housed the embroiderers, Baba stooped and picked up something from the dirt. It was a needle made of gold. It caught a beam of light and shone brilliantly.

'Baba, this is Savitri's favorite needle! She has been looking for it everywhere! She will be so happy to get this back!' Duni Chand exclaimed, eagerly reaching for it. 'It is made of solid gold and made by one of our famous goldsmiths.'"

"I have a favorite needle, too; this one!" one of the women at the Trinjan cries. "I have had it twenty years. I keep it pinned to me. I packed it in my dowry, pinned it to my wedding dress, in fact, as a symbol and reminder to mend the tears between my husband and myself as soon as they showed themselves. But that night I forgot it and my husband screamed out because it pierced him."

"He got poked while his needle was poking you!" Shai Tani jokes. Some women laugh out loud while others are offended.

"This needle is easy to thread and it is so smooth it never snags on the cloth but goes in and out easily," the woman continued.

"Goes in and out so easily!" Shai Tani repeats.

There is more laughter and more annoyance.

"The shadows are lengthening. Let me go on with my story," Bebe Nanaki says. "Duni Chand was about to run back to the house to tell Savitri about the happy recovery of her needle when he stopped and said, reluctantly, 'But Baba, since you found it, keep it. My wife has others, I know, because I got some more made from the goldsmith and she loves them."

'I don't want it,' Baba said.

'I insist,' Duni Chand said magnanimously.

'Alright,' Baba said, taking it and looking at it. 'But keep it for me for the time being. I don't have a place for it. I will take it from you in the afterlife.'

Duni Chand laughed at the joke, took the needle and pinned it to his shawl for safekeeping. Later that evening, Baba and Mardana sang for several hours and were about to retire for the night when Duni Chand returned, accompanied by his wife.

Savitri fell at Baba's feet.

'Thank you,' she said. 'Thank you for opening my sewn shut eyes.'

Duni Chand explained in a confused sort of way.

'I took the needle to her and explained how you had found it and how I had offered it to you and you had said, 'I will take it from you in the afterlife.' She looked at me blankly, her jaw dropped, her eyes grew wide, and she sat totally still for a while. 'What's the matter with you?' I asked her, and she cried 'you fool! You fool. Don't you understand that we cannot take anything with us? Not even a needle? There are no pockets in shrouds, nor in our bodies?' 'I'm not a fool,' I replied. 'I know that!' 'No, you don't! You say you know it but you don't,' she cried, casting away the shawl she was embroidering and ran to you.'

Duni Chand's wife began to take off all the jewels she was wearing and heaped them at Baba's feet.

'Bibi, sell them and do some good with the money,' Baba said.

'You're a wise, enlightened man,' Duni Chand said. 'Baba, please show us a way so we never have to part with our wealth. Look at all these expensive things I love so much! If I put them in storage before I die, could you ensure that when I reincarnate I can have them again?'

'You can take untold riches into your next life, but not these baubles,' Baba replied. Duni Chand fell at his feet and prayed to know how his wealth might accompany him. Baba Nanak answered, 'give some of it away in God's name, feed the poor, nurture the sick and the feeble with your funds, and that portion shall accompany you.'

'Baba,' Savitri said, 'give us your understanding and wisdom. Teach us how we may live well in this life and in the next.'

Baba said, '*She alone is known as the Lord's bride who embroiders her gown with the Name. If a woman becomes virtuous and turn her heart into a thread, the Beloved will string Himself on it like a priceless gem.*'

While Duni Chand was still disturbed at the thought of leaving his treasure behind one day, Savitri was really affected by Baba's words. Baba was affected, too, for his eyes closed, and his face became softly emotional as *bani* came to him."

"Daadu Jaan took out his *rabab* and sat down, like this," Aziza demonstrates, holding her *rabab* and playing the alaap of Siree raag.

"Savitri and Duni Chand did exactly what Baba told them to do," Nanaki says, picking up her *rabab*. "They built smaller buildings for the poor, opened schools, hospitals, free kitchens and also a shelter for stray animals."

Both of them play chords to whose accompaniment Bebe Nanaki explains the meaning of the *shabad* they are about to sing: '*When the pitcher of the body bursts, there is terrible pain; those who are caught by the Minister of Death regret and repent. Crying out, "Mine! Mine!" They depart, leaving their bodies, their wealth, and their loved ones. Without the Name wealth makes you lose your way.*'

After her translation and explanation, Bebe Nanaki and Aziza play and sing together:

ghat binsai dukh aglo jam pakrhai pachhutaa-ay,
mayree mayree kar ga-ay tan dhan kalat na saath
bin naavai dhan baad hai bhoolo maarag aath

The shadows are beginning to melt and they all know their

Trinjan day is fast coming to an end. Shai Tani picks up her *dholak* and says in her characteristic way, "come, come, this child Bissy is about to get married. Let's prepare her for what is to come with some songs."

Many earthy, gutsy, exuberant, bawdy songs are sung to much merriment. In the middle of their singing, Bhai Buddha walks into the Trinjan. All the women look up. It is highly unusual for a male to walk in. His face looks drawn and sad. He stands and looks at the women, his gaze moving from Mata Sulakhni to Nanaki, who are sitting close by. He hesitates a moment, then walks up to them and whispers. Mata Sulakhni screams while Nanaki stands up, her dupatta and thread falling to the floor. Bhai Buddha escorts them out, the women collapsing on either side of him.

A flutter of fear, a shudder runs through the women as they whisper to each other, "Something has happened. Something dreadful has happened to their family."

CHAPTER 22

Winged Horse

Lakhmi Das is dead. Nobody quite knows how, though it is clear that it happened after a fight with his older brother, Sri Chand. Lakhmi had returned after a hunt the evening before, and while he was skinning and cutting up the doe, two fetuses were found inside its belly. Seeing this, Sri Chand attacked Lakhmi Das and a raging fist-to-fist fight ensued that ended when Sri Chand's followers broke the two apart. In the verbal battle that followed the physical one, Sri Chand swore that Lakhmi would have to give an accounting of his actions to God, that he would be found wanting and be condemned to the deepest, darkest hell. Lakhmi Das retorted that God himself created animals of prey. Impetuous as he was, he said he would go give his accounting right there and then. He grabbed his son, Dharam Chand, mounted his horse, and spurred it towards the jungle outside Kartarpur where he hunted. Sri Chand, whose prophetic powers saw what was going through his brother's mind, shouted:

"Don't you dare end our clan!"

People who saw the incident swore that Sri Chand's arm lengthened and extended as if it were made of some fictile, rubbery material, and with it, he intercepted the galloping horse and plucked Dharam out of his brother's embrace. He wanted Nanak's lineage to continue through generations and millennia to come.

He himself, being celibate, would have no progeny.

Lakhmi Chand's horse had later returned to the dera, rider-less. The men had been searching everywhere for him and the horse for two days without telling the family. Though no body had been recovered, they agreed the family must be informed.

The women of the family and the Sikh community at large are devastated by the event. Baba Nanak weeps; Nanaki cries, grieves, and acknowledges her sense of relief that the death her soul had anticipated was not Nanak's, though she is wise enough to know that all such relief is temporary; Mata Sulakhni and Lakhmi's wife, Dhanvanti, wail, howl, and are inconsolable. Sri Chand leaves the Dera and is not seen again for many years.

Some say Lakhmi Das drowned or killed himself in some other way; others, more inclined to fantasy, say he flew to heaven on the horse and then sent it back because it was not the horse's time to die yet.

What makes it difficult for everyone is that sudden deaths are all the harder for being unexpected. Moreover, there is no body to say goodbye to, no customary rituals to lay the dead to rest and allow the living to have some closure by channeling their grief into prescribed practicalities.

Expected deaths follow an ordered sequence: right before death the person is carried from the bed to the floor, already prepared with a paste of dung and grass, his feet turned towards the north to ensure he/she doesn't become a ghost; the body is bathed, often with curd; ghee is applied to the body, hair, and poured into the cavities of the mouth, nose, ears, both as a sign of respect and love, and to make the burning easier and quicker so that, in Kabir's words, 'the hair burns like a bale of hay, and bones like a bundle of logs;' the corpse is clothed in the best outfit, placed on a bier and covered with a shroud; widows and children touch the feet; the ceremony of *deeva batti*[133] is then performed: dough, shaped into a lamp, is filled with ghee, a cotton wick placed in it and lit near the head or on the right palm of the deceased to illumine his/her journey to the other world; professional female mourners come to the house, lamenting, beating their breasts, wailing loudly, giving voice to the grief that family members are unable in their shock and grief to express; relatives and members of the community visit, sit around the body, offer condolences to family members and keep them company in their hour of need; others go into the jungle to collect wood to make a pyre for the cremation; women cook meals for the visitors who come from out of town; Hindu men shave their heads; widows take off all their jewelry, break their bangles, remove all make-up, never to wear them again; their lives, even if they don't commit *sati*,[134] are over; a widow is a non-entity without a husband; the *Nain*, the maid, combs and ties the hair of the widow and people give her much-welcome money since she is not to have a source of income from now on and must be entirely dependent upon family members and relatives. If a married woman dies, she is adorned with jewelry, nose ring, bangles and the parting in her hair is colored vermilion as a sign of her good fortune in not surviving her husband. An old man's death is cause for celebration. His shroud is bright red and his bier, shaped like a boat, is decorated in gold and red ribbons; his body is then escorted to the sounds of drums, stringed instruments, gongs, and conch calls, to the cremation grounds. Flower petals, coins, dry fruits and other edibles are thrown over the body that the poor await eagerly to collect.

The corpse is then carried out of the house, feet first – contrary to head first from the womb – to the cremation ground on the shoulders of four close relatives and placed on the already prepared

---

133 Lamp and wick.

134 The practice of women burning themselves along with their dead spouses, a custom absolutely forbidden by Guru Nanak.

pyre. More wood is then piled on top of the deceased. A family member, generally the oldest son, breaks an earthenware jar full of water to symbolize that the form has broken and shapeless water returned to the soil. Usually the eldest son sets fire to the wood logs, starting at the head, clockwise, reciting prayers. Midway through the burning he lifts a club and breaks the deceased's skull, the thickest, hardest part of the body, to facilitate its disintegration into ash.

On the way back mourners bathe at a pond or well, wash their clothes, wear new ones as a gesture of purification from death; then, they sit on the ground and pluck a blade of grass. The priest chants and instructs the gathering to break the blade of grass into two and throw it behind them over their shoulders to sever their ties with the dead one. Of course, this ritual never serves its purpose, for the dead continue to live with the living in one form or another.

After the body is charred to ash, the bones are collected from the pile of ash in a ceremony called *phool chugna,* meaning 'picking flowers.' The bones are washed in milk, placed in a bag or an earthenware jar and consigned to a river, always to a river, that brings, takes away, and brings again.

A feast follows, and many more ceremonies and rituals are performed to ensure the deceased a good afterlife. Food, grains, sugar are given away in charity in the hope they will reach the loved one; a cow is given away so that the dead man can clutch its tail and cross the wide river to the other shore. Brahmin priests, who receive the cow, assure the family that the cow will perform this important function for the dead man and also feed him milk in the afterlife.

Though Baba Nanak forbade *sati,* discouraged the many rituals of death and the elaborate ceremonies that often put poor people into debt, they persisted in rituals to placate their conscience and the inevitable regrets and guilt of the grieving.

In Lakhmi's case, they could do nothing and were left with a vacuum that was hard to fill.

When the kirtan sessions resumed upon Baba's insistence a few days later, he sang many songs about death: '*We, bubbles of breath, live for the briefest moment; we do not know the time or place of our departure. O Nanak, serve the Deathless One to whom our soul and breath belong.*'

His music and words soothed the community and evoked reflection and wonder in many: who knows where we come from, materializing out of invisibility, sound out of silence, living out our seemingly solid, bounded existences, then returning to the folds of that Mystery beyond our comprehension, beyond gender and categories, beyond the bounds of space and time, at once infinite and finite, invisible and palpable, unbound and bound, beyond and within the life that surrounds and inhabits us, like air; the Mystery none has named, no eyes seen, no tongue uttered, no hand touched, but glimpsed briefly, ever so briefly, when Death opens its Door, humbling us in our knowledge that we do not, and may never know, though we have felt it beating in our hearts as the unfathomable sea upon the shores of our consciousness.

Mata Sulakhni and Dhanvanti, Lakhmi Das's wife, cloister themselves in their sorrow. People spend long hours sitting by Baba and Bebe Nanaki, finding their presence consoling. Bebe Nanaki talks about grief as a gift from the Beloved. The death of someone close to us opens Death's Door and allows us a glimpse beyond. People tell their own stories of remarkable coincidences and dreams following a death. Nanaki explains how dreams are a different dimension in which connections with the dead can be made. Death, she says, always wrenches from their hinges the doors of the heart, confronts us with our mortality, and allows us to see and experience life from the vantage point of mystery.

People who are convinced Lakhmi Das has committed suicide

want to know whether it is a sin to do so. Nanaki says everything that happens, everything we are helpless in the face of, is *hukum*; that we must accept it fully and not judge people for what their destiny makes them do.

She also explains that those who believe he rode off into heaven are happier and calmer than those that make reason the measure of their knowledge. Bhai Buddha asks Bebe Nanaki the difference between the two.

Sometimes, Bebe Nanaki explains, when 'reality' becomes too much for us to bear, the universe gives us ways of thinking that are just as true as 'reality;' that there is a Reality, accessed through the Imagination, that is so vast it contains both reality and fantasy. This whole world is Akaal Purukh's imagination and fantasy, Vishnu's dream, she says. She repeats Baba's image of how all of creation flows from one fantastical Word written by Akaal Purukh. From the womb of that primeval Word, rivers, mountains, trees, earth, soil, sky, water, people, creatures, flowers, plants, insects appeared. We too, are utterances, words, vibrations emanating from His Mouth, she says. The world is a vibration, a wave, a breath, a sound given a body, form and shape that returns to the original Vibration when it dematerializes.

Bebe Nanaki goes on to say that those who cannot bear 'reality' must find refuge in the arms of Winged Imagination, that God-given Truth, Mother, who lives beyond the reach of constricting reason shackled to the senses, and feeds balm from her teats to the torn and bleeding heart. The imagination transforms blood into roses, and the bones of the dead into flowers. Even literally, she says, bones and ashes make good fertilizer for plants, and one way or another, we return, since God's energy is deathless. Who, she asks, in their right mind would not step beyond the mind – not denying its harsh imperatives – but choosing this other, more beautiful way to think and live? It is hardly the coward's way; much courage, especially from those who live through their brains, is required to enter here, she says. The simple peasant who believes in miracles knows more than all our knowing. Miracles, in all their literality, she adds, speak of those Truths that lie beyond plodding, ponderous, reason.

So, dear readers, let us follow the fantasists' footsteps, knowing the realities and rituals surrounding the diseased, yet choose consciously to see reality in another light, in the suffused flame of myth. Here, people fly up to heaven on horses and leave no residue behind, except flowers. Death comes for all, even for our prophets and heroes, and flesh, clothed in which we enter the realm of matter, must be shed like a garment specific to this dimension.

Nanaki's words are uttered on the threshold of a wave of deaths that pass through Kartarpur following Lakhmi Das's death. They prepare the listeners and gift them a path to prefer as they are swept up and out in it. Every death affects everyone that comes into contact with it because, as Nanaki says, we exist in a fabric and a web we share with everyone else, and with every death a part of us dies. With every death, she says, we must turn again and again towards the Deathless One in whom we exist and never perish.

All year it was fall in Kartarpur. It was time for lives, like leaves, to shed, float down the currents of air to the soil from which they sprang. It was all part of *Sehaj*, the natural order of things, though the human, so removed from this order, mourns and weeps. We inherit weeping and mourning from the moment of the Great Spirit's incarnation into flesh – the vessel that contains the uncontainable Spirit which laps at the shores of our boundaries and in the very nuclei of our cells – till death, spirit's summons, finally frees us from the cage we call the body.

Many we have not even heard of in this narrative, having played their parts in the Drama of Life, moved into the wings where the River waited without ever ceasing its flow, to carry them away – who knows where? Even Baba, always humble enough to know he did not know, admitted in a song: *some are cremated, some buried, some eaten by dogs, some thrown into rivers, O Nanak, it is not known, where they go and into what they merge.*

Daulatan Masi, on a night of thunder and lightening found the energy within her frail body to leave the house and stumble towards the dera with a single intent: to die in Guru Nanak's arms. Guru Nanak, too, sensing her urgent need, went out in the pouring rain to meet her half way, his arms spread wide. She walked into them, and with a beatific smile on her face, exhaled her last breath. Clasped in his loving embrace, she returned home to the infinite spaces that a kiss of the awakened one's lotus feet had transported her before her time; she died in a dream and never returned to that which most of us call 'reality,' her soul returning to those vast, boundless spaces that her mortal frame and sanity could barely bear.

Since we are on the topic of death we might also mention the deaths of Nanak's parents who perished long before this: Mata Tripta died in her son's embrace; Mehta Kallu died a contented man, having given up his small expectations of life, he had an inkling of the invaluable gift he had been given in Nanak; unlike mortal kings who become but a word, a footnote, or a name in history books, his son would live forever, and he along with him.

It is time now for Mardana, who had given death the slip so many times during his adventures with Nanak, to die.

CHAPTER 23

Final Hours

Mardana has always wanted to die in good spirits. "Allah," he has prayed repeatedly, "when it is my time to die, please let me come to you joyously. Let me come to you, in Baba's image, like a bride comes to the bridegroom."

But as Mardana's death approaches, he is in anything but good spirits. He finds himself praying for an extension instead. "I have loved your life, Allah! Enjoyed your wonderful senses. Can you give me a little more life, please?"

But the answer comes to him clear as a bell: 'No. It is time to leave, Mardana.'

Food has lost its taste; even the halwa he loves so much tastes like ashes in his mouth; he can barely feed himself; he can't bathe himself because his arms and hands are too weak to pick up the *lota* full of water. He has reduced the quantity of water in the lota, but now even the minimum amount is an effort, and worst of all, Fatima has to escort him, shaking and stumbling, to the outhouse, and has even, upon occasion, to clean him.

Unable to lie in bed, or to get up, all his limbs aching, he mumbles a verse from Baba Farid: '*Fareedaa baar paraa-i-ai baisnaa saa-ee mujhai na deh; jay too ayvai rakhsee jee-o sareerahu layh:* My Love, *do not make me dependent on others. If this is the way you are going to keep me, then go ahead and take away my life and body.*'

Fatima, hearing him from across the courtyard, comes, makes eye contact, as if to ask, are you dying? There are no tears in her eyes, but a fullness indicating the tide is not far behind.

Mardana clutches her thumb desperately, urgently, with his index and middle finger. He realizes at once he is clutching too much, once again doing what Baba has told him to beware. 'Hold life and death lightly, Mardana. It is a dream.' Besides, clutching costs him too much energy and he relaxes his hold. As he settles under the covers, life's stubborn, alluring dream flares up in him once more.

"Take me to the *meihkhana*,"[135] he whispers to Fatima, sitting up.

"What?" cries Fatima. "You can barely walk!" She had never approved of it, but she knows she has to hold her disapproval in abeyance. *Nothing matters but pleasing him and giving him ease*, she thinks.

"Help me put on the clothes I wore on my wedding," he says in an irritable, grumbling tone that had always irritated Fatima. But over the years she has learned through much suffering and observation that his grumpiness is the voice of his powerlessness. She forgives him instantly in her heart, but says quietly, lovingly:

"Our wedding."

Mardana is too of full of his own frustration with the state of his body to hear her. The journey he must make, its contract signed and sealed when he was but a thought in the universe's brain, has begun in earnest. From here on he must proceed alone, unaccompanied, naked into the awaiting womb of death.

Fatima turns towards the old wooden trunk she had received as a dowry, its polish gone, just the grains and whorls of wood where hands habitually touched it, around the shackle, and all the other places children had played upon it, rubbed to a fine shine. Seeing the unlocked shackle, in an instant she reviews the history from locking it so jealousy in her youth to leaving it open. *Who would*

135 Tavern.

want to steal these rags? She chuckles to herself.

As she lifts her own worn wedding dress – a torn red taffeta *garara*[136] to get to his, in an instant her post-marital history presents itself in quick montages: from the trauma and anticipation of her wedding, on through its abysses and peaks, and the present gift, yes, '*gift*,' she names it to herself, of old age. She can't articulate to herself in what the gift lay. Perhaps, she thinks, in arriving at a certain spaciousness in her life and relationships she had not experienced before; a spaciousness that had flowered when she had stopped pushing and pulling to change the people and events of her life, or even her own undeniable proclivities. She had, somewhere along the progression of her aging, loosened the reigns of her mind and surrendered to the breath that lived her. No one and nothing was *hers* anymore. They were all their own, Allah's, mysteries to be marveled at. What did she really know about this man she had spent her life with? He had depths she could never reach because he himself had not touched them. *So much of me remains beyond my comprehension because I am a part of the mystery of life, part of the whole.'You are the ocean without boundaries. How can I, just a little fish in it, know anything about you?'* She recites one of Baba's *shabads*.

She brings the cream-colored, embroidered, worn clothes they had both been loath to cast away these many years, and dresses him, *like a child,* she thinks, fumbling to ensure his limbs enter the right passageways, head, arms, legs.

After Mardana is ready, he finds himself too exhausted to do anything but lie back down on his bed again, his mind lingering on memories of his past visits to the *meihkhana*: his buddies joking and laughing as the scantily dressed village *saakis*[137] passed the opium and *charas* hookahs around and served roasted goat and fowl. The last time he had drunk more than he should have and

136 A flared split skirt worn by Muslim women.

137 Saakis: females, hetaeras.

had to be carried home, Fatima had made him drink four glasses of buttermilk to help him get over his dreadful headache.

At least I got a poem out of it! He chuckles to himself. *My very first, and last.* Lying in bed, he recites it to himself. *The barmaid's name is Misery, the brand of wine is Lust; False and Covetous are the company. Fool, make right thinking, good conduct, humility your meat and drink. These, O Nanak, dispel sin and sorrow.*

Mardana had surprised himself when he ended the *sloka*[138] the way Baba Nanak ended his, by signing off as Nanak. Was this pride, he had wondered, but understood in a flash that whoever sings Baba's *shabads*, ending with 'Nanak says,' is Nanak! How often he had signed off his songs on those two words! *Yes*, he had thought, *whoever transcends his lower nature, sings Baba's shabads with humility, becomes Nanak!*

He had sent the poem to Baba Nanak through Bhai Buddha and told him to explain to him that it had just happened and that he wasn't being arrogant. Bhai Buddha had told him Baba had laughed out loud at the poem.

How long ago was it? Yesterday? Two months ago? Two years? Time's string has begun to fray, split, break in his mind. Only events remain in his memory without the interim between them, without the chronology. *What happens to the time in between*, he wonders. *Soon time itself will end and I will enter timelessness. And my time-bound body?* He can't think anymore, and doesn't care that he can't. *How little the mind knows of where I am going.*

The effort of thinking and questioning is altogether too much for him, even though he thinks in fragments, snippets, images, inchoate feelings instead of the syntax and sentences that make thought coherent to others. He allows his brain to rest and linger on the memory of his last visit.

Mardana's desire to taste some more of the wine of life makes him

138 A metered, rhyming poetic verse; a song.

turn in his mind to the *saakis*, dressed in provocative clothes, lips painted an alluring red, eyes lined with kohl. Suddenly, a vision so compelling presents itself to his mind's eye that he sits up in fright. The bodies of the seductive *saakis* disintegrate before his eyes: rosy cheeks wither, turn to hides, taut limbs turn to pulp, separate from the bones, fall in a cloud of dust, dirt and ash.

"Baba!" he cries out aloud. Nobody comes. His fright turns to anger. *Why hasn't Baba come to see me for so long? Is this all I mean to him after I gave him my life? And where in hell is Buddha? I want to see Baba once more! I won't die till he comes!*

Simultaneously with this thought he sees the tip of a blue turban across the courtyard wall, followed by a white turban, and then a green one. His heart flutters wildly like a bird in a cage as strength surges in his frame.

[illegible] in his hand to the soldier dressed in protective clothes [illegible] [illegible] his red eyes [illegible] with [illegible] [illegible] [illegible] [illegible] [illegible] right [illegible] [illegible] [illegible] [illegible] [illegible]

“Oh!” he [illegible] nobody [illegible] [illegible] [illegible] [illegible] [illegible] [illegible]

[illegible] across the [illegible] and [illegible] and then [illegible] [illegible] [illegible]

CHAPTER 24

Into God's Great Heart

Baba Nanak and Bhai Lehna, carrying *rababs* on their shoulders, accompanied by Buddha, walk through the open gate and proceed towards Mardana's bed. All Mardana's anger evaporates as he totters shakily out of bed and stumblingly falls at Baba's feet. Bhai Lehna tries to pick him up, but Mardana clings to his feet, and kisses them, tears flowing in rivulets down his wizened cheeks.

Fatima, Aziza and Shehzada come running to touch Baba's feet and put Mardana back in bed. Nasreen, aware of the gravity of the moment, says nothing to Buddha, and brings *peedees* for them to sit on.

Pale and trembling, Mardana lies back on the pillows. Baba Nanak sits by him and takes his skeletal frame in his arms. Mardana turns and clings to him like a child, sobbing. Tears begin to flow down Baba's cheeks and he lets them. There is no movement to push them away or hide them.

So profound is the drama that is playing out before their eyes that the rest of them are stunned into silence. Having caught the contagion of tears, they weep too, especially Shehzada, who, on the verge of loss, realizes what an opportunity he has missed in not being close to his father. Their relationship, though distant, yet had an element of a dark and unfulfilled attachment.

Baba holds Mardana near his heart; no barriers between spirit and spirit remain, though the body still imposes its own. They stay thus together for a while. There is no need to pull away. Mardana's labored breathing quietens down till it becomes the same pace as Nanak's. Their hearts synchronize their rhythms till they become one. It feels very much like music to Mardana, the moments when they played and sang together and no distinction remained between their voices and the voices of the wind, tree, water, and bird. It was all one.

"Thank you for being my Beloved's gift to me, Bhai Mardana," Baba says.

Mardana's heart lurches upward, trying to escape through his throat. He splutters, half in anger, half in a joy that is almost unbearable.

"What… took you… so long… to say this? Couldn't you… have said it… earlier when all those years… I went around feeling… like your fool?"He stammers, haltingly, with pent up passion.

"I accept your blame, Bhai Mardana jee. Forgive me. The Beloved forgot to remind me to say it before."

"Go ahead… blame your Beloved… for everything," Mardana gasps.

Nanak and Angad laugh heartily. Mardana feels offended at first, then joins in the laughter, and ends up coughing. Baba gives him a drink of water, then lays him down, and strokes his forehead.

"Rest, my friend. Rest," he says, softly.

"I'm afraid to die," Mardana whispers.

"I'm afraid, too. I am not too far behind you, friend," Baba says.

"You're a liar!" Mardana says, in yet another burst of energy. "I've… never known you… to be… afraid."

Baba turns to Bhai Lehna. "*Rabab chaid, Lehnaiaa.*[139] Let us entertain our Master of the *Rabab* who has pleased us so very much and so very often." And then, looking at Aziza, he adds,

---

139 Awaken the rabab. 'Lehnaiaa' is an affectionate take on his name.

"bring yours too."

Aziza wipes her tears and runs in to fetch her *rabab*, stumbling in her excitement, thrilled beyond words that she would accompany Baba, confused with the simultaneous presence of joy and sorrow in her heart.

Bhai Lehna awakens the *rabab* with a few strokes of his fingers and Aziza follows the chords. Mardana shuts his eyes when the *alaap* begins. The three of them sing together, their voices spiraling out as one voice in different pitches. After a long *alaap*, they begin to sing the refrain: *Na jaanaa haray mayree kavan gatay. Ham moorakh agi-aan saran parabh tayre kar kirpaa raakho mayree laaj patay: My Friend, I don't know what my condition shall be. I am foolish and ignorant, I know nothing, I seek Your Sanctuary. Sometimes, my soul soars high into heaven; sometimes it falls to the depths. Pre-ordained, Death comes to all; my Beloved, the burning fire is coming closer! Nanak prays: bless me with Your Name; it shall be my help and support in the end."*

The sound and sense echo Mardana's state of mind as he hovers over the fuzzy border between the two dimensions of this and some other state, beyond words and description, whose increasing gravity he resists with the density of regret.

"I'll never… make music with… you again!" He cries. "I'll never… hear your… voice again! Can't you… save me… once more? You did… so many times… in the past? *Help this drowning stone swim!"*

"No more swimming now, Mardana. It is time to fly. This time I have to let you spread your wings and go to the Beloved's marriage bed. Listen. He is calling you."

"'*Mahal bulaa-irhee-ay bilam na keejai: The Beloved has called you to the Mansion of His Presence – do not delay!*'" Buddha quotes Baba's words.

"Go with gratitude, my friend. How blessed we are to have sung the Great Spirit's praises! How much we have been given, what wealth that allowed us to live and watch this wonderful dreamlike drama, to have so many adventures together. But the best one awaits. Die with courage and excitement, my beloved minstrel, as you embark upon a new journey."

"But you… yourself said… we don't know… where we go," Mardana stutters.

"It's true. But we must die with trust and utter surrender. Surrendering with sorrow and regret is not surrendering. Let go."

Mardana listens with intent and wants to believe every word of Baba's. But his incorrigible humanity asserts itself once more and he says,"I fear… my death will be the end… of me. The world… will forget me!"

"Marda na, Marda na, Marda na,"[140] Baba's rhythmic words are spoken with a smile as he holds Mardana and rocks him gently, like a mother her child. "You will never die. Here, too, on this planet, your name and story will be remembered, my hero. A time will come when our own terrible times will seem peaceful to the coming generations, and a need will arise for Sikhs to engage in war. Heroes will be needed who will not be afraid to die doing the righteous deed. Then your words – the poem you sent me through Bhai Buddha – and mine, Mardana, will be part of a Granth – enshrined under canopies of gold, lovingly wrapped in silken scarves – full of magical, holy words, sense and sound, reminders, names of our Beloved, lamps in darkness."

A sudden peace perfuses Mardana. He shuts his eyes and lies back again on the pillows. Above and beyond the gratification and assurance of knowing he would leave an indelible trace behind, not due to any worth of his own, but on account of being a small but important part of Baba, is a certainty that his life, and death, had meaning. Looking back on the entire arc of his life from the vantage point of its end, he sees the pattern and, yes, perfection

---

140 'Marda-na,' when separated into two syllables, means, 'won't die'.

in it. He is, he knows now, having traversed the path to the other side of doubt, an indispensible part of the design of the limitless fabric of the universe.

"So, tell me, my friend, what I should do with your remains," Baba asks Mardana. Fatima and Aziza, witnesses to an intense encounter between Mardana and Baba, can remain detached no longer. They burst into tears and each hold on to Mardana's feet and kiss them. "Shall I bury you like a good Muslim and erect a stone tomb in your honor? It will endure, for a little while at least, and generations will come to pay their obeisance to the famous musician."

"No," Mardana gasps out his words. "This body… has been… my tomb. Why shut it… up in another? You… have taught me the spirit… can't be contained… in any house. Like air, I will be… everywhere now. Do what you want… with my body. Make slippers… for your feet… from the skin… of my heart. Let me… touch your feet, always."

"That, my friend, I will not do," Baba chuckles. "But we will never be parted. I will return you to the river from which we all come, like seemingly solid waves."

"Just… put your… hand… on my heart and leave… it there."

Baba does so.

"We will meet again in God's Great Heart, my dearest friend," he says, holding Mardana's hand with his other hand.

Mardana relaxes. All his nerves, taut like the strings of a *rabab* when it is finely tuned, slacken. He knows with knowledge replete with feeling and the gnosis of infallible intuition the truth of Baba's words. He is assured that as long as men and women long for stories and songs that help them find their path in darkness; as long as stories are as staffs to the blind, mother's milk to wailing infants, light to lost travelers, Mardana's name would forever be linked with Baba Nanak's; that wherever his soul might journey in or outside time, Baba Nanak's hand would always be in his.

Guru Nanak's eyes are oceans sloshing over with brine. Mardana feels himself falling into them, like a man diving into turbulent waters from a broken and sinking ship. Just as panic begins to surface in him again, he hears the words,"Sleep, Mardana, sleep and awaken in the Beloved's Heart."

The churning waters become still. Mardana sees his horizons widening. A ship with wings for sails swims into his vision. Baba's words whisper faintly in his fading ears: "Go play your *rabab* for God, Mardana. Play the melody that never ends."

Then he hears and sees no more. His breáthing ceases as he merges with the light that casts no shadows.

CHAPTER 25

A Friendship Begins

Some years later, Aziza sits in her Hermit's hut, spinning. Tears of gratitude pool in her eyes at the many memories of her grandmother teaching her the skill.

Each time she sits at the loom, she recalls how she had found her grandmother slumped over her loom in the hut one day in the heat of summer. Fatima had spent more and more time after her husband's death at the hut, teaching all aspects of the art to Aziza. It had given her focus and a purpose for several years, and Aziza was an eager and enthusiastic learner. In dying, Fatima had bequeathed her incomplete weavings to Aziza as models to follow.

Though *rabab* playing is her primary passion, Aziza has come to love the entire process of the art of spinning, dying and weaving. She spends most of her time at the hut in the company of her dog, Motia, singing as she goes about her tasks. Buddha would come sometimes, not as often as she would have liked, and tell her what was happening at the dera. Each time he would bring her the words of Baba's new *shabads*; she would compose them in the suggested raag and play them for him when he came the next time.

The sound of familiar footsteps makes her stop suddenly and listen. She runs to the mooda by the hole in the wall, and waits. Shortly thereafter, she hears his voice.

"Sat Kartar!" Buddha says, cheerfully. This has become the

greeting and parting phrase in Kartarpur for a while. It means, 'True is the Creator'. Though for many the words had become just a habit, words people mimed on meeting and parting, for many devout people it served as a reminder several times a day that the Invisible, Beloved Creator was the truest thing in existence.

"Amro has been in town," Buddha says. "Do you want to meet her?"

"Why should I want to meet her?" Aziza asks, irritably. The time she spent alone in the hut has made her reclusive.

"You have so much in common," Buddha replies.

"I don't have anything in common with anyone," she says curtly.

"You both play the *rabab*. You both sing."

"Is she better than me?"

"No one can be better than you. But you could sing together. Maybe you could teach each other a few things."

"Oh, alright, though I don't think she can teach me anything," Aziza responds, reluctantly consenting to meet her sometime.

"She's waiting by the peepal tree by the well. I will go get her," Buddha says. The peepal is close by and Aziza feels sudden trepidation and annoyance at the thought of meeting another good friend of Buddha's, and at such short notice.

Soon, the two arrive. Buddha sits on the moodaa by the hole, and Amro opens the door and comes inside.

"You don't have to be jealous of me. I don't want Buddha. I can't have him anyway, so I would rather not want him. I am quite firm about that," Aziza blurts out her feelings to Amro as soon as she steps in. After a brief silence, Amro, who tries to figure out what Aziza is saying, starts to giggle. Soon both of them are giggling and laughing out loud. Buddha is also quite amused.

"He is like a brother to me. I will only marry the man my father and mother pick for me, and they have already picked Jasso," Amro explains.

"Aren't you the good one!" Aziza says, not without sarcasm. "So obedient!"

"I know from my dreams and my desires that I can be quite bad! That's why I like to submit to an understanding superior to mine: Baba Nanak's, my father and mother's, and my friend, Nihali's. I think that all our desires must be subservient to our desire for the Beloved."

"I don't think that surrender to a superior wisdom is the way we are meant to live our lives. I hope one day we will have more choice," Aziza says with conviction.

"Not even to the Highest Power? I think that if we surrender ourselves to Her, She will do what is best for us."

"Why do you call Him Her?" Aziza asks, astounded.

"I believe in both Ma Durga and Akaal Purakh. They are the same, you know, only Ma Durga is an image that we can see and Akaal Purakh a concept we can hardly imagine. Sometimes I need the comfort of a female presence, sometimes a male's. Baba Nanak also calls this Energy Mother Father God. So sometimes I call Him Her and sometimes Her Him."

Aziza doesn't know how to react to this radical idea. Her image of a female deity is someone like her mother, stern and prescriptive, while her concept of a male is more like her grandfather and Baba. "I think I prefer Akaal Purukh, Allah, or Krishna."

"They are all names for the Energy that has no name," Amro says. "My favorite name is… You."

"You," repeats Aziza, shutting her eyes. "You. Yes, it certainly brings Him closer. *Ham tum beech bhayo nahee koay.*"

"I love those lines of Kabir's," Amro says, translating them. "'*No one, nothing stands between You and me.*' Kabir goes naked into the Beloved's arms."

"You can use that metaphor. *You* don't need to live in the spaces of your mind, like I do. You will marry, have children, live a *real* life, and forget all about singing."

"What would be the good of marriage and children if I couldn't sing?" Amro asks.

"Exactly," Aziza replies.

"My father wouldn't marry me to someone who wouldn't want me to sing," Amro says, with assurance.

"Lucky you. You'll have everything. Jasso will let you sing, you will have babies, too, and lead a blessed life. When you can't live in the flesh, you have to live in the mind."

"It doesn't have to be that way," Buddha interjects.

Amro looks troubled, sad, her heart opening wide with compassion. She looks at Aziza, opens her arms and Aziza walks into them, like a child, and allows herself to be held as she sobs. Amro, generous hearted Amro, weeps, too, for her sister and her difficult destiny. She has heard her story from Buddha and her heart is wide open to her.

"Phapa jee says, 'don't be anxious, don't worry. You will be provided for, just as everything else in the universe is provided for.' As for marriage, we are, all of us, essentially alone," Amro consoles. "My friend Nihali, who is an orphan and who didn't marry, says that if you are not connected to the Beloved, no matter how many friends you have, you will be alone. She leads a humble life and is the happiest person I know. She owns a cow, sells milk, buttermilk, ghee, makes cow dung patties that she dries on the outside walls of her hut, and sells those, too, as fuel. When she gets a little lonely she visits us. One needs just a few connections to be happy, she says. She is much older than us, as old as my mother, maybe even older, but she is very childlike at heart. She talks to God all the time. I have learned to do that from her. Make God your Friend, Aziza. Talk to Him and He will be the best friend you will ever have."

"Let's talk about other things," Aziza says, a little irritably. "Let's talk about music!"

"No, let's not talk about it; let's play and sing!" Amro replies.

Aziza fetches her *rabab*. With her back to Amro she thinks *I am certain I am better than her! I will show her!*" Aloud she says, "No matter how bad things get, if I can play and sing, everything becomes instantly alright. Let's start where I always start when I play the *rabab*, with raag kalian."

"I always start with a *shabad*," Amro says.

"I love the notes themselves, sheer sound devoid of meaning, yet meaning enough," Aziza replies.

"Yes, it's important to know our notes, but it's also important to remember that the notes are just a ladder to something else."

"Sometimes they are the destination for me."

"I like sense with my sound. I only want to know as much music as will connect me with the Divine."

"But raags are your tools! If you want to become a better singer you must perfect them! It's not enough to be good, you have to become great!" Aziza responds, taking some joy from opposition.

"I don't want to be great. Then I will become proud. I only want God to be my audience."

"Liar!" Cries Aziza.

Amro laughs out loud at Aziza's candor.

"Of course one wants to be heard, but I know the pitfalls. My one desire is to turn people towards the Source. Shall I sing first? I have been practicing a small composition by my father."

Aziza is disappointed because she wants to show off her skill first, but pretends to consent. Reluctantly, she offers her *rabab* to Amro, who shakes her head.

"But don't you sing with the *rabab*?"

"I do, but I prefer to sing while I go about my tasks, milking the buffalo, churning the curdled milk, the sound of the rope around the matki's neck and the turning of the churn providing the rhythm. I only sing with the *rabab* at the congregations sometimes when my father or other kirtanias are not available."

Aziza is filled with envy at Amro's freedom, the liberality of her parents and religion that allow her to sing in public.

In a beautiful voice, like a lark's at daybreak, not highly trained, but full of feeling, like a koel's call, natural, spontaneous and heart piercing, Amro sings two lines, repeating them in pleasing patterns and variations. Aziza is enchanted despite herself.

'Jay sa-o chandaa ugvahi sooraj charheh hajaar, aytay chaanan hidi-aa gur bin ghor andhaar: If a hundred moons were to rise, and a thousand suns appear, their light would be pitch darkness without the Guru.'

After a respectful silence, Aziza reaches for her *rabab*, her ego resurging, and says, "Now let me show you how I would sing those two lines."

She sits on the *daree* with her *rabab* and begins, lingering on each note, on each word, drawing it out like yarn from a spindle, bending, stretching and texturing it. Amro, sitting by her, shuts her eyes and goes into a deep meditative state. While she herself has sung those two sentences in a short time, Aziza's *alaap* extends and unwinds organically, slowly, meanderingly, like a river that has widened in its journey through the planes and slowed down till it almost seems still. There is a deep, resonating silence when she finishes. Aziza opens her eyes, sees Amro drying her tears with her veil, and is pleased.

"Buddha, hey Buddha," Aziza calls through the hole. "What did you think of that?"

There is no sound from him. Putting her ear to the hole Aziza hears a faint snoring.

"Wake up! Wake up!" she shouts.

"Oh!" says Buddha, sleepily. "What happened?"

The girls laugh, even though Aziza is a bit offended.

"I did something I have never done before and you fell asleep?"

"You can't imagine how much peace your voice gave me, Aziza, and I fell asleep after many nights staying awake. So much has been happening at the dera lately."

"Tell me. Tell me everything," Aziza says, moving her *mooda* closer to the hole.

CHAPTER 26

Transmission

"Guru Angad is in town," Buddha begins.

"Who is Guru Angad?" Aziza asks. "Is he a new character in our story?"

"An old character with a new name and new form," Bhai Buddha explains. "Let me start at the beginning. When I met Bhai Lehna, accompanied by Amro in the street of Kartarpur, I asked him, 'what brings you here?' He hadn't been in the dera since Baba had asked him to leave for Khadur after the trouble with his sons, a long time ago. He replied, 'Baba Nanak came to Khadur to get me.' I was surprised to hear this though I didn't say anything. I had been with Baba Nanak the whole time and I swear he hadn't gone anywhere lately."

"But he *did* come. I saw him," Amro says. "He came several times to Khadur in the past few years."

"There are many things I don't understand," Buddha admits. "The strange events of the past week have twisted and bent my brain. The evening after Bhai Lehna arrived, Baba Nanak wore some dreadful looking dark clothes, a ragged black chola that made him look like an actor playing an *asura*[141] or a thug. Holding a crooked staff that looked like a snake in one hand, a fierce-looking hunting knife in the other, his hair and long white beard disheveled

---

141 Demon.

and blowing in the wind, he proceeded towards the jungle."

"I thought he looked like a dark form of Durga Ma, Kali herself, our Lady of Destruction," Amro says.

"You were there?" Aziza inquires, envious that Amro is free, like a male, to go wherever she wants.

"I go everywhere with Phapa jee. Though Buddha looked uneasy, I knew that Baba Nanak's behavior had a purpose. Whenever Kali gets angry and fierce, it is to destroy and establish something new on the ashes of the old."

"Yes, I can see that now," Buddha agrees.

"The folds of his ragged, dark *chola* swishing about his ankles above his bare feet," Buddha resumes, "Guru Nanak proceeded into the jungle as if to hunt. Sri Chand, who had also shown up from his wanderings, was enraged at his father's absurd actions. Some other Sikhs were so shocked that they decided to leave the dera, thinking they had been fooled by Baba into thinking he was a peaceful and gentle sage. I, however, followed him, as did Bhai Lehna, together with Amro, several other Sikhs, and Sri Chand, too, out of curiosity. It was a dark and thunderous night, lightening zigzagging across the skies in which the moon sometimes sailed between the clouds, revealing our path through the darkness.

With his long strides and fearful face, Baba flew into the forest energetically, and we had a hard time keeping up with him. In a clearing between trees, lightening illumined the forest floor strewn with glinting copper coins. Some Sikhs who had accompanied us collected them in their pockets, took off their shirts, piled the coins in them, made bundles and returned home, feeling they had been amply rewarded for their service to their guru.

Baba went deeper into the jungle, the rest of us following him, a bit afraid, for we were entering the territory of the leopards. In a grove lightening revealed silver coins shining among the fallen leaves. Some Sikhs congratulated themselves for not being content with copper coins and collected as many as they could in their turbans and shoes and returned to Kartarpur. But Baba was not done. In another clearing, gold coins sparkled on the ground, and the few remaining Sikhs, thrilled beyond measure that their devotion to Baba Nanak had earned them such wealth, gathered as many coins as they could and returned home to enjoy the fruits of their spirituality.

Baba went further. Now only I, Bhai Lehna, Amro, Sri Chand and a few of Baba's Sikhs who knew the rewards Baba bestows are far beyond material wealth, remained.

Further into the forest, we came upon a lurid scene: flashes of blue lightening tearing the fabric of the sky to the accompaniment of thunder that pierced our bones and reverberated in the chambers of our heart revealed a pyre stacked with wood. Near it, on the ground, lay a corpse in a shroud, reeking of rot."

"I was quite scared at first," Amro admits.

"Baba turned to us, his eyes reflecting flashes of lightening, and said, pointing to the corpse, 'whoever wants to follow me any further can do so after eating this.'"

"I and the other Sikhs almost retched at the thought. Sri Chand turned around in disgust at his father's madness – he, a vegetarian, now asked to eat the flesh of another human! – and went home."

"But I knew what Baba meant," Amro interjects. "Eating something to renew it, to give it new life, is an old rite. All of us eat something to renew our lives daily, and in renewing ours, we make what we eat into ourselves. The eaten *becomes* us. Even as I saw the reality of the corpse and the pyre, I knew in my heart that we had all been transported to another dimension where we were privileged to witness a cosmic drama, a dream scene playing out in the shadow lands of the mind. We had been taken to a space where everything is possible, where things are more real and not real at the same time. I felt we had reached Ma Durga's mythic domain."

"All of us, except Bhai Lehna, were disgusted at Baba's words. Baba knelt down reverentially and removed the shroud. We all gasped in shock and turned away from the sight though we couldn't help but look at what the moon revealed. The body beneath it, its flesh rotten and mingling unrecognizably with the dirt beneath it, its white bones visible here and there, had the unmistakable face of Guru Nanak himself. Our brains were befuddled at seeing Baba both alive and dead, standing by us and looking at himself lying dead before his eyes."

A long pause follows, in which Bhai Buddha sighs deeply.

"If we had all been as conscious as Baba Nanak, the sight before us would not have shocked us in the least. Isn't this the preordained fate of all flesh? Baba was looking at it without flinching, with full acceptance of his own destruction as an act of that Supreme Energy, personified as a Being, he has worshipped all along, the Energy that creates *and* kills. He has sung repeatedly of the dual nature, or rather, the non-dual nature of Akaal Purukh, whom we, torn and conflicted as we are, see as dual. I could see in his eyes that in this encounter with his own death Baba experienced the truth of his message: *jis kaa kee-aa tin hee lee-aa ho-aa tisai kaa bhaanaa: That which creates, destroys; All is Its Will.*

He, who had offered himself as a sacrifice to the Beloved daily, hourly, was finally being commanded to sacrifice himself. And he was ready."

Aziza starts to sob. She loves Baba with a passion, has prayed to him whenever she finds herself lost and bewildered. Amro puts her arm around her shoulders.

"My heart was gripped with a sorrow I had never experienced before, mingled with the fear of loss of that which had been my eyes, my legs, my mind and heart," Buddha voices Aziza's thought. "I could not imagine the vacuum Baba's death would create in my life. I, who knew from a very early age that death could come at any moment, found myself unprepared for it to come for someone I adored so much. It was a moment of Truth for all those who were present. Though we had all thought of the possibility of Baba's death, none of us were ready for it.

By his condition that we walk no further with him till we partake of his corpse, he was asking of us the same obedience to his will that he himself had rendered his Creator. And we all failed. Except, Bhai Lehna. He wanted to follow Baba Nanak wherever he may lead, do whatever he might command, passionately, unconditionally, with no reservations and conditions. For Bhai Lehna, Baba Nanak's will was Akal Purakh's Will. He folded his hands, bowed, and asked, "Master, where should I begin? The head, or the feet?"

"Oh! Oh! What… surrender! What… purity… what… utterness!" Aziza stammers, fumbling for words.

"Baba pointed his staff at the corpse and in another flash of lightening we saw that though the corpse had rotted away, the heart, the brain was palpitating, alive!"

"And the throat!" Amro adds. "The throat through which he has sung to his Beloved all his life!"

"Baba's staff pointed at the corpse's beating heart.

'And may I share it with those present?' Bhai Lehna asked.

'That's what it's for, sharing,' Baba replied, 'I know you will continue sharing for generations to come.'"

"I knew at that point that Baba's death was not far away, that Phapa jee was part of a very primeval rite, that by eating Baba's heart he was getting nourishment and keeping Baba Nanak alive. Phapa jee was regenerating his own and Baba's body and soul. Phapa jee cupped both his hands, knelt by the corpse, and scooped out the heart.

As we looked at his hands, before our very eyes, the beating heart turned into Prasad!" Amro exclaims.

Aziza gasps in surprise, stunned beyond words.

"Baba laughed loudly, wildly!" Buddha continues. "Bhai Lehna took handfuls and distributed it to all present. It was delicious, like *amrit*, a particle of which would nourish us all for the rest of our lives. It was like eating courage. All our fears vanished."

"Why didn't you get some for *me*?" Aziza cries in agony. "Why was *I* left out? Why am I always left out?"

"Aziza, my dear friend, Aziza," Buddha says lovingly. "Do not despair. You *have* it. You have it in Baba's words, which it is now Bhai Lehna's task to keep alive and disseminate."

"Do I? Do I? I feel so left out, and *impure*!"

"Listen to the rest of the story, my sister, and you will see how Baba and his Prasad is available to all of us. Whatever happens to him, with the transmission of his power, he will be alive for all time," Amro reassures.

"Baba turned to Bhai Lehna and said, 'you are now blood of my blood, body of my body, soul of my soul, limb of my limb, my *ang*.[142] I rename you, Angad."

"I saw a flame, like a beam of lightening, pass from Baba Nanak to Angad," Amro adds.

"Oh, you saw it too!" Buddha exclaims. "I thought maybe I had imagined it! So it was true!"

"And then?"

"Bhai Angad fell at Guru Nanak's feet. Baba lifted him up and as he embraced Angad I rubbed my eyes. I thought I was dreaming when I saw the boundaries of their bodies blend and merge."

"You didn't imagine it. I saw it, too."

"And then we returned to the dera somehow, although I have no memory of the physical journey back. It was more like we were transported back from whatever place we had been transported to," Buddha continues. "I went to Bebe Nanaki right away and told her what had transpired. She listened, calmly, without reacting. I

---

142 An inseparable part; a limb.

wondered what she was thinking, feeling, but received no clue. I have noticed, even before I told her of these happenings, that she has had an intensity about her lately. She has been very happy, childlike, living each day as if it were new. She's been hugging everybody she comes into contact with, and I have wondered at her behavior.

The next day, Baba wanted to perform a formal investiture to declare Angad his spiritual heir. He took me aside, put both his hands on my shoulders, and said,

'You, too, Bhai Buddha, will carry my flame and be my voice for generations to come. You will become the tree that grows so tall it towers above all the others and sees things from a height that others can only guess at or glimpse. You will become a Gurmukh, turning in your troubles to face the Light that throws our shadows behind us. But beware; beware of taking your life for granted. Age and wisdom will be yours only if you stay on the path, my Buddha, or at least return to it each time your ego makes you stray away from it.'

Then he put me in charge of the ceremony and instructed me to take care of the details. Under the *peepal* tree where Baba usually sits, discourses and sings, I erected an umbrella."

"Oh, does he still sing?" Aziza asks.

"Daily. Not only does he still sing, he's still composing as well. His voice is a bit feeble now, a little jagged and raspy, but none of the love and intensity has diminished. Sometimes your father and sometimes the *sangat* sings when Baba feels unwell, and since Amro has been here she has also sung a few *shabads*…" Buddha bites his tongue, knowing what a sore point this is for Aziza, and returns to the story. "I bought a coconut and a small container of red powder, put a five pice[143] coin in my pocket, and informed everyone to be there for the morning service, that something important was going to happen.

---

143 One pice was the smallest denomination of money.

The dera, teeming with Sri Chand's followers, was anything but a peaceful place. They showed up at the appointed place, and Sri Chand was very angry.

'What have I, your son, your flesh and blood, done that you do not recognize *me* as your heir?" He shouted.

'Being a guru is not a hereditary post. It passes to the one who is most deserving of being a guru,' Baba replied calmly.

'How is Lehna so different from me? I *worship* you," he said, holding up a statue of Guru Nanak that he always kept with him. 'You, my father, who I consider an *avatar*[144] of God.'

Baba snatched the statue and dashed it to pieces on a rock.

'It is not a clay statue I wish my followers to worship. I am not an *avatar* but a slave of the slaves of Akaal Purukh, Formless, Timeless Being beyond images who is the only One worthy of worship,' Baba said, and I could see the sparkle of rage in his eyes that his son had not grasped the basics of his message. 'If I am anything, I am a poet, a peddler of His Name.'

'I worship your words, I sing and propagate them!' Sri Chand said, holding up a *pothi*.

'Sikhs must engage with every aspect of existence and not withdraw from their duties and commitments as human beings, as you teach your followers to do, Sri Chand,' Baba said in a voice that was at once firm and kind. 'They must not be compelled to do anything their God-given natures will not allow them to do. They are to fulfill themselves in every way, lead a fully engaged life. Your sect has too many rules. Your followers *must* be celibates; they *must not* eat meat; they *must* distinguish themselves by a particular garb, woolen cords, caps, gowns with colors you mandate, white or ochre, carry drums and other instruments, keep their hair matted and uncombed, apply ashes on their bodies. There is too much ritual in this sect you have created, my son. Sikhs will be unfettered by

---

144 Reincarnation.

rules and not congeal around rituals, doctrines and superstitions. My successor will leave humans as free as The Free Being intended them to be, as free as the wind and as the rivers we become when we devote ourselves to Kartar who beats in every heart, each atom of our beings, and in all of our experiences. Sikhs must be true *shishyas*[145] of the Guru – their hearts and minds open to learning, about themselves, first of all, to seeing through man-made, false divisions between all beings and creatures with whom we share the Earth, regardless of religion, caste, class, color or difference. The only religion I endorse is the religion of love and devotion for Akaal Purukh, whatever His name, and love and compassion towards all fellow human beings and creatures.'

'My followers come from all castes and religions, father. Can't you see that?' Sri Chand asked.

'And that is good, my son,' Baba said.

'How can you, who preach love for all, be so intolerant of me and my ways?'

'I accept who you are. I not only tolerate but love you. I just can't make you the guru,' Baba said, turning his back on him, and calmly proceeding with the ceremony.

Just as the sun arose, before a large gathering Baba put Angad on his seat under the tree and asked me to put a red *tilak*[146] on Angad's forehead. Baba placed the coconut and 5 pice coin before Angad, and bowed to him. Everyone knew what Baba meant by that gesture: Bhai Lehna was now Guru Angad.

Nanaki was the first to fall at Guru Angad's feet and kiss them;

Sri Chand's followers made a big noise and tried to disrupt the ceremony. In the swirling of dark energies all around us, the rest of

---

145 The word Sikh goes back to the Sanskrit sisya, meaning a learner or disciple. The Punjabi form of the verb is sikh, learn. A Sikh then is a perpetual student of learning in all its forms.

146 Dot. As a mark of spiritual sovereignty.

us were transported to the eye of the storm, the heart of eternity where something momentous was taking place.

Sri Chand and his followers left in a jealous huff, resolved to strengthen and institutionalize their own sect of the *Udasis*. Mata Sulakhni, who everyone knows has lost some part of her sanity since Lakhmi Das's death, kept repeating, 'but what about my sons? Lakhmi Das is a good boy. He will take care of his mother. And Sri Chand came out of my flesh, his head and body all bloodied.'

She looked anguished and burst into sobbing. I held her for a long time and then I told her about the events of our miraculous night. As she listened I saw the same look in her eyes that I saw when she had seen the mud on Lehna's white clothes turn to saffron stains before her eyes."

Silence falls in Aziza's hut. Then Aziza asks Buddha:

"And how do *you* feel about all of this? Any jealousy, regret?"

Buddha laughs loudly, heartily. "How rare, the rarest of the rare – so rare you often doubt he even exists – is the person who can step into Guru Nanak's shoes! I was disappointed when I asked myself the question when I realized Baba Nanak was ready to die: would I confront my death the same way? I, who have been so conscious of the presence of Master Death from an early age? Would I turn to my Maker if He should command me to return immediately? And the answer was, no. I wanted to fulfill Baba Nanak's prophesy for me, I wanted to be a hoary old Bodhi tree. I wanted more life!"

The shadows have melted and it is time for all of them to go home. Buddha and Amro leave first. Aziza puts things away in a distracted and less than graceful way, and grabs her *burqua*. Motia, seeing the sign of leaving, gets up and follows her with stiff and aged legs. As Aziza is locking the cottage to return home, she stops in mid-act to acknowledge the voices of dark feelings in her soul.

She gets to go where she wants and to sing with Baba while I'm stuck with an uneducated mother and an unsupportive family!

Locking the door she turns and faces the path to the village snaking its way from twilight into darkness. She hears Amro's voice in her head: 'Nihali is very childlike at heart. She talks to God all the time. I have learnt to do that from her. Make God your Friend, Aziza. Talk to Him and He will be the best friend you will ever have.'

Aziza falls to the ground, genuflecting in no particular direction, and cries aloud: "Ya Allah! Send me your angels! Let them cut open my chest, like they did Mohammed's, take out my unclean heart, pluck out the black clots in it and wash it in a basin full of pure white snow! Help me; help me to turn to you in my afflictions!"

She lifts herself. *Yes,* she thinks as she walks into the village. *Buddha is right. I, too, have had the Prasad by listening to their story. I, too, have access to the miraculous, magical Energy that pours into my ears through words and stories. Wherever I am, in whatever circumstances my fate brings me, I participate and partake in it all. I am supremely connected.*

CHAPTER 27

Why Quarrel with a River?

Nanaki walks into Baba Nanak's study in the dera, where he sits on the ground hunched over his small wooden desk, transcribing his latest composition in the *pothi*.

How frail he looks! She thinks, as a spasm of pain shoots through her heart. She doesn't want to disturb him so she stands by the door, her eyes shut, basking in his presence.

"Nanaki," Baba Nanak says, turning around. "How long have you been standing here?"

Nanaki can't tell. It seems like a very short time, though it has been a while.

How pale he looks, she thinks, walking towards him.

"Vir jee, I have come to ask for something. Please do not refuse."

"Would I ever refuse you anything?" he smiles.

"Do I have your assent?"

"Of course. Anything you want."

Nanaki takes a deep breath, looks into his eyes, and says, "I would like your permission to leave before you."

Baba is silent. Then he says, almost sternly,

"My death is *hukum.* It must be accepted."

"How can what I am feeling now so strongly, that I have no control over, also not be *hukum?*" Nanaki asks bravely. "How can this also not be His? He, who causes all events, even those *we* seem to choose? All my wisdom is twirling like twigs in a tornado. I *know* I won't be able to bear your leaving. I don't want to. What I want is for you to light my pyre with your hands."

"That's too much wanting and not wanting, Nanaki. There's too much 'I' here," Baba says harshly.

"I know. May the Beloved forgive me."

"You think I will be able to bear your death?" Baba asks.

"You are a lotus. Nothing sullies your petals."

"And you are not a lotus?"

Nanaki's face quavers with emotion as she speaks.

"I have been preaching and practicing detachment, acceptance, obedience to *hukum,* telling those who come for advice to drink joyously from the chalice of suffering. But I am a fake and a failure. Your death is one chalice I know I will be unable to look at, leave alone drink from."

"I may survive you yet, dear sister!" Baba laughs. "You never know His ways!"

"Even before Bhai Buddha told me what happened in the forest, I had a dream. Before you were born, I kept dreaming over and over of rivers. The night before you were born, I had a dream in which the river came to our doorstep, broke open the door, and came in, like an honored guest. It filled our house and I was swimming in its waves: happy, happy, happy! And when it left, I was surprised that our house was not wet, but clean, and nothing at all was washed away. Instead, the river had left treasures in our house, on the bed, in the kitchen, in the courtyard, on the trees; everything was sparkling like diamonds and jewels. They were not ordinary treasures but magical things, the wealth of angels. In my last dream, the river that brought you to me, to us, came again, but this time it took you away, carried you away in its arms; on the horizon I saw you, a great white swan with wings like clouds that spanned the sky, and in a mighty, muscular, flapping of wings you flew away into the waiting heart of God."

"What a lovely dream, Nanaki. Why quarrel with a river?"

"My faith will be tested."

"Faith is not faith unless it is tested. You have passed all tests, Nanaki."

"I will fail this one. I will drown in this sorrow. My voice has been telling me, 'you will be uprooted, Nanaki, root and all. You will be unable to bear it and I will be helpless to help you.'"

"My sister, my sweet, honest sister," Baba says, looking at her with tears in his eyes.

"Wait. There was more of the dream, I remember now. A Muslim and a Hindu came to you. The Muslim wanted to bury you and build a garden around your mausoleum; the Hindu argued to cremate you and build a temple on the site. There were flowers, lots and lots of flowers."

"A mausoleum! A garden! A temple!" Baba laughs delightedly, and then returns to his momentous discussion with Nanaki, and his attempts to dissuade her from her intent.

"You bore a long separation from me when I was gone for so many years! This interim will be brief compared to that one."

"That was different. When I really longed for you, you came. How many times I gasped for your presence, to just see you, but more than anything, hear your voice, singing. I disobeyed you when you came with Bhai Mardana that time and camped outside Talwandi. He told me you didn't want to see any of us. But I followed our parents when they disobeyed you, and came, laden with food and promises to convince you to give up your wandering and return home."

"I didn't see you there," Nanak says, surprised.

"No, because I hid in the trees. I told Bhai Mardana, 'beg him to sing, please, just let me hear his voice once more.' You did, and it sustained me for years."

"Oh, so that's why Mardana started strumming the *rabab* after our parents left! I didn't want to sing but he insisted. He said he had a tickle in his throat that told him he needed to sing along with me!"

"Your voice poured into my ears as I sat in the bushes, like the song of the rarest of birds!"

"It's scratchy and raspy now! I get winded after two lines of the *sthai*."[147]

"For my thirst it is ambrosia."

"I'm not God, Nanaki, and ambrosia comes only from Him. Turn in your sorrow to the Deathless, Timeless One. Don't mistake a human for God."

"Humans need images, something concrete to pin their faith on."

"Mistake. Mistake," Baba says. "Images *must* break."

"I couldn't survive the breaking of this image with any grace. I *know* God is formless, know it in my head, heart and soul. During our separation I learned to transfer my adoration for you to the Beloved. I knew, too, that was the purpose of our separation. You had touched my head and said to me before leaving, 'you will suffer separation. But that suffering shall be your salvation.' But I am older now," Nanaki continues, "and know the limits of my suffering. Do I have your consent?"

"You had my consent even before you asked. You tricked me."

"I am a coward."

"You are no coward, Nanaki, but a warrior. You go to death with your arms wide open, as to a bridegroom. *Death is the privilege of the brave.*"

"I lack your certainty."

"My certainty wavers, Nanaki. I too am afraid even though I know without a doubt that it is only our egos that are bound by space and time. Do you think I will feel nothing when I light your

---

147 The refrain of a song.

pyre, you who have been as a mother to me all my life?"

"You are stronger than me and can bear far more, so do you, my brother, my child, bear my leaving before you."

A pause follows her words.

"I fear we will never meet again," Nanaki begins to sob.

"I had meant these words for the One. But now I sing them for you, Nanaki," Baba says, clearing his throat of phlegm.

In an unaccompanied voice, Nanak begins to sing in a quavering voice. Nanaki joins him and brother and sister sing together: *nadee-aa vaah vichhunni-aa maylaa sanjogee raam: the rivers and streams which separate are united again in the Ocean of His Heart.*

It is a magical moment and has the intensity that only the proximity of death can bestow. Both of them know that words would only be a sacrilege of its sanctity.

Nanaki kisses Nanak's feet, bathing them in her tears. Then with an abrupt movement, as if she can no longer trust herself to stay, she gets up and leaves the room.

It is past ten at night and Nanaki sits at her desk, writing out her will. Jairam is next door, asleep. After much thought, she has decided against telling him. He would be distraught. She shuts her eyes and thanks him in her heart for being her earthly husband, companion, friend, and family. She could not have wished for any better. He has been perfect in every way, and as far as it is possible for her to adore a human other than her brother, her guru, her god, she has adored Jairam and given thanks over and over to the Merciful One for gifting him to her. She writes a note to this effect and explains that it is time for her to say goodbye; that she knows they will meet again in God's Great Heart. She leaves a note for Sri Chand, too, thanking him for his presence in her life.

Like her brother, she believes in taking care of all business before departure. It is one's dharma.

My rabab, to Aziza, she writes. *Five hundred rupees to Shai Tani, to buy herself a home and for the education of her children.* She wants to ensure these two things and knows Jairam would take care of the rest, for they have already discussed leaving their assets to the functioning of the dera both in Kartarpur and the one that has already sprung up around Guru Angad in Khadur.

She puts aside quill and paper as a wave of certainty washes over her: *Jairam will not survive me for long. If there is an afterlife, then, dear husband, may the Beloved give you to me again!*

She gets up, ready to take the bath for which she has already prepared by laying aside her old wedding dress, the red salwaar kameez embroidered with gold, and filling the bucket with warm water. Recalling her wedding to Jairam, she thinks, *our worldly weddings are metaphors of the real Union.* She hums Baba's words as she bathes: *Kar kirpaa apnai ghar aa-i-aa, taa mil sakhee-aa kaaj rachaa-i-aa; khayl daykh man anad bha-i-aa, saho vee-aahan aa-i-aa.Gaavhu gaavhu kaamnee bibayk beechaar; Hamrai ghar aa-i-aa jagjeevan bhataar. When by His Grace He came to my home, then my companions met together to celebrate my marriage. Beholding this play, my mind became blissful; my Husband Lord has come to marry me. So sing. Yes, sing the songs of wisdom and reflection, O brides. My spouse, the Life of the World, has come into my home.*

As she bathes and sings she thanks her body, each and every part of it, and all her senses for having served her soul so well. There is no regret, none.

Your eyes have seen enough, Nanaki, your ears heard the hearable, your heart felt every human emotion you were sent here to experience, everything the Maker sent in His mercy. It is enough. Know, Nanaki, that you are tied indissolubly to those you love. Wherever they will be, you shall, too. Die consciously, Nanaki, go into this with your eyes as open as they can be before you shut them forever. This is what your preparation and practice has been, as it has been his. Now you must journey to the land of the Invisible to see unseen things, hear harmonies beyond the scope of these ears.

She wears her clothes, combs her hair, parts it in the middle, and puts *sindhoor*[148] in the parting. She looks around the room, and says aloud: 'Death is such a private affair. Today is a good day; now is the time; this is a good place to die!'

She has no doubt she is returning to whence she came; no doubt, none, that her Beloved would be there with open arms.

She sits down to meditate, bliss radiating from the core of her heart to the edges of her being. First, she recites the *Japji*[149] attentively, with full devotion before entering a wordless silence in which she sits, calm and serene, in the presence of the Beloved. Soon, she exhales through the thousand petaled lotus on top of her head; millions of luminous particles of light emanate forth as Nanaki's soul flies out of the prison of her body, and merges, as water merges with water, becoming indistinguishable from it, with the Soul of the Universe.

Jairam found Nanaki's body, upright in a meditative pose, the next morning. True to her prediction, he survived her by only three days; as desired so fervently by her, Guru Nanak lit her pyre.

---

148 Red powder married women wear in the parting of their hair.

149 The first composition of Sikh scripture.

CHAPTER 28

Light Merges with Light

Dear reader, we come to a moment in our history that must come to all, a moment that is difficult for us to contemplate and recreate. The difficulty of confronting Baba's death, which the so-called writer of this particular story has put off for two books, must be overcome by the remembrance that though our beloved Baba Nanak dies in this chapter, he is alive and with us, now and for all time, through his words, which are like stepping stones in the marshes of our mind to reach that Beloved, beyond the power of words, whom Baba, the divine poet, revealed and made manifest in his undying songs. Words were dear to Nanak, all words, sung and read and heard, the best of which, he never failed to remind us, is the *anahad*, unheard and unknown Word and Sound of His Name.

The Beloved, he told us, loans us our lives, which we must surrender with joy when the summons comes; that the only way for us to be grateful for the tremendous gift of life is by sacrificing ourselves willingly to the Universal Will, whatever and whenever it might be.

We can also console ourselves with the knowledge that Death, which most of us fear and shun, had been Guru Nanak's Companion and Guide throughout his life, illuminating his paths, bestowing insight. He knew his Beloved would come to him in the guise of Death. When it came to gather him up in his arms and take him into

God's Great and Waiting Heart, Baba was not only ripe and ready for it, he looked forward to his reunion with the Other – that was also himself – from whom he had been seemingly separated at birth.

Let us witness his passing without sadness or grief, though there must have been grief for those who survived him, to whom he was so very dear, and for us for whom his life means so much that he continues to live with and illumine generation after generation. Let us not forget to rejoice that such a being as Baba once walked the Earth, all over it, in fact, in his desire to see and observe the far-flung geography of His creation.

We will meet him again in the pages of following books, in the stories about him yet to be retold, and words, his words that are alive as Guides that will show countless men and women the path through the wilderness that life can become.

Let us take comfort and courage from the fact that the word 'history' has 'story' in it. With the aid of that Arch Seamstress, the Imagination, let us mend the rents in our knowledge. She can reach with her deft fingers into the mists of time, tear them, and reveal – in part, only – the details we long to know. With her magic needle and thread, let us come to the date and time of Baba's arrival at the Portal of Invisibility where he sheds the cloth and garment of his body and walks naked into the embrace of his Lover.

It is a few days past 22 September 1539, a date that history has preserved for us as the day that Baba Nanak returned Home. Let us hear about that day as Buddha, sitting by a hole in the wall of a hermit's hut, tells it to Aziza.

"Has he gone?" are Aziza's first words to Bhai Buddha when he takes his place on the mooda.

"Yes."

Aziza bursts into tears. Buddha at first tries to console her but soon he is sobbing too, his whole frame heaving with pent up emotions. When the tide passes, at it must, since everything shifts and passes in the great river of life, they both quiet down.

"Tell me everything," Aziza requests.

Buddha wipes his tears, and begins.

"He died a conscious death and was alive through every moment of it. I think he knew, though the rest of us were blinded by hope. I watched him sleep peacefully the night before. At that moment, neither night nor day, but both, when stars still shine in a cobalt sky on the verge of changing its color imperceptibly into the colors of dawn, and the winds the sages call *malyanil* blows as if from eternity, Baba awoke, as he had always awoken at this holy time. He sat and meditated with his beloved Guru Angad by his side. I was sitting right behind them. As the day dawned with the brilliance of these fall days, bright and crisp, with a slight nip in the air that gives intimations of the approach of winter, the congregation started to gather around them.

Guru Angad, who too must have known, so attuned he was to every pulse of his beloved Master, turned towards Baba and said in a whisper:

'May God take my life and my body and give it to you.'

'Better I have your body and life,' Baba laughed heartily. 'Mine is falling apart. Come, Lehnaiaa, come, my soul, my spark, my son, and sing along with me as I sing once more like the swan that sings even as it dies.'

I got up and sat in the congregation before they began to sing. Baba's eyes were twinkling in the first rays of the sun as he looked at us, and at Guru Angad, who reached for Baba's *rabab* and handed it to him. Then he reached for his own and began to tune it. Accompanied by Angad, Baba sang in a voice that was strong, clear and sparkling. There was no trace in it of feebleness. So much so that I was very heartened, and I know the *sangat*, was, too, that Baba was recovering his strength and would stay with us yet."

"Which *shabad* did he sing?" Aziza asks, eagerly.

"A new one: '*Vismaad naad vismaad vayd. Vismaad jee-a vismaadbhayd. Vismaad roop vismaad rang. Vismaad naagay fireh jant.*' [150] It was as if Baba, standing on the threshold of invisibility looked over his shoulder and burst into praise of every aspect of every particle of existence.

His great paean to life celebrated all of it, excluding nothing: sound, words, music, silence, form, colors, tastes, our scintillating senses, each and every species on Earth, every force of nature, both creative and destructive – wind, water, fire, earth; people, straight and eccentric, no one excepted; all of human existence and the varied and colorful ways in which it is lived; the nadir and zenith of human experience, shadow and light, the sad and joyous human condition; procreation, attachments, together with detachments, closeness and distance, union and separation, hunger and satisfaction, wilderness and the path. There was no 'or' for Baba anymore, only 'and' as he stood at the door sill of the Great Silence, the country without a name that borders life on all sides, like the Great Ocean from which we come and into which we flow again. The refrain of his song was 'Wonderful! Wonderful! Wonderful!' The word bounced off every visible thing in sight and resounded all around and within us. His wonder and awe at every bit of creation, positive and negative, all came together in a blessed, holy marriage, the bliss of a union that nothing could ever tear apart or separate, the bliss attained by those who are blessed with the best of fortunes.

After the singing session, Baba lay down on his manji under the dead and withered acacia tree at the dera."

"Oh! The beautiful umbrella-like acacia from which Guru Angad collected gum to make ink, died?" Aziza asks with anguish.

"Hold your sorrow till I finish," Buddha advises. "Yes, it died, and so lovely and majestic it was in its death, its thick, dark trunk

---

150 Summarized and translated liberally by Buddha, below.

tall like a spine, an axis towering and thrusting upward from the dirt, its gnarled, black branches fanned out against the blue sky in a symmetry that included crookedness, that none of us had the heart to cut it down though many said we should and make furniture out of the wood, something useful, for the dera.

Baba spent the afternoon under it. Angad sat by his feet, massaging them; Mata Sulakhni, as if in a daze, walked aimlessly through the langar; Amro," Buddha pauses in his narration, knowing this little detail will upset Aziza, but knowing what he is about to say to her after his narration, carries on. "Amro went about her tasks, milking the cows, churning milk, singing; Sri Chand, who had arrived a few days earlier, and who had an inkling of what was to come, tried hard and vociferously to persuade Baba Nanak to practice techniques and exercises to extend his life, but Baba held up his hand and quietened him.

A sheikh showed up and said since Guru Nanak was a *pir* for the Muslims, he had put aside a large tract of land and would build a garden around the mausoleum where Baba would be buried; a rich Hindu merchant offered to make a *samaadh*[151] at the place of his cremation, since Baba was a Hindu saint. A fight broke out between the two, each claiming Baba for his own religion. Baba laughed, and I laughed along with him. They obviously didn't get Baba's message of Oneness; they couldn't see that Baba belonged to no religion but was a phenomenon of Nature, like a river, like the moon, like wind and fire and air. They didn't have enough sense to be quiet in his presence during such a sacred time. Baba quietened them by saying, 'let the Hindus place flowers on my right, the Muslims on my left. Whoever's flowers are fresh in the morning may do with my body as they please.'

Baba looked around at everything and everyone, and his look had a smile in it, almost laughter. I was reminded of the story your

151 A small temple on the site where a holy person is cremated.

Daadu told us a long time ago that Daulatan Masi told him: when Nanak was born, he didn't cry like other infants but giggled and laughed!

And then, imperceptibly, like the coming on of light at dawn and its disappearance at dusk, Baba exhaled his last breath, which mingled with the formless and everywhere present air he had materialized out of at his birth. His pilgrimage on this planet was over."

After a pause in which Aziza is unusually silent, Buddha picks up the thread of his narrative.

"The Hindus heaped flowers on the right side of his body – lotuses, jasmines, marigolds, and the Muslims roses, roses, roses of all colors and hues on his left. Someone draped a shroud over Guru Nanak's body. I felt myself sinking like a stone into my sorrow. Just then, my gaze was pulled towards the dead acacia tree, and Aziza, I saw tiny green shoots on its dead limbs! The sap that had dried has risen again!"

—

Let us pause here for a bit before Buddha resumes his tale. History has preserved no details about what happened to Baba's body after he died. Perhaps it was bathed and the rituals, described earlier in the book, followed; perhaps his body was cremated or consigned to the river that had brought him to us and took him away. Let us take recourse to legends and myths that sprang up in the wake of Guru Nanak's passage from form to formlessness. Let us use the language of the Imagination that conveys essential truths in images that speak to our senses directly and unmistakably. Legend tells us that when the sheet covering Baba's body was removed, there was nothing beneath it – just a heap of Muslim and Hindu flowers, still fragrant, still fresh, still in bloom.

In Guru Nanak's memory the Muslims built a masjid and the Hindus a *samaadh* on the banks of the river. In time, the River Ravi, in a raging flood of laughter, changed its course and swept both of them away with its mighty, muscular waves.

—

Buddha and Aziza are silent a long time before Buddha resumes the story.

"A lot of suffering followed Baba's passing. You see, it is one thing to *think* death a good thing, inevitable, ordained, and quite another when it comes to human *feelings*. Suffering and wisdom, when we see them from the perch of the high perspective that Baba saw them from, are one. Both help us on this journey. Wisdom gives us perspective, and suffering softens us, like rain the earth; it gives life to seeds that have been dormant, if not dead; they stir again, send out tiny shoots below and above, push through the soil and begin their transformation to blooming and fruiting."

Aziza is silent.

"I know that one loss summons others that arise from the dead and haunt us again," Buddha continues, knowing intuitively that Aziza's silence indicated her suffering – that the ghosts of her grandfather and grandmother were present in her present grief over Baba's death. She had done then exactly what she is doing now: withdrawing so far into the darkness within her that no one can reach her. People who had seen her beneath her burqua reported that she looked half crazed after her grandfather and grandmother's deaths. The grief for her grandfather lasted longest. Buddha doesn't know how long her present grief would last, but he endeavors to shorten it.

"Baba, too, suffered at the death of his parents and at Nanaki's death. I know, because for days he didn't sing. But then his *rabab* called to him and he was rescued. Singing to the Beloved, pleading with him, asking for his aid, remembering him, gave him an intensity and passion that couldn't help but evoke that Presence in whose embrace he was safe, happy, and at peace."

Buddha hears Aziza moving away, and worries. He feels relief, and a warm, loving sensation in the region of his heart when she returns and he hears her fingers on the strings of the *rabab*, bequeathed to her by Nanaki. It is to the sound of her chords that Buddha continues his recounting.

"Yes, on the wings of song he flew instantly to that high perch that the fortunate attain."

Aziza maintains the harmony even though Buddha's narration becomes discordant once more.

"Sri Chand's followers armed themselves and took up positions to secure the dera against those who had accepted Nanak's command that Angad be guru now; Angad, unconcerned about the gaddi, but distraught by the death of his master, has disappeared, God alone knows where. I sent some Sikhs to Khadur, for I was certain he was there. But they have sieved through the whole town and he is nowhere to be found. Mata Khivi, who had accompanied Guru Angad to Kartarpur, didn't seem overly worried about her husband's whereabouts and went about ministering to the needs of the visitors who had come from far and wide; Mata Sulakhni goes about saying 'Forgive me! Forgive me!' to the air; Sri Chand broke down and cried like a baby; the congregation was inconsolable, weeping, grieving that their guru, their Father, had died and now there was no one to guide and console them. Women wailed and beat their breasts.

At first I grieved along with them but then, Aziza, I saw in an instance how stupidly we were all behaving.

'How foolish to grieve like this!' I cried, standing up from the ground where we sat on darees, wallowing in our grief. 'Blind and ignorant fools! Can't we see he is all around and within us?'

'*We* don't see him,' they cried.

'And yet you followed him when he took you to our Invisible Beloved! Don't let doubt paralyze you. Think with your heart instead of your head and you will be wise. There is no separation, ever. We are all connected in a web that transcends visibility,' I said.

'We are creatures with eyes. We need to see something to believe. We could see and touch and hear our Guru Nanak. But now we are blinded by his absence,' they cried.

'Then it is time for you to take the first step towards trust and faith in the Invisible Yet Everywhere Present. Do you see the air? Do you see love? Do you see faith? Do you see breath? The eyes conceal more than they reveal. Become good Sikhs. A Sikh is always a humble pupil who knows he knows very little, surrenders to his Guru, his Guide, and remembers his lessons well. Guru Nanak exists in a different form now, in our Angad,' I reassured them.

'But where is he? We don't see him anywhere. He should be consoling us.'

My own heart plummeted in despair.

'We will find him,' I said, almost as much to myself as to my audience. 'We must trust Baba who gave him to us. Without this trust, we are doomed. Trust he will return, and in the meantime, let Baba's words and music guide us to the only Reality in this seemingly solid world of ours, the only Power that can accomplish that which we are incapable of. Remember Baba's message. Life is a game, and only those who drink from the chalice of Love, and offer it to others, win it. We can drink from it by drinking the ambrosia of his words.'

'But we don't understand his words,' someone cried.

'Repeat them, and they will bring solace to your hearts in the hour of need; their sound guides beyond understanding. This is what Baba meant by 'Jap. Jap. Jap.' That is why our first prayer is called 'Japji'. Also, if you don't understand the words, study them. Go to someone who does. Come, instead of mourning Baba's death, let's celebrate his marriage to the Deathless, Timeless One. Come, let's sit under his tree, recite and sing *kirtan Sohaila.*'"

Aziza tunes her *rabab* and begins to play the notes of Raag *Gauri Deepki.* In a voice saturated with feeling, she sings Baba's Song of Praise of the Fearless One. It was this *shabad* that had pulled her up from the dark depths of her sorrow at the death of her grandparents.

'*In that house where the praises of the One are sung and the Doer of all is contemplated and celebrated, pour oil on the threshold for the pre-ordained wedding and sing songs of union with the Beloved. Bless death, which is a wedding! The summons comes for all. Remember the Summoner, and turn your sorrow into praise!*'

When the last notes of her song merge with silence, Buddha continues with his narration.

"Mata Khivi was there and began to prepare a feast for all, and all joined in the preparation. Everyone found such relief in activity. Our sorrow was channeled into celebration.

Some of the elders and some from Sri Chand's entourage grumbled and said, 'Where will the funds come from?'"

Buddha laughs heartily and repeats their fears. "'Where will the funds come from? You will deplete the dera's resources!' Ah, but ingredients, funds, food poured in! Some brought large buckets of ghee, some sacks of flour, sugar, rice, corn; others brought cartloads of fruits, vegetables, nuts of all kinds – almonds, raisins, cashews. And what a feast Khivi prepared! People started calling Khivi 'Mata Khivi.' Even though she is young. Though she is small in size, she is large and generous; she participates in and contains the largess of creation itself. She is another of those beings whose luminosity dispels shadows. O, what a great, delicious feast it was!"

"It sounds very much like the story that Daadu once told me about the feast that was given by Baba's family at his birth," Aziza adds. "There was such expectancy and joy that day, like a divine holiday! Children didn't go to school but ran off in the fields to play; the women did not go out to collect fodder and yet miraculously there was no dearth of fodder; the teachers didn't teach, the housewives didn't scrub pots or pans and yet they were all clean. It took no energy at all to do them. The halwai of Talwandi couldn't understand why he was making so much mithai so joyously. His milk supplier had dropped by with buckets of milk because his cows gave so much milk that he didn't know what to do with it. Everything was free. Children and strays dogs converged upon his shop and everyone was fed. That day, spontaneously, on the birth of the Child of Nature, a feast had taken place in Talwandi."

As Aziza tells her story excitedly, Bhai Buddha mulls in his mind what he wants to say to her today. He coughs nervously and begins: "I have been thinking for a long time that there is a solution to your isolation. Marry me. I will become a Muslim or you will become a Sikh, it really doesn't matter. We will continue to be the people God meant us to be. But there will be more advantages in your becoming a Sikh. You won't have to wear a burqua and have far more freedom than a Muslim woman. You can sing wherever you want. We can move to Khadur. I will return in a few days. Think about it"

And then Buddha is gone.

[illegible] that day, like a little [illegible]
[illegible] bridge, [illegible] light on the [illegible]
[illegible] other [illegible] since then [illegible]
[illegible] there was [illegible]
[illegible]
[illegible] there. [illegible]
understand why he was making so much of this [illegible]
[illegible] and [illegible] with [illegible]
[illegible] didn't know what [illegible]
[illegible]
[illegible]
[illegible]
[illegible]
[illegible]
[illegible]
[illegible]
[illegible] we will [illegible] people
[illegible]
[illegible]
[illegible]
[illegible] Thank

[illegible]

CHAPTER 29

Storm

Still reeling from Baba Nanak's death, Aziza is hurled into a tempest by Buddha's words. Unable to stay still, she dashes out of her hut without wearing her burqa, with the aged Motia at her heels. It is mid-afternoon of a cool winter day. Motia splays out in the sun, too weary to follow her mistress. Aziza walks without intention or awareness towards the village, then abruptly turns around and follows the footpath to the forest on the opposite side. Realizing she has walked too far from her hut, she turns around, returns to the hut, and wanders aimlessly in circles around it. She feels herself tumbling helplessly, without direction, in a flood of emotions and thoughts.

"Aziza, Aziza, calm down!" she berates herself. "Go play your *rabab*!" But the thought does not attract her in the least. She sits on the sill of the door, puts her head on her knees and cries:

"Help me, Ar Rashid!"[152]

Lifting her head, some weeds in the front vegetable garden catch her attention. She gets up, fetches her trowel and digs them out. Soon she sees others, and begins to pull them out, one by one, till the storm ebbs, only to come back full force periodically. Feelings she did not know she had, though she had felt them in her unconscious and in her dreams, make her stop and acknowledge

152 The Guide: one of the many names for God in Islam.

them.

"Aziza, what are you thinking, what are you feeling?" She speaks aloud to herself. "You will get sucked into a whirlpool in seeking the kind of love a moth seeks but rarely finds to burn itself to death. You will love him so much you'll become his servant and his slave; you are in danger of making him your god and worshipping him. This unbound love can only be given to the Unbound One. You will have babies and forget all about your real lover: your *rabab*, music, the One with Many Names who fits your soul so snugly. Never, Aziza, never make *that* mistake. Remember Bharatrihari, child."

She surprises herself by addressing herself as 'child,' and realizes she is speaking to herself in Fatima's voice. Feeling her grandmother's invisible nearness, she grows calmer, as if a strong hand has reached out and plucked her out of darkness.

"Buddha is a thinking sort of person. 'I have been thinking,' he said! Not, 'I have been feeling.' 'There is a solution to your isolation.' Solution! It is a mental decision on his part, a sort of business arrangement to help out a childhood friend, an act of compassion, not passion. His passion flows only and forever into Akaal Purukh. He will never fulfill your female longings. No man can fulfill them, Aziza, no one! He will only arouse your hungers. You will become a clinging vine: 'why don't you ever spend time with me, love me, as I need to be loved? Why are you away so often? Why do you spend so much time at the dera? What about me?' You will be disappointed in him as a lover, or a husband, and become a bitch and a nag, hit him over the head with a rolling pin or chase him around the courtyard, broom in hand!"

The image makes her laugh and cry out loud. Memories lurking in obscure recesses of her mind unfurl one by one as she tends the roses, snipping off the dead heads. She recalls the stories Buddha had told her about Mata Sulakhni with Baba Nanak; her grandfather's abandonment of her grandmother for decades;

her parents' relationship, or rather, non-relationship. She is not encouraged by any of the marriage models in her mind.

The flood of confusion, somewhat quelled by her digressively relevant recollections, is back in spate.

How much work it takes to keep a relationship half-alive, Aziza thinks, fetching saplings from a shady spot behind the hut, and planting them in a prepared bed. *Who knows, Buddha might get it into his head to travel like Baba and leave me, pregnant. His mother will tyrannize me, like Mata Sulakhni tyrannized Dhanvanti. All mothers-in-law want their daughters-in-law to be sweet and obedient. Do this, do that, and keep your mouth shut! And when Buddha returns, the children will not know him and fight with him constantly! How badly Abba got along with Daadu, and Sri Chand and Lakhmi Das with Baba!*

"No," she says aloud, standing up.

Who knows, Buddha may tyrannize me, too, she thinks, pulling up male bhang plants from their roots. 'Unfertilized females are strongest,' she hears her grandmother, who had grown it for her grandfather, say. *He will tell me like he told Daadu that eating and smoking bhang is a dirty habit. Or I'll have to lie to him about eating my halwa.*

She works some more, removing dead leaves, staking plants that need support, digging the hard soil around the roots till it becomes loose and soft. She fetches manure and spreads it on the earth around the roots.

"When he comes again I will say, 'no.'" The decision brings another tempest. She does not understand why, so she stops, trowel in hand, to examine her feelings and the thoughts accompanying them: regret, jealousy and sorrow.

How easily he will forget me! He will marry someone else and make babies with her. She will be just a woman to him, to love occasionally and leave to her tasks, like Abba leaves Ami. Abba doesn't even come home many nights and she is not to ask him where he goes. Buddha will spend all his time at the new dera in Khadur, listening to kathaa and kirtan, engrossed in the affairs of the institution the Sikhs are becoming.

But oh, how will you hear his wonderful stories? She asks herself, despairing. She takes a decision, but the decision does not hold and she totters to the other side of the scale, back and forth, back and forth between 'yes' and 'no,' enumerating benefits and disadvantages of each.

I won't have to wear my burqua. But then I have become used to it. No, I like it, love it even. It gives me anonymity. It is my fortress, my cocoon.

Working outdoors ebbs her conflict somewhat, but the tide returns and robs her of her peace, putting her in the meat grinder of conflict.

Stop it, stop it, stop it, Aziza, she screams, stamping her feet on the ground. *It is your ego that is grinding you down, child, deluding you into thinking you have a choice to make. You cannot make it. Turn to the Goddess of the Crossroads instead. Become a Gurmukh, child, and you will be taken in a boat that glides on calm waters to your predesigned Destiny in which all is forever well if you set your compass to the Great One. S/he will give you the power and skill to navigate yourself to your one and only desire: to be, to live always in accord and harmony with the Cosmic Will. This is the first and last lesson that Baba has taught us. Whatever happens will be for the highest good. Go meditate, child, and surrender, surrender, surrender.*

Aziza stands still for a while and then goes indoors.

She sits cross-legged on a daree.

I have come to You, All Knowing. I give myself to You, Al Alim,[153] *Al Haadi,*[154] *in trust that You will guide me into the right decision.*

Almost instantly Aziza falls into the eye of the storm, into blessed, blessed calm. She sits thus for a while, and when she opens

153 The All Knowing.

154 The Guide.

her eyes her gaze falls on one of the looms. It is one of the unfinished ones that Fatima had bequeathed her. Two warp threads of browns, the color of earth and the many shades of natural wool, alternate with hints of madder red, burnt sienna, pale yellow and ochre in the weft. She recalls how her grandmother had made the browns from the bark of horse chestnuts and the soot of burnt, resinous wood. She touches it. Motes of dust arise and dance in a beam of light streaming through the speaking hole on the west of the hut.

Aziza's heart leaps as she wonders if this is a sign for her to go ahead and accept Buddha's proposal. Or, her mind whispers, as she looks at the loom, a sign to stay in her solitude?

The question put her once more in the mouth of conflict but almost immediately she remembers to surrender and sit still in the center of it. Trusting she will be led to the right decision, she turns with an empty mind to the loom, and begins to weave in silence.

her [illegible] gaze fall upon one of the [illegible]. It [illegible] unfinished [illegible] that Fatima had [illegible]. Two [illegible] of earth and the [illegible] of [illegible] in [illegible] stone [illegible] in the [illegible]. She [illegible] she had made [illegible] from the [illegible] and the [illegible]. She [illegible]. More [illegible] on the [illegible].

[illegible]

[illegible]

CHAPTER 30

The Parting

It is another cold day in a spell of unremitting wet, overcast winter days. Aziza is slowly, lovingly, painstakingly working at the loom when she hears a step outside the hut that makes her stop, bobbin in hand. She keeps sitting at her loom as she hears Buddha move the mooda closer to the mouth in the wall that serves as their speaking hole.

Her heart leaps into her mouth and she sits absolutely still.

"Aziza?" Buddha calls. She says nothing. He calls her again.

Buddha hears her picking up the mooda and placing it near the hole. An awkward silence follows in which Buddha clears his throat, and asks,

"Well?"

Aziza, who had prepared by utter surrender to what would happen through her when this moment came, says, quietly, almost in a whisper,

"No."

She truly hadn't known that this was the word that would enunciate itself. And yet, here it was, as if whispered to her by her angels that had spoken in the voice of her soul. A space, wide, vast and silent, opens up within her. She knows at that moment that being single is her destiny; that she must accept it, not begrudgingly, but with Wide Openness, for that alone would make it sweet. She knows, too, that the decision belongs to a power higher than her mind and that though her path would be difficult and often beset with doubt, this quiet space would be the perch that she would strive and pray again and again to return to.

A long silence follows.

"May I know why?" Buddha asks.

"I'll never make the kind of wife you need."

"How do you know?"

The knot she has been in loosens itself and she feels her heart opening to Buddha in a love that had always been there but which, in their struggle to change it from friendship to romance, had faltered and failed. She feels an energy surging within her that is at once lighthearted, clear, and detached.

"Let me give you an example. You will come home from the fields or the dera, doing important things – for you will be an important person, I know – and ask, 'Aziza, where is my dinner?' And I will say, 'I'm sorry, Jaan,[155] I didn't make any. Raag Dhanasari carried me away.' And you will turn around and slap me."

"Never. Even thinking of it hurts my heart."

"Or get angry, or stay hungry."

"We can both serve and eat at the dera."

"But I may not want to do that. Here are some more examples. I will be glorying in my solitude and you will bring guests and say, 'make them a meal.' And I will say, sweetly, of course, 'I don't feel like it. I would rather sit at the loom, or garden.' But who knows, I might become a shrew and shout it, like Shai Tani often does; you will expect me to be social when I want to withdraw, and shut me up when I am feeling social; I may not wait for you to eat first, as women do, and eat before you because I am hungry; you will want me to look pretty when I won't even want to comb my hair."

"I know you rarely comb your hair."

---

155 Meaning 'life.' Used as an endearment.

"But it's getting worse since I started to wear my burqua. My eyebrows have grown bushy and I have bristles on my chin. All women have them, you know, beards and moustaches. I know I'm going to take after Daulatan Masi, that I will become her. She didn't marry or have children, she was half mad, but really, she was happy. She was the only happy one in our family. I never saw her get angry at anyone, only at phantoms inside her head to which she would shout, 'go away!' 'Leave me alone.' I want to be free, like a butterfly. I will be a rebellious wife, Buddha, not the quiet, loving sort that always thinks of others first. You need someone supportive, loving, and subservient to the great being that you are and will become. Besides, I wouldn't give you children. I would hate to have a girl... I mean, I would love to... but why? In this world? And you would not be able to follow Nanak's injunctions to be a householder."

"One way or another I will be a householder. My parents are arranging a marriage for me and I thought I would ask you first."

Aziza feels a pang at the thought of Buddha marrying someone else, but almost instantly steadies herself by the thought that at least he would have a fulfilled life.

"We won't have a wall between us," Buddha says, hitting the wall with his fist.

"There will always be a wall between us. There is always a wall between people. It is called the skin. Even in the womb a caul surrounds a fetus. It is only in our relationship to the One that the wall crumbles."

"You're right. But it will make your life and our relationship easier," Buddha persuades.

"There will be nothing easy about it. We will be shunned, ostracized by both our communities. A Muslim woman and a Sikh boy! I will lose whatever remains of my family. Isolated, our love will suffocate and die. Love cannot thrive when it is surrounded by hate."

"Perhaps it will thrive more. Perhaps that is its only test," Buddha suggests.

"Idealistic. Not on this planet where love is as much under assault as true faith. Baba's message that there is only one caste and one race, the human race, and only one religion, the religion of love, will have to wait centuries, maybe hundreds of centuries to bloom."

"I will become a Muslim, then. I truly believe that the Muslim, Hindu and Sikh God is one and the same though we call Him by different names."

"Will you get circumcised?" Aziza asks, and bursts into uncontrolled laughter and giggles.

Buddha does not laugh. His silence is serious.

"There, see? That's the kind of woman I am. I make fun of things and mention things I shouldn't. You'll be ashamed of me."

"Never," Buddha replies. "I was just wondering how serious I am about this proposal… I mean, not about marrying you, but about becoming a Muslim," he hastens to add. "I couldn't, for example ever believe as most of the Muslims I have met personally and from the history of the Moghuls in our country that Islam is the only path to God; that the rest of the people must be converted or killed. Look at how they are razing all the Hindu temples, building mosques in their places, converting Hindus by the sword, beheading those who refuse, burning libraries, toppling sacred Hindu images and sculpture and bathing them with the blood of Hindus; look at Ala-ul-Din Khilji,[156] his cruelty in the name of Islam. He killed all the male Hindu inhabitants when he invaded a city, and took all the women as slaves. He once asked his qazi[157] what the Muslim law was for Hindus, and he replied, 'if a Muslim wants to spit in a Hindu's mouth, the Hindu should open it wide. The Prophet, may

156 Ruler of the Khilji dynasty. Ruled from 1296-1316.

157 Islamic judge.

peace be on him, has ordained that if Hindus do not accept Islam, they should be imprisoned, tortured, killed, and put to death.' We also heard from your grandfather how Babar treated Hindus."

"Well, I am not that sort of Muslim, either. I was trying to think of a name for what I am and I couldn't think of it. HiMusikh? HiSikhlim?"

Buddha loosens up and laughs.

"I will call my religion Sikhlimish after I convert!" he says. They both burst into laughter.

"And our babies will be Sikhlimings!" Aziza says, giggling almost hysterically.

They both laugh till tears stream down their faces. Buddha's laughter ends with what sounds to Aziza like a sob.

"Let me take care of you," he pleads.

"We are both in God's hands."

"So you will marry a Muslim?"

"Heaven forbid! I will marry no one. I don't want to belong to anyone but the One who leaves me free to live my life in my own way."

"Your life will be difficult."

"I know. But I think marriage would be more difficult for me."

"How do you know?"

"How many lifetimes have I been married? In one of them, I was married to you and in one of our fights, we smeared each other with cow dung; in another, I killed you because you tried to keep me in a cage; in yet another, I gave you the fruit of immortality and you gave it to your whore! No, it is my destiny not to marry in this one. Don't worry about me, Buddha. I don't worry about you, for you are Guru Nanak's child, as am I. Your allegiance must and will be only to him and to Akaal Purukh. I am just a creature made of ash and bones. Make my memory the grain of sand in the oyster's heart. He will wear you near His heart. Those who obey Him in all things, as Baba Nanak says, become that jewel. Our desire for a perfect love in the flesh exists as a phantom on the stages of our mind. We are meant to see it for what it is – something unreal, created only by a desire never to be fulfilled in the flesh. We would be fools to seek it with another human. Our souls live us, and we must obey its pull towards the Vaster Life that lies beyond the edges of this one. But oh!"

The exclamation is wrung out of her as she feels her heart sinking into a well like a bucket of lead without a rope. Lest Buddha mistake it for regret and a change of heart, she hurriedly adds:

"But don't exclude me from the ongoing story! Don't abandon our speaking hole! Come back and tell me where Guru Angad is. I know Baba Nanak will lead you to him when you begin your search in earnest. I must know. The life of my soul depends upon it."

She hears the sound of the mooda being pushed back as Buddha stands up.

"I promise," he says.

"Between the life that never was, or can be, there is a space where we will never be apart," Aziza says with a catch in her voice. "Let our separate lives reflect our friendship with the Friend. Go, Buddha, and do not look back."

As she hears him get up and walk away, a silent sea of stillness springs up and fills her. Space returns to her heart, a silent and still space in which the colors of the loee she is weaving leap up towards her eyes, thrilling them. She knows in that instant that solitude would be her companion; solitude in which she would be free to enter the cage of Love.

But O, what a long and unknown journey lies ahead of you, Aziza! But stay in the moment. Stay here, child. As Baba says, 'mat man jaanai kal:' Let not your mind think about tomorrow.

CHAPTER 31

Into the Swamp

His eyes focused on the mud on the path that is carrying him away from a dream and a desire, Buddha half walks, half runs furiously, blindly, thoughtlessly towards the forest, as if to outrun his rage. It is a new feeling and he doesn't like it. It erodes everything he thinks he is and wants to be.

He breaks a branch from a tree, strips away its tiny branches and its bark, and with it thrashes everything in his path – bushes, branches, trunks of trees. He goes off the path, stomping on the soggy undergrowth, stamping on young plants, beating at the wet foliage.

"Why," he asks, kicking a stump and crying out loudly in pain. "Why, why, why is Your life so full of frustration? Why do You give us dreams and desires only to squash them beneath Your feet? Why do You tantalize us with unfulfillable desires? Why is life so very difficult?"

He does not know how long he walks in an effort to leave his demons behind. The root of a vine trips him and he falls into a thorny bush that grows at the edge of a swampy pond. His face and hands lacerated by the thorns, his feet still entangled in the vine, he falls headlong into the cold swamp.

In that instant, he is plunged from his angry thoughts into the moment. He feels very alert, very alive. He looks around and sees he is in dangerous territory, full of poisonous snakes and other predatory animals. None from the village come here unaccompanied, without weapons. He berates himself for having left his sword, bow and arrows behind. He had not thought it appropriate to carry a weapon on a mission of love. He knows, too, that the tangled roots of the vine that his feet are trying desperately to shake off can drag him down and drown him. A part of him wants to end the pain in his heart. A part of him knows that if drowning is his destiny, so be it. The words, 'in an instant let go that which you hold most precious. Your life, your very life,' come to him, and he relaxes.

And the relaxation catalyzes his energy. Not a thought remains in his head except the imperative to survive. He *has* to. Not just for himself, not just to become the Ancient, Great Tree that Baba has predicted he would become, but to find Angad. Much depended on it. He could not fail the community now.

His habit of prayer before every endeavor infuses him with courage and gratitude. He is alive, strong, and a good swimmer, having often accompanied Baba – in warm weather – into the river. Casting off his wet, heavy loee and his soggy shoes, he renews his attempts to use the less entangled foot to push down the roots around the other foot.

It takes a while but one foot is finally free. He swims to the edge of the marsh to find a place to climb out, but every ledge he clutches crumbles in his hands and falls into the water. He swims around the periphery of the pond till he finds a thick root, one end of which is still anchored to its mother tree. It feels to him like an arm has reached down into the freezing waters to rescue him.

Slowly, he hauls himself up after several failed attempts, to solid ground. Spent, covered in dirt and the mulch of rotten leaves, he sits on the muddy ground; his anger turns to sorrow and he weeps, feeling very mortal, enmeshed and embroiled in the sticky web of attachment, in the human condition he thought he had transcended. No wisdom, no perspective comes to his rescue.

He wants to lie down and go to sleep but knows that danger lurks all around and within him. He must get up and move away, retrace his steps to safety. He has to get some warmth, and soon. The cold is creeping into his chest and congealing it.

The sky is so overcast he can't tell the position of the sun. Long accustomed to examining the adverse incidents of his life as signposts guiding him through the marshes of his mind, he knows at once that his actions and feelings have led him astray. He is lost, literally and metaphorically. He knows he must calibrate his direction, and return to the path once more.

With another prayer he takes his first tentative steps away from the swamp. Barefoot and cold, he begins to walk in the first direction that presents itself. Regardless of thorns and sharp pebbles, in pain, he keeps walking on the forest floor, grateful for soft mud that cushions his feet whenever it appears. He walks for quite a while – it seems, in circles – when he is startled by the smell of smoke. He turns this way and that, sniffing like an animal, till he sees in the haze an unmistakable, thin filament of smoke rising in the distance.

As he hurries towards it, Buddha suddenly bursts into laughter. *You fell into the swamp. It wasn't hot and boiling, like Baba's swamp of attachments in which people get stuck and drown, but cold. Same thing. Buddha, Buddha, how did you think you could avoid it? You, the witness, fell into the web of His Drama!*

He recalls how Baba, too, was enmeshed that night he had followed him into the forest after the battle in his family. The memory of that night recalls Baba's words.

'No one can avoid the shadow of flesh! How it takes us away from Perspective, bakes us in fire and slices our hearts with its knife.'

By now he has discovered the source of the smoke. A figure

bundled up in a blanket huddles by a smoky fire lit with damp wood. At his approach, the figure turns his head. It takes Buddha a while to see that it is his friend, Jodha.

"Buddha!" he cries. "Where have you been? I came from Khadur and you were nowhere to be found! I got cold looking for you and tried to make a fire to warm myself."

"Did you find him?" Buddha asks eagerly despite his enfeebled state.

Jodha shakes his head, sadly. "We have looked everywhere, under every hay stack. I looked everywhere for you, too. I went to your room and your sword and bow and arrow were there. I waited a long time, then went here and there and even to Aziza's hut, and she didn't know where you were. But she told me what happened. I came looking for you. Come, come, here, take this blanket and warm yourself," he says, wrapping Buddha in his blanket. "You look like a swamp rat! Warm yourself first, and then you need to eat and sleep! There, now I'm cold. This won't do. Let's get some warmth." And with one powerful movement of his arms he hauls Buddha up on his shoulders and hurries into town.

CHAPTER 32

Bhai Jodha

Jodha deposits Buddha in front of a polished wooden door with brass studs, and knocks on it.

"Who lives here?" Buddha asks, sneezing and coughing violently.

"Basanti."

Jodha has mentioned her to Buddha before as one of the women he frequents. Buddha turns around to walk away.

"Oh don't be so high and mighty. You are no different. Look at yourself! This is what you have done to yourself over a woman?"

"Aziza is not *that* sort of a woman."

"Question your principles, Buddha, and don't be rigid. Basanti is enlightened. I will tell you why after we get inside."

Buddha tries to guffaw but falls into a fit of coughing.

The latch of the door is lifted from the inside but Buddha has already turned away.

"You either clutch on to your dogmas and die, or survive to go on a quest with me to find Guru Angad," Jodha says forcefully.

The door opens and a female servant looks at Buddha and smiles at Jodha who takes Buddha's arm and brings him inside. Buddha is too weak to resist.

"Something hot to drink at once, a warm bath, a fire and food," Jodha commands urgently, walking in. A fire is already roaring behind a grate. Buddha collapses on a mattress before it. The servant leaves to fetch something hot to drink.

"I'm going to your room for warm, dry clothes," Jodha says, grabbing a red velvet blanket and wrapping himself in it. Buddha looks at him pleadingly.

"She's is not in the habit of seduction, she's not going to eat you up. I'll tell her maid to tell her not to visit you, you prig," Jodha says, and is gone.

Having reached safety, Buddha falls into a feverish delirium. He is vaguely aware that he is fed something warm, bathed by Jodha, wrapped in blankets, clothed, and put into a bed. A hakim is brought in who feels his pulse and prescribes herbs and potions. Wheezing and coughing, Buddha drifts in and out of consciousness, waking and dreaming. He can't tell for how long he has been there, but wakes into consciousness in a warm bed. He lifts himself up and tries to get out of bed, but collapses back on the pillows again, fragmentary images of incoherent dreams drifting in and out of his memory.

Someone writing something… a slate… a chariot made of bones and ash… Aziza in the chariot… hovering in the air…a charioteer. Who? Looked familiar, a peacock feather in his cap; flying off into the sky… smiling… who's smiling so sweetly? I am vomiting… jewels in the vomit."

"Enough of illness. Get up and be well again. We have an important journey to make in search of our Guru."

Buddha half sits up in bed and focuses his eyes on Jodha.

"What's all this mumbling about jewels in the vomit?" he asks, propping his friend on pillows and feeling his forehead. "No, no fever; fuzzy-brained, but on the whole, well and healthy. Basanti's maids have fed you good food and labored over herbal recipes. And don't worry; nobody has violated your virginity. Can you hear me?"

Buddha nods.

"Can you understand what I am saying?"

"Yes," says Buddha, sitting up without the support of pillows. "I must leave here immediately. What will people think?"

"Now let me ask you: hasn't Guru Nanak said the Light shines in everyone, without exception? Didn't he say that the definition of a religious person is that he, or she, thinks of everyone as equal? Do you believe that?"

"How can I not believe what my Guru tells me?"

"Then let me tell you a story. A saint… oh, what's the use? I'm not a storyteller like you, but a singer and a warrior. I have forgotten the plot. I only remember that someone went all around a town to find holy men, and found only two: one was a prostitute and the other a butcher."

"How can that be!" says Buddha.

"The butcher, because he killed animals with compassion and kindness, in full acceptance of the necessity of his profession and the knowledge that every death, including his own, is a sacrifice and a sacrament; and the prostitute because she does not distinguish between the caste, economic and social status of her customers. If there is one thing I have learnt from Guru Nanak it is this: our concepts cannot contain His greatness. He is vaster than our vastest conception. You laughed when I said Basanti is enlightened. She is. She lives with her arms open, never puts demands on me, welcomes me whenever I come, and bids me goodbye sweetly when I leave. No recriminations, no quarrels, no attachments. That is a great quality, one of the greatest."

"Bhai Jodha, our Baba would not approve."

"How do you know? Baba has said God himself created this colorful world with its diversity of people, the different species and the manifold variety of Maya: *rangee rangee bhaatee kar kar jinsee maa-i-aa jin upaa-ee.*

"But Baba overcame all temptation and stayed true to his wife with whom he had, in his own words, 'exchanged hearts.'"

"But he was tempted. Don't be a zealot, Buddha. Understand

your religion. Understand Baba."

Jodha begins to hum, and then sings lines from Baba's *shabads*: '*jaytaa samund saagar neer bhari-aa taytay a-ugan hamaaray;*' '*kahay na jaanee a-ugan mayray*: *My sins are as vast as the water in the ocean; my demerits cannot be counted.*' These are Baba's words. If Baba can have sins, surely I'm allowed some, too."

"Everyone is tempted. We are human," Buddha begins, at first slowly, and then gaining mental momentum as he proceeds. "But if you want to be more than a mere human, you have to carve out a path for yourself, after examining and analyzing it thoroughly, of course, and commit to it. A path by its very definition is limited, confined, but if it is a true path, as Baba's is, then its limitations bestow upon us unimaginable freedom and peace. Don't use Baba's words to justify your own sins, Jodha. Baba surrendered his shadows, his temptations, his human sins to Akaal Purukh who navigated him through the maze of his attachments. Attachments are more than just strings that tie us to people and things, power, position and wealth. The worst of them are webs of thoughts we do not want to examine or change."

Jodha is silent, then scratches his beard for a while in silence before saying, "You know, I have this weakness in me. I love women. I have tried, at times, to be like you and Baba and *have* had pangs of conscience. But so far I have been unable to do anything about it, or change. Perhaps I am like the pig's tail that can't be straightened? But don't make me feel bad. I don't like to feel bad. How can I be so bad when I was the instrument of bringing Guru Angad to Guru Nanak in the first place with my song?"

"I don't want to make you feel bad, Jodha. I just want to remind you of your potential."

"I do feel connected to Akaal Purukh whenever I sing Baba's *shabads*. Want me to sing a few lines that I have composed to a lovely melody?"

"Yes," Buddha says, lying back down on the pillows in a fit of exhaustion.

"The melody just came to me one day. In it, Baba sings praises of Word, in all its spiritual and secular manifestations. His name, Naam, the highest mantra that we have, a word, a magical word, uttering which conjures the Magician who, with one glance of his eye, can transmute dross to gold, suffering to peace, *koord*[158] into roses, illness into health, madness into sanity; who, with one wave of his finger can calm our storms."

"Calm *and* cause them," Buddha corrects.

"Of course. But that is another discussion. There, you have just made me forget my eloquence. But I won't let you because He just blessed me with a glance. I will return to Word, coruscating Word that bounces off our eyes, like light, and shows us His Magnificence and Power. The world is made of words. The 'l' in 'world,' stands for liberty, love, labyrinth, ladder… er, come on, help me with more 'l' words…"

"Lame, lace, lamp, lines, land, lavatory, lechery… my head hurts," Buddha says.

"Let me just finish it off with lamp, luminescence, the light of our glorious senses, our magnificent, marvelous, material world! Baba says, 'our destiny is written on His tablet with words; we are the words of the Writer of all Writers. He, alone, free, unwritten, unbound, unattached, blooming eternally in beauty and joy, can, with one word emanating from his glance bless us with freedom from all shackles. I adore the last line of this stanza in which Guru Nanak says *every thing in this universe is created by the sound and vibration of a sound, a word, the echo of His Name! Jaytaa keetaa taytaa naa-o. vin naavai naahee ko thaa-o.*'"

"Jodha, what's come over you? I have never, ever heard you speak like this before."

---

158 Dirt, filth.

Jodha begins to sing. Tears come to Buddha's eyes as he looks at Jodha's youthful, bearded face, his eyes shut as he sings in his deep, rich, resonant, lyrical voice, the sounds of the words reverberating not just in his throat and lungs but every atom of his being. His singing, like Aziza's, transports him at once somewhere else and here, as close as within, in his very skin, bones, and organs.

Buddha understands, not just with his mind but with his whole being, Baba's passion and adoration of words, song, and singing. Singing to the One Energy with All Power, which Baba personalized and personified with a Name, brought it closer from the infinite inner and outer spaces of existence to nestle in the fibers of the heart.

For an instant, regret arises in Buddha that he had given up on kirtan long ago, but immediately upon the heels of that regret comes the knowledge that singing was not his destiny. The closest he could get to it was by listening and *jaap*. He resolves to teach himself, with the aid of Jodha, who he loves, to make his recitations of prayers as melodious as he can.

This is what Jodha must have meant by the Glance that saves, that turns dross into gold, koord into roses, Buddha thinks. *It must have been the Magician's glance that turned, almost immediately, my regret into resolution.*

May Your Glance penetrate mine when I look at the circumstances of my life, Buddha prays. *It will be difficult; it will bring suffering that I cannot understand, but help me return here, to this home, this perspective where I see everything in Your Light, instead of in the darkness of my ego.*

The words Baba had spoken to him after he had gone off to the fields at night, and returned after singing his beautiful *shabad*, *merai jeearaya, paradesia,* float into Buddha's consciousness. 'But ah, how wonderful losing our perspective seems when we arrive at it again! How wonderfully sweet this union after each separation! It is enough to make you want to court separation, sing it!'

Jodha is done singing. He turns to Buddha and says, "Now, tell me about your dream. About jewels in vomit."

Buddha relates the fragments of his dream to Jodha. And as he does so, he sits up in bed and exclaims, excitedly.

"Of course! Makes perfect sense! Something written on a tablet! Even the few lines you just sang… nothing is a mistake. This rejection by Aziza – it was written, ordained, hukum!"

"What about the chariot? I haven't seen one, but when I think about one I think about Arjuna[159] in the Mahabharat," Jodha says.

"And Krishna was his charioteer. Krishna carrying away Aziza? A god carrying her away? Yes, a god carried her away. How can I compete with that?"

"But what about jewels in your vomit?" Jodha asks.

"I don't know. Sometimes dreams are just nonsensical."

"Maybe. But let me analyze it some more. Throwing up something you have eaten, or something you did not digest and got rid off, but what you are getting rid of is something precious."

"What?"

"I don't know, either. Tell me, how did you feel when you saw the jewels in your vomit?"

"I felt bad that I had thrown out something precious that I should have kept safely. Now they lay in the vomit and mud."

"Does Baba say anything about eating?" Jodha asks, his brow contracted in concentration.

"Let me see… 'eat the Given.'"

In the pause that follows, both men look at each other. Jodha slaps his thigh and an 'aaaah,' escapes Buddha.

"Of course!" Buddha exclaims.

"Okay, tell me," Jodha says, his face beaming. "I know what you are going to say!"

"I did not eat the Given. I did not accept hukum. I thought it

159 A hero in the great Indian epic, the Mahabharat.

was just Aziza who had rejected me but I couldn't see that it was the Universal Will that spoke through her. I rejected her rejection; I rejected the Universal Will and became angry instead. By eating it, by accepting it, I would have turned the dross into gold, the mud into jewels. But it isn't too late. No, it is never too late. I accept it. I accept it fully, and gratefully. There is a Design here that I am too blind to see. I struggled to change Aziza's destiny, but I am helpless to do so. The universe's design for her life will be fulfilled, as will mine. I do not know what it is, and may never know, for only the All Seeing, the Timeless, knows it."

"I knew you would say this," Jodha beams. "Here, put on your clothes and let's be on our way."

As Buddha puts on his clothes, he feels alive, new, reborn from the womb of his recent suffering. A memory flashes through his mind of Aziza as a waif of a child, her short, greased hair framing her face, her eyes bright and sparkling. She had cut her hair herself one day, very badly, so it was uneven and wispy at the edges. Skipping to the guava tree in their courtyard, showing him the cocoons hanging under the broad leaves, she had shouted, 'worms can become butterflies! But they have to be very still as they cocoon.'

Buddha feels his heart dilate and expand. He realizes that his ego, lurking in the shadows of his brain like some ancient behemoth that has made itself invisible by some magic, is watering the dark flower of hate by whispering 'the bitch has rejected you, you weren't good enough.' He knows his ego has to be harnessed and made to serve the higher purpose; that he and Aziza would always be together as friends in the Great Heart of the Friend. That their love – whatever form it took, whether close or distant – would transform each of them.

"Hurry up. Let's embark on our adventure!" Jodha says, adjusting the sword at his side.

"No, Jodha. We must not hurry. I have learnt from Baba to move in a way that is neither hurried nor slow. There is a tempo where the two meet in the vast spaces of Sehaj. It is the tempo in which Baba lived and sang. Something is whispering to my soul that we will find our guru. How can we not?"

Buddha laughs long and hard. Jodha laughs along with Buddha's infectious laughter, though he admits to himself he does not understand what Buddha means by "How can we not?"

When they stop laughing, Jodha admits to Buddha that he is afraid they might not find Guru Angad. What if something has happened to him? What if one of Sri Chand's zealous followers has harmed him?

"Fears are weeds in the garden of our minds, Jodha. We can only get rid of them when we turn all our fears into fear of Him."

"Why should we fear Him? I want to love Him, not fear Him."

"How can you love Him without knowing that you know nothing at all of His Power? When things change in the blink of an eye from this to that, His Hand is at work. Never doubt it. But because we are creatures who have many fears, how can we not? We are reminded again and again as we move through our lives about the many who perish at the hands of demons and fears inside their heads; of those whose lives were inexplicably and brutally cut short; of those who suffered unimaginably, and died without turning to the Power that lives and breathes us – our only resort is turn to Him in all humility and trust. That is why Baba turned his ire on the doubters, the *saakats* of life who let their minds interfere with the truths of the heart. Let your Fear of Him be sweetened by the Prasad of trust. Let your love be humble before such Power. Fears and other illusions and temptations have to be corralled, circumscribed, mastered. I could tell you the story of when Baba met Kaliyuga, but it will have to wait. I can only tell you that Baba picked up his staff, waved it at the phantoms of fears, and shouted, 'Illusion, stay in your place!' Baba lived like a warrior, keeping the sword of his agile mind ready and sharp to cut down the weeds that grew in the garden of his mind. Let us follow his path."

Buddha opens the door and steps out with Jodha behind him.

"Please thank Basanti for taking care of me," he says. "And thank you, Jodha, for widening my heart to include her in it."

"So, is the tempo and the time right for us to begin our search?"

"Not yet. I have to go home first and tell my parents I accept the match they are arranging for me."

"Have you seen her?" Jodha asks.

"No."

"But what if she is ugly, like this?" Jodha asks, twisting his face into a hideous grimace, shutting one eye, squinting the other and walking with an exaggerated limp.

"Then so be it. I will accept my destiny. There will be purpose in it. I am going wherever I am taken."

"I'll come with you to your parents' home, and then we can start our journey."

"No, Jodha."

"Don't you care?" Jodha asks, angrily.

"Very much. But I must seek guidance from the Guide."

"And how will you do that?"

"By cocooning," Buddha says, striding ahead. "I will call you when I am ready."

The friends part ways. Buddha goes to see his parents, and Jodha leaves for Khadur.

Epilogue: Transformation

True to his word, Buddha returns once more to the speaking hole to complete this section of the story.

"Have you found him?" is Aziza's first, eager question. Peace spread like concentric circles from the center of her being to its edges, expanding them with a quiet joy and gratitude. Buddha has fulfilled his promise to her! Even though her inner voice had whispered 'trust, trust,' a sharp thorn of fear and doubt had been chafing the flesh of her heart.

She had struggled to say to the Fulfiller of Desire, 'if it is Your Will he come no more, teach me to accept it." Though she had said it several times, each time her surrender and prayer seemed insincere and shallow. She felt anything but resigned. She sat on the daree on her knees, her hands folded, to say something truly heartfelt. She began her prayer with the same plea she began all her prayers with: "if it is Your Will he come no more, teach me to accept it" but before she could put the full stop on that sentence and thought, her soul burst out of her mouth: "but Oh, do not deprive me of my friend who brings news about the Guides in whose footsteps I trustingly follow the path to You; in whose words and songs I fly with open wings into Your Great Heart. Send the teller who ever whispers Your Name to me!"

Now, sitting on the mooda, her open hands resting on her knees, she feels utter peace at what has transpired between them, and knows he will return whenever he can.

"Let me tell you the story from the beginning," Buddha says, with no hint in his voice of the suffering he has undergone. The suffering has already transformed itself into a pearl he wore, gratefully, close to his heart. He wonders for a brief moment if they would ever get to the point of being friends again but knows at once that there might be danger in it. He wonders very briefly if he should stop visiting her, but knows he couldn't betray his promise to Aziza. No, he determines, he would never jeopardize his chosen path. And the choice, like a line in stone, has been made. He trusts and knows it is the right one. There is no place on this path for regret.

He had said 'yes' to his marriage with another, and would be with her as his wife in God; he would exchange hearts with her, abiding with her through his life. His worry about Aziza had dissolved from the moment he had made his decision. That thread, too, had snapped: not in any hardening of his heart, but in trust that though she was beating her own path through life in her rebellious way, she would be protected and safe in the hands of the One who would lead her, through the voice of her rich soul, to where she needed to go; though she would stray, as all must stray, she would be connected to the Friend with a bond that would hold firm and fast. Buddha knows that all is well, as it always is, though we are sometimes too blinded by our humanity to see it.

"As you know," he resumes after a brief pause in which his many thoughts jostle simultaneously in his mind, "the Sikhs who had gone in all directions from the dera at Kartarpur, now taken over entirely by the Udaasis, returned empty handed and empty hearted. Guru Angad was nowhere. I could tell from their slumped postures and drawn faces that despair had settled in their souls. The Udaasis, jealous of Guru Angad, in their loyalty to Sri Chand, were glad about Angad's disappearance; now Sri Chand would be guru. This much can be said in Sri Chand's favor, though: he has retained all his father's raagis, including your father, who sings Guru Nanak's compositions. I know without a doubt that no matter how different Sri Chand is from his father, he will keep his father's voice alive through the centuries. I also understand that Sri Chand did not want to surrender his entire self, ego and individuality, and merge with Baba, the way Angad did, because he wants to keep a corner for himself where he can have his dramatic differences with his father. Take celibacy, for instance. He makes no concession or room in his austere path for human nature and need, the way Baba did."

"There's nothing wrong with it if you choose to be celibate," Aziza objects.

"But you can't institute it and make it mandatory, you have to leave room for differences," Buddha replies.

"Yes, everything is different from everything else. Though the Ravi River is always the same river, the patterns of the water and waves on the shore are always different each time I observe them."

Buddha hopes his wife would be reflective, like Aziza, and that he would be able to communicate his innermost self with her.

"To get back to our story. Before I began my search with Bhai Jodha, I remembered something you had said about how worms need to cocoon to become butterflies, and I knew that I had to isolate myself somewhere, be very quiet. A pool becomes clear when it is still and calm. I had to meditate to discover Guru Angad's whereabouts. I did not want to be disturbed so I looked for rooms to rent where no one could find me. In my head, I heard Baba's voice singing '*man ray, thir raho; mat kat jahai jeeo*: *oh my mind, stay unmoved; don't go hither and thither.*' I was not to look outside for our guru, but inside.

I rented rooms on the other side of town, told no one about it, and requested the landlord to put a lock on the door so no one would know where I was.

On the fifth day I had a vision. Baba Nanak came to me and pointed with his finger at a small hut, with a straw roof, its outside walls plastered with cow dung patties, a lock on its door. I saw a path in my vision that I knew I had seen before but couldn't place in any town. I struggled to remember, but remembering the futility of struggling, I fell once again into silence. And then suddenly a powerful spirit, like a gust of wind, entered and shook my mind, causing many pieces of the mystery to fall into place all at once: I saw Mata Khivi's calm and undisturbed face as she went about preparing the langar after Guru Nanak's passing, and Amro, going about her tasks, singing. I knew they knew where he was, safe, unharmed, though I knew they would not betray his whereabouts to me. Then I heard Amro say about her friend, Nihali: *She owns a cow, sells milk, buttermilk, ghee, makes cow dung patties, which she dries on the outside walls of her hut, and sells them as fuel.* Simultaneously, the thought blew into my brain: *of course! Guru Angad is doing exactly what I am doing: cocooning!*

And then, Aziza, in a flash I knew where he was. I left the room, called the Sikhs, and left for Khadur."

"But the Sikhs had sieved through all of Khadur, you said!"

"Yes, but they didn't know where to look. I first went and fetched Jodha.

'Is the quest underway?' he asked, strapping on his sword when he saw me and the other Sikhs that were accompanying me. In his eagerness to find Guru Angad, he had made all preparations for a long journey at a moment's notice. I laughed at him when he said, 'several horses with saddles and saddlebags stand ready in their stalls. Let's go find him!'

'Come,' I said. 'We don't need to go very far in our search.' Jodha and the others followed me as I let my insight guide me, like a star, through the streets of Khadur. Soon, we were standing before a wall plastered with cow dung patties and a lock on the door. I stood before it and knew I had found him. I touched the lock and saw that though it looked locked, the shackle was open by the width of a hair. I opened it, and went inside.

At first I saw nothing, for the room was stacked with hay. And then in the light of the open door I saw him: sitting in a corner, his legs crossed, his face pale, gaunt, but with a strange glow upon it, as if it was coming from within.

He opened his eyes, briefly. There was a burning, aching longing in them. He said nothing, and shut his eyes again. I went near him and picked up the little pothi that he had been writing in. On the first page I read the words: *jis pi-aaray si-o nayhu tis aagai mar chalee-ai, Dharig jeevan sansaar taa kai paachhai jeevnaa*: *Die before the one you love dies; life is a curse without him.*

He was grieving profoundly; he missed his master; he felt guilt at surviving him. I understood and empathized with it. But I could see from his face that his grief had thrown a thick veil on his consciousness and made him forget the most important thing of all.

"You miss him?" I asked.

Tears began to roll out of his eyes. Suddenly I felt myself shaking with the same spirit that had visited me earlier at the close of my long meditation. It entered, took possession of me, and I felt a spontaneous, God-given, power rising and shaking me. Though I was far younger than Angad, I felt old, very old and hoary as I towered above him where he sat, and said in a thunderous voice that sounded like a loud drum beating on the tympani of my whole being:

"You miss Nanak? You fool, you *are* Nanak!"

Aziza gasps in awe.

"Angad's head came up and he looked me directly in the eye," Buddha resumes. "It was a sharp, inquiring gaze that looked as much at me as into his innermost, questioning self. It was a gaze

– how should I describe it? No, it is indescribable though I can use ineffectual words like 'illumined,' 'light,' 'knowing beyond knowing.' I will only say it was the look of a man who was on the verge of becoming divine. He knew, and he knew that he knew that the moment had arrived for him to make the leap Baba Nanak had trained him for: into the wide-open arms of Akaal Purukh, with unswerving, unconditional, trust.

The truth, the proof of his physical transformation that both Amro and I saw in the passing of the flame to him, became fully manifest to Bhai Lehna now. He began to luminesce with a bright, holy flame. All of us present could see it. We all felt the transformation. We knew that Nanak's spirit had returned to us in the body and form of Guru Angad who was Angad no more, but henceforth: Nanak.

As he arose, at once majestic and humble, powerful and meek, we bowed our heads in unison."

A long silence followed Buddha's words before he concluded his narrative.

"He will stay in Khadur from now on. The Sikhs have already begun migrating to the dera in Khadur. Donations are pouring in for the construction of a kitchen, langar, gurdwara, dharmasala. He has commissioned many scribes to write down all of Baba's *shabads* and to collect and write down all the stories of his wanderings and life. Many musicians and kirtanias have arrived from far and wide to sing both Guru Nanak's and Guru Angad's *shabads*. Yes, I will copy them and bring them for you. Many *shabads* are springing out of Guru Angad, like energetic, bubbling, streams. Here are some I brought for you," he says, passing some pages through the hole. "He is signing all his compositions as 'Nanak.'"

Aziza takes them, gently, gratefully. Holding them with infinite care, she holds them to her breast, thinking, *music and meaning, Love and the guru, married in my heart! What more can I ever ask for?*

Bibliography

Bal, Sarjit Singh.1984[1969]. *Life of Guru Nanak*. Chandigarh: Panjab University Press.

Bedi, Sohinder Singh. 1991. *Folklore of the Punjab*. New Delhi: National Book Trust.

Cunningham, Joseph Davey. 2003. *History of the Sikhs*. New Delhi: Rupa and Co.

Duggal, K.S. 1989. *Sikh Gurus: Their Lives and Teachings*. Honesdale, Pennsylvania: The Himalayan International Institute of Yoga Science and Philosophy.

Goswamy, B.N. 2000. *Piety and Splendour: Sikh Heritage in Art*. New Delhi: National Museum.

Kohli, Surinder Singh. 1978. *Travels of Guru Nanak, 2nd edition*. Chandigarh: Panjab University Press.

Macauliffe, Max Arthur. 2008. *The Sikh Religion: Its Gurus, Sacred Writings and Authors, Vol 1*. Delhi: Low Price Publications.

Singh, Harbans (ed.). 2002. *The Encyclopaedia of Sikhism*. Patiala: Punjabi University.

———. 2011. *The Encyclopaedia of Sikhism, 3rd edition*. Patalia: Punjabi University.

Singh, Kirpal. 2004. *Janamsakhi Tradition: An Analytical Study*. Amritsar: Singh Brothers.

Singh, Puran. 1977. *Sisters of the Spinning Wheel*. Patiala: Punjabi University.

Thind, Kulbir Singh and Khalsa, Sant Singh (trs.). 2000. *The Electronic Sentence-by-Sentence English Translation and Transliteration of Sri Guru Granth Sahib*. Arizona: Hand Made Books. Available at http://old.sgpc.net/CDN/Gurmukhi%20to%20 English%20translation%20&%20transliterat%20of%20SGGS,%20

About the Author

KAMLA K. KAPUR is well known as a poet, author, and playwright. Her previous work includes *The Singing Guru, Classic Tales from Mystic India* and *Rumi's Tales from the Silk Road*. Kapur has also published two books of poetry, *As a Fountain in a Garden* and *Radha Speaks*, numerous short stories, and a series of award-winning plays. Kapur was on the faculty of Grossmont College in San Diego, California, for eighteen years and taught courses in playwriting, poetry, creative nonfiction, fiction, mythology, Shakespeare, and women's literature. She and her husband, Payson Stevens, divide their time between the Kullu Valley in the Indian Himalayas and Southern California.

For more information visit kamlakkapur.com